Praise for *India's Unending Journey*:

'The quintessential foreign correspondent, informed, even-handed and practically a native.'

The Times

'A labour of love, written by a man who has witnessed the worst of India and yet can still find hope and optimism, someone who sees beyond the disunity in diversity and finds a unique balance.'

India Today

'A warm and engaging guide.'

The London Paper

D0048987

By the same author:

No Full Stops in India
India in Slow Motion (with Gillian Wright)
The Heart of India
Amritsar: Mrs Gandhi's Last Battle (with Satish Jacob)
From Raj to Rajiv (with Zareer Masani)
Lives of Jesus

INDIA'S UNENDING JOURNEY

FINDING BALANCE IN A TIME OF CHANGE

Mark Tully

RIDER

LONDON SYDNEY AUCKLAND JOHANNESBURG

1 3 5 7 9 10 8 6 4 2

First published in 2007 by Rider, an imprint of Ebury Publishing
This edition published by Rider in 2008

Ebury Publishing is a Random House Group company

Copyright © Mark Tully 2007

Mark Tully has asserted his right to be identified as the author of this Work
in accordance with the Copyright, Designs and Patents Act 1988.

The Random House Group Limited Reg. No. 954009

Addresses for companies within the Random House Group can be found at
www.rbooks.co.uk

A CIP catalogue record for this book is available from the British Library

The Random House Group Limited supports The Forest Stewardship
Council (FSC), the leading international forest certification organisation.
All our titles that are printed on Greenpeace approved FSC certified paper
carry the FSC logo. Our paper procurement policy can be found at
www.rbooks.co.uk/environment

Printed in India by Replika Press Pvt. Ltd.

ISBN 9781846040184

Copies are available at special rates for bulk orders. Contact the sales development
team on 020 7840 8487 for more information.

To buy books by your favourite authors and register for offers, visit
www.rbooks.co.uk

The author would like to thank the following for permission to use
copyright material: Bloodaxe Books for permission to quote 'Freedom' in
Poems by Michael Siadhail (Bloodaxe Books, 1999); William Clowes &
Sons Ltd for lines from Summoned by Bells by John Betjeman (John
Murray, 1976). Every effort has been made to trace all copyright holders but
if any have been inadvertently overlooked, the author and publisher will be
pleased to make the necessary arrangement at the first opportunity.

CONTENTS

ACKNOWLEDGEMENTS

THIS book is about living with the uncertainty of certainty, about accepting the limits to what we can know, and being willing to question our beliefs. This uncertainty doesn't just apply to religious beliefs or, indeed, beliefs hostile to religion. In the book I also suggest we need to be much more open to questioning our economics, our business practices, the way we educate our children, how we live as members of communities and citizens of nation states, and how we live our individual lives. But the book started from my belief that the Hindu tradition of acknowledging there can be many ways to God could help Christians to question those of their beliefs which have led them to deny the validity of other faiths, and all too often the validity of other Christian traditions than their own. I had never considered putting the thoughts that were buzzing around my head down on paper until the organisers of the Teape Lectures asked me to give those lectures in 1999. The lectures, to be given that year in the Universities of Cambridge, Oxford and Bristol, had to relate to the *Upanishads* and the Catholic Church. Previous lecturers had all been outstanding theologians, including my former tutor Robert Runcie, who later became Archbishop of Canterbury. I am no scholar so I was very reluctant to accept this invitation. But finally I decided to face up to the challenge. So my first debt of gratitude goes to the organisers of the Teape Lectures, not only for taking the risk of breaking a scholarly tradition, but also for the generous reception they gave to my lectures, which encouraged me to go on reading and writing abut the ideas I had expressed.

My second debt of gratitude goes to my editor, Judith Kendra. There would be no book if she hadn't asked me to consider writing it. I did not leap at the opportunity because I was far from certain that my ideas could stretch to a book, but I gave her a copy of the Teape Lectures to give her a clearer picture of what would be in it if it ever materialised. She came back after reading the lectures with an encouraging reply and at all stages in writing the book she has continued to encourage me, reading different drafts and making invaluable suggestions for improvements. I am also very grateful to Judith's colleague Sue Lascelles, who took over the editing at the last stage.

This book covers many different subjects, in none of which can I claim to be an expert. I am therefore particularly grateful to those people who are experts in their fields and who have allowed me to test my ideas on them. In particular I am grateful to my old friend Chaturvedi Badrinath, who was the first person to awaken my interest in the uncertainty of certainty and who has helped me to build on that start. The scholar of Eastern philosophy Chakravarthi Ram-Prasad read the first draft of the chapters on Hinduism and made many invaluable suggestions. Madhu Khanna with her knowledge of Sanskrit and her deep understanding of the Tantric Hindu tradition, the art historian Shobita Punja with her knowledge of Hindu mythology, and the Jungian psychologist Rashna Imhasly-Gandy all helped me find a way through the mine-field of the chapter on sexual mores. Alvaro Enterria, a publisher and long time resident of Varanasi, read the chapter on that city and made valuable suggestions.

My knowledge of the modern developments in Christianity has been enriched by the many theologians and other Christians I have interviewed during the eleven years I have been presenting the BBC Radio 4 Programme *Something Understood*. I am grateful to the BBC for giving me this opportunity and particularly grateful to my producer Eley McAinsh, a wise Christian herself. I have for many years now been a regular reader of the Irish Dominican journal, *Doctrine and Life*, and it has opened my eyes to the breadth of Christian, particularly Roman Catholic, theology today. The editor of the journal, Bernard Treacey, organised the whole of my visit to Ireland. While not hiding the concerns he had about the Irish Church he did his best to ensure that I presented a balanced picture of it. I hope he succeeded.

Many of the ideas in the chapter on economics came to me through the network of the Centre for Holistic Studies. Barbara Panvel, who set up the UK network and Molly Scott-Cato, a fellow member, gave me invaluable advice on the economics chapters. Rajiv Kumar, Director and Chief Executive of The Indian Council for Research on International Economic Relations, gave up several hours of his time to talk to me. He encouraged my belief that there can be economic growth with a more human face, and that criticising certain aspects of market capitalism does not mean advocating a return to the full rigours of socialism. Will Hopper allowed me to read an advance copy of the book he and his brother have written on the failings of modern capitalism and he read a draft of the chapter on business management in my book.

Lastly, I must mention two people to whom I owe a deep personal debt. Richard Wilkinson, my friend since my schooldays, organised my visit to Marlborough College where we both studied. I am grateful to the Master and staff for making us welcome, although they knew that I did not rate my education at Marlborough very highly. I am grateful to Richard for far more than the visit to our old school. For well over fifty years we have discussed issues raised in this book. A deep faith and many years of teaching have given Richard wisdom far beyond mine, and I have benefited greatly from it. The second person is Gillian Wright, my partner. She has also been a partner in all my books and this one is no exception. She has frequently disagreed with what I have written, and more often than not she has been right. She has worked tirelessly on various drafts to tidy up my incompetent typewriting, to improve the punctuation, and of course the contents too. This book is unlike anything I have ever written before, so there have inevitably been moments of doubt and of despair. Gilly has always encouraged me to keep going. But just as Gilly still does not agree with everything I have written, I cannot hold anyone else responsible for the views expressed in *India's Unending Journey*.

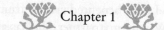

Chapter 1

PURI: EXPLORING
THE OPPOSITES

I WAS asleep under my mosquito net in the BNR Hotel in Puri, a temple town on the east coast of India, when I was suddenly woken by loud explosions, sharp, ear-splitting cracks and the swoosh of rockets shooting up into the sky. It was still dark and my mind, befuddled by sleep, couldn't fathom what was happening. Then, from the loudspeakers of a nearby temple, shrill pre-recorded *bhajans*, or hymns, began blasting out at all and sundry. That's when I remembered that this was the festival of Kartik Purnima, which marks the full moon of the month of Kartik. It's considered an auspicious day for worshipping ancestors or praying for success in a business venture. I had been told that Hindus eager to indulge their insatiable appetite for festivals would start the celebrations before dawn, and so realised that the booms and bangs must be the sound of fireworks.

I had not intended to come to Puri at the time of a Hindu festival. Rather, I had come for a few days' holiday, and to wallow in nostalgia for my British Raj childhood. As a child, I had spent winter seaside holidays at the BNR, or Bengal Nagpur Railway's Hotel, in Puri with my parents and an ever-increasing number of brothers and sisters – I was second in line and by the time we left India there were six of us. My grandfather also used to join us for the holidays.

Lying in bed now, and trying unsuccessfully to ignore the fireworks and the *bhajans*, all my worries bubbled up in my mind, as they usually do when I can't sleep. One of them was whether I would ever be able to write this book, which I had promised to my publishers. It was to be a book describing how nearly forty years of living in India had changed me and my outlook. I was worried that this would seem very arrogant, and one of the lessons I have learnt from India is to value humility. Others are to avoid thinking in black and white, to be suspicious of certainty, to search for the middle road and, in particular, to acknowledge that there are many ways to God. But it's so much easier to argue in black and white, to come down wholly on one side or another, and I worried that my book would be muddled and unconvincing.

I had finally run out of excuses for not starting to write, but I had no idea where to begin. Then suddenly it occurred to me: maybe the coincidence of being in Puri during Kartik Purnima meant that I should start the book here. India has taught me that coincidences are often significant, and this coincidence certainly appeared to symbolise the forces in my life that were driving me to write the book. The more I thought about it, the more it seemed to me that the BNR Hotel stood for my very British upbringing, an upbringing that was designed to keep me apart from India, whereas the festival stood for my adult life, of which India has become an inseparable part.

Holidaying in the BNR hotel of my childhood was a very British affair. I don't remember any Indians drinking their early morning tea on the BNR Hotel's long, wide verandas, with their red concrete floors polished as bright as the toe-cap of a sergeant major's boot. My grandfather was fascinated by the colour of the white *sahibs* and *memsahibs* who arrived in the dining room for breakfast after a night on the Puri Express. He would embarrass my mother by loudly criticising some individual or another for being 'pasty-faced', adding that the poor unfortunate looked as though he 'spends too much time in the office, and doesn't ride and get out in the fresh air'. Of others, whose ruddy complexion may well have been the result of getting out and about, he would say, 'Look at him – red as a beetroot. He must be spending too much time in the bar.' We were all fascinated by a man who sat on the beach buried up to his neck in sand, in the belief that this would cure his rheumatism.

For me, holidays at Puri were part of a childhood designed to ensure that my siblings and I in no way 'went native'. The Indian servants considered essential by every European family were thought to pose a particular threat to their employers' children. In her book *Children of the Raj*, Vyvyen Brendon describes one *memsahib* who recommended the employment of English nannies to guard children against 'promiscuous intimacy with the native servants'. However, Rudyard Kipling's parents did not take that line and Kipling had an Indian *ayah* rather than an English nanny. He spoke to her and the other servants in Hindustani; in fact, he had to be reminded to speak English to his parents when he went into the dining room. When Kipling returned to India after his education in Britain he was surprised to find his Hindustani coming back, which was a great help to him as a journalist.

I was not so lucky. My childhood custodian was Nanny Oxborrow from England, and I remember being slapped by her when she found the driver teaching me to count in Hindustani. 'That's the servant's language, not yours!' she snapped. Years later, her zealous protection very nearly prevented my career in India from getting off the ground. When, in my twenties, I came up before a BBC Appointments Board to be interviewed for the post of Assistant Representative in the Delhi Office, one member said, 'You must remember a lot of the language from your childhood.' Perhaps because I was overawed by the occasion I blurted out, 'Not really, but I can recite "Humpty Dumpty" and "Little Miss Muffet" in Hindustani.' (Much to Nanny's annoyance, Grandfather had taught us these nursery rhymes.) To this day I don't know why that didn't ruin my chances.

The only Indians I remember on the hotel's stretch of the beach during my childhood were the lifeguards. We all had our own bare-chested fisherman, with a number painted on his white pointed hat. Without these men to watch over us, the breakers crashing onto the beach and the undercurrent as they retreated would have made bathing far too dangerous. Just down the road from the BNR beach was Puri itself, a Hindu temple town throbbing with pilgrims. But I knew nothing of that – I never went there.

Now, as I lay listening to the fireworks explode, the celebration of Kartik Purnima seemed to represent the India I had been isolated from all those years ago. The press estimated that 500,000 people had gathered on the beach at Puri to bathe in the sea this year, yet, when I joined in the festivities later that day, there was no one in charge to tell the devotees who to worship or how to worship them, and there was no one to turn me away for being a foreigner and a Christian. Neither was there any line drawn between the sacred and the secular. Hawkers shouted their wares – candy floss, ice cream and Indian fast foods; plastic windmills and other toys; vermillion powder, coconuts and small clay lamps, as well as all the other accoutrements of Hindu worship – their cries competing with the bellowing of sacred conch shells and the mournful sound of women ululating as they remembered their ancestors.

A circle of women from a fishing village made no objection as I watched them pat little mounds of sand into shapes like temple towers. Beside the mounds, they placed small boats made from the stalks of banana trees, bearing marigolds, betel leaves and sacred *doob* grass. After lighting the short sticks of incense that formed the boats' masts, the women bent double, huddled together and charged down the beach like a rugger scrum, their ululating tongues wagging furiously, to launch their boats on the sea. The boat symbolised the legend of seven brothers who had crossed the seas to trade and bring prosperity to their homeland. There was no hint here of the old tradition that Hindus who cross the 'black water', as the sea used to be called, become polluted or ritually impure. Women dressed in traditional black-and-red checked cotton saris, together with others in saris of more modern designs – an array of yellows, greens and pinks, scarlet spangled with gold, and purple spangled with silver – squatted on the beach alongside girls in equally colourful *shalwar kameez*, all delicately splashing their hair with sea water and washing their arms and shoulders. Behind them, young boys leapt over the breakers and bobbed up and down in the sea. One less bashful middle-aged woman rolled in the waves, expertly managing to keep herself covered with her drenched cotton sari despite the pull of the breakers. A senior police officer paddled in the shallow water. Although he did not venture into the deep, he still required the company of two life guards and a security escort to prevent him from being swept out to sea. Amidst all this activity, a barber quietly shaved the head of a young boy with a cut-throat razor to prepare him for his naming ceremony.

Observing this celebration of Kartik Purnima, where everyone was doing their own thing, I was again reminded that Hinduism is a pluralist religion. When I have spoken about this pluralism in the past, or recalled other lessons I have learnt from Hindu traditions, it has often been assumed that I have converted to Hinduism myself and that I am suggesting others should convert too. This is not so: I remain a Christian. I agree with Mahatma Gandhi's advice to one of his closest disciples, Mirabehn, the daughter of an English Admiral, that she should not convert to Hinduism but try to be a better Christian. Anyhow, conversion to Hinduism is only allowed in certain sects because traditionally Hinduism is a way of life that people are born into.

However, I do believe that we should all listen to each other and learn from each other – and that includes those who do not adhere to any religion. In my opinion, no single religion has a monopoly on the truth or is without blemish, nor can any religious tradition survive if it remains static. Those who reject all criticism and are not open to developing their doctrines do a disservice to their own traditions, often ending up defending indefensible practices or outdated prohibitions. In the particular case of Hinduism, it is quite clear that the practice of untouchability is indefensible. While Kartik Purnima brought to mind my experiences of Hinduism's admirable tolerance of different doctrines and different philosophical schools, including atheism, I was also reminded in Puri that Hinduism can be exclusive.

Puri is one of the major pilgrimage centres in India because it is the legendary home of the god Jagganath, or Krishna. He is an incarnation of Vishnu, who, with Brahma and Shiva, is one of the Hindu Trinity. But Jagganath's great temple at Puri is not inclusive. Non-Hindus are not welcome to enter the temple precincts or to have a *darshan*, or sight, of the god. This meant that while I was in Puri, I had to stand on the roof of a dusty and apparently little-patronised library in order to peer into one of the forecourts of Jagannath's temple. Before the high conical tower under which Jagannath sits, there were two halls separated by courtyards with high walls, so I really couldn't see much from my roof-top perch. However, I knew from reading that inside the courtyards and the halls there were lots of smaller shrines where pilgrims worshipped before going on to the ultimate *darshan*. A priest of another temple once told me that the gods in the minor shrines in temples were a little like secretaries and personal assistants sitting in the outer offices of government ministers: you had to gratify them before you could get admission to the great man.

The English word 'juggernaut' derives from the deity Jagannath's massive wooden chariot. Once a year the god comes out of the temple on his chariot, which is pulled by devotees to another temple at the far end of the wide avenue that runs through the centre of Puri. There, Jagannath enjoys 'a holiday for nine days'.

In the late nineteenth century, this Car Festival, as it is known, appears to have suffered from an acute form of a malaise that can all too easily afflict any religion: it was priest-ridden. In his book *Memoirs of a Bengal Civilian*, John Beames (the British official in charge of the district at that time) records that Brahmin priests, known as Pandas, used to fan out to all corners of north India in order to persuade pilgrims to come to Puri for the festival. Beames called them 'touters'. The Pandas were, he says, 'naturally' more successful with women. He describes the plight of those who fell for their sales talk:

> It used to be a common sight to see a strong, stalwart Panda marching along the road, followed by a little troop of small, cowering Bengali women, each clad in her one scanty, clinging robe, her small wardrobe in a palm-leaf box on her head, with the lordly Panda's luggage on her shoulders. At night they put up at one of the chatties or lodging-houses which are found all along the road. Here his lordship reposes while his female flock buy his food and cook it, spread his couch, serve his dinner, light his pipe, shampoo his limbs, and even if he so desires, minister to his lust.

When the women reached Puri, the temple priests fleeced them of what little money they had left after the ravages of the Pandas. As for the Pandas, they deserted their pilgrims and left them to find their own way home. What a miserable journey that was, according to Beames:

> Far from their homes from which they have in many cases started surreptitiously, purloining their husbands' hoard of money, these

wretched women have to tramp wearily back through the rain, for it is mostly for the Rath Jatra (Car Festival), in the rainy season, that they come. What with exposure, fatigue and hunger they die in great numbers by the roadside. Those whose youth and strength enable them to survive the journey are often too much afraid of their husbands' anger to return home, and end by swelling the number of prostitutes in Kolkata. '*Tantum religio potuit suadere malorum!*'

Beames was a scholar of Indian culture and languages, and so he is unlikely to have been as prejudiced as many British of his time. If his account is accurate, the Puri Car Festival of the nineteenth century was not an event that Hinduism could be proud of. But it can be proud of what is the world's largest religious gathering today – the Maha Kumbh Mela. It is, like Kartik Purnima, a bathing festival, and it is held every twelve years at Allahabad, where the two sacred rivers, the Ganga, as the Ganges is known in India, and the Yamuna, meet.

In 1989 when I attended my first Maha Kumbh Mela, I had been deeply impressed by the millions of pilgrims who thronged to Allahabad. Their strong faith reconfirmed my belief that Hinduism still had deep roots in India, for it clearly gave the pilgrims the courage and determination to make long journeys in buses and trains filled beyond bursting point, to queue for hours and walk for miles before getting to the riverside, and then to ignore rumours that there might be a stampede on the most sacred bathing day. Nevertheless, when I wrote about the festival, to offset any impression that Hinduism faced no challenge from modern materialism, I found myself quoting a warning by R.C. Zaehner, the former Professor of Eastern religion and Ethics at Oxford: 'With the spread of Western education right down to the lowest strata of society and the progressive industrialization of the country the whole religious structure of Hinduism will be subjected to a severe strain; but such has been its genius for absorption and adaption that it would be foolhardy to prophesy how it will confront this new and unprecedented crisis.'

Industrialisation has indeed spread rapidly in India since the 1980s, and now almost all Indians want their children to have a Western education and to be taught in English. Yet the Maha Kumbh Mela and – on a smaller scale – Kartik Purnima in Puri demonstrate that Hinduism is continuing to stand up well in the face of the crisis that Zaehner forecast, precisely because of its 'genius for absorption and adaption'. In that, it is unlike Semitic religions for, as Zaehner has also written:

> Hindus do not think of religious truth in dogmatic terms: dogmas cannot be eternal but only the transitory, distorting images of a truth that transcends not only them, but all verbal definition. For the passion for dogmatic certainty that has racked the religions of Semitic origin, from Judaism itself, through Christianity and Islam to the Marxism of our day, they feel nothing but shocked incomprehension.

It's that genius for absorption and adaption, and in particular that 'shocked incomprehension' in the face of dogmatic certainty, that I want to write about in this book. I would like to suggest that dogmatic certainty isn't just a trait of religion and philosophy, but can be characteristic of attitudes in politics, economics and society as a whole. In my own life time, the governing school of economics in the Western world has made a 180-degree swing, from the certainty that socialism is the ultimate and absolute truth to the conviction that market capitalism is the only guarantee of prosperity. Left-wing politicians, civil servants, nationalised industry employees and trade unions once espoused a socialism that came to dominate us in the West, and government became a vast vested interest. Now big business is dominating us because we have been led to believe in market economics with absolute certainty. In Chapters 8 and 9 I will be considering the limits of economics and looking at ways in which India can help us to redefine growth.

It's not just our economics but also our sexual mores that have swung by 180 degrees, from one form of certainty to another. As I will explain in more detail in Chapter 2, I was educated in the fifties and so belong to the last generation brought up in the repressive Victorian tradition of sexual behaviour, taught to believe that any diversion from the strict Christian code of sexual morality was a heinous sin. Later in the twentieth century, however, we veered to the opposite extreme. Now sex has become a commodity.

In charting the course of *India's Unending Journey*, it is not my intention to offer startling religious or philosophical revelations, new directions or full-stops to old ways; there will be no green or red lights, but several ambers – perhaps not much more than warnings. All the same, attempting to observe those warnings has made a deep difference to my own thinking and, indeed, my life, and I sincerely believe them to be relevant to the Western world. As I believe that modern Western culture tends to ignore those warnings, much of this book is a discussion of religion, politics, economics, business and sexual mores in the West. Nevertheless, I believe that these warnings are also relevant to India, which is in danger of ignoring its own traditions and rushing headlong into the adoption of modern Western culture. As this book is based on my personal experiences, I will be writing about the two Western cultures I know best – the British and the Irish. I realise that when it comes to religion, the position of America is very different.

In Britain and Ireland, the decline in the influence of Christianity has not meant that the passion of dogmatic certainty has diminished. Modernism was the secular counterpart to dogmatic Christianity. Modernism's dogma was rationalism and rationalism's offspring, science. Modernism regarded true knowledge as being universal and believed its validity could be proved with absolute certainty. Modernism held that we were capable of discovering truth, and established dogmas that were irrefutable. The seventeenth-century philosopher René Descartes is regarded as the father of modernism. In his work *The Passion of the Western Mind*, the philosopher Richard Tarnas notes that Descartes was a mathematician and says, 'By applying such [mathematically] precise and painstaking reasoning to all questions of philosophy, and by accepting as true only those ideas that presented themselves to his reason as clear, distinct, and free from internal contradiction, Descartes established his means for the attainment of absolute certainty.'

Some might argue that the arrival of post-modernism has meant that the passion for dogmatic certainty and Descartes' method for discovering absolute certainty have gone out of the window. Post-modernists tell us we live in a world of uncertainty, in which it is accepted that nothing final can be said, no view can go unchallenged and all dogmas are up for grabs. Yet I wonder just how deeply post-modernism has penetrated, how willing our allegedly post-modern society really is to absorb and adapt, and whether we are not actually still bound by certainties, even though they may not be the certainties of Semitic religions and Marxism that Zaehner spoke about, or even the mathematical methods of Descartes. At the very least, it seems to me that we still want to believe in absolute truths, even though, as post-modernism has suggested, those who claim to know those truths often use them to try to dominate us.

As I see it, one of the reasons for the decline in religious observation in Europe is an aggressive secularism that is as dogmatic as any religion and which has become the dominant philosophy of life in the West. The philosopher John Gray has pointed out a strange reversal that has taken place in modern life. In his foreword to *Straw Dogs*, he argues:

Today religious believers are more free thinking [than their Victorian predecessors]. Driven to the margins of a culture in which science claims authority over all of human knowledge they have to cultivate a capacity for doubt. In contrast, secular believers – held fast by the conventional wisdom of the time – are in the grip of unexamined dogmas.

Advocates of the conventional wisdom are not just dogmatic; they are also afraid of religion. The Archbishop of Canterbury, Rowan Williams, spoke in an interview of the 'agenda of nervous secularists', which he said was creating 'hostility to religion'. The religions that the secularists fear are fundamentalist, yet ironically it is their own dogmatism that plays a major role in creating the dogmatism that they fear. The world got warning of this with the Iranian Islamic revolution against the Shah, the darling of the West. The Iranian professor Ahmed Fardid coined the term 'West-toxication' for the poisoning and pollution that Iranians felt was afflicting them. Fearing what they saw as extreme materialism, many Iranians naturally took refuge in an extreme form of Islam.

In India today there is a corresponding battle between Westernised secularists and those following an extreme and dogmatic form of Hinduism, a form that is quite contrary to Hinduism's traditional dismissive attitude towards dogmatic certainty. As a result of this battle, anyone who speaks of Hinduism is likely to be accused by secularists of being a fundamentalist. A few years ago I made a film suggesting that Mahatma Gandhi had the answer to the current shouting match. The Mahatma said, 'My Hinduism teaches me to respect all religions.' He was assassinated because he insisted on Muslims being respected and fairly treated. Being quintessentially Indian, he advocated a middle way between a theocratic state and one that gave the impression of having no time for religion, which is what the word 'secular' has come to signify in the minds of so many. He advocated a state that was avowedly proud of being multi-religious and hoped India would 'live for this true picture in which every religion has its full and equal place'. But when I advocated that same view in my film, many of my secular friends accused me of supporting fundamentalist Hinduism. An article in one of India's national dailies went further, claiming that I had advocated a theocratic state, which was the last thing I intended, or that Gandhi would ever have wanted. Such is the nervousness of secularists in India.

We have become convinced that liberty is the supreme value in life, and so have lost sight of the other side of that coin: the fact that we are also social animals. The result is that the individual has become more important than society. We are forever hearing about rights, but we don't hear much about duties. In *The Dignity of Difference*, Chief Rabbi Jonathan Sacks writes of 'the collapse of moral language, the disappearance of "I ought", and its replacement by "I want", "I choose", "I feel".' We have to have something to want, something to choose, so we need perpetual change, perpetual so-called 'progress'. However, as Jonathan Sacks goes on to say:

> Bad things happen when the pace of change exceeds our ability to change, and events move faster than our understanding. It is then that we feel the loss of control over our lives. Anxiety creates fear, fear leads to anger, anger breeds violence, and violence – when combined with weapons of mass destruction – becomes a deadly reality. The greatest single antidote to violence is conversation, speaking our fears, listening to the fears of others, and in that sharing of vulnerabilities discovering a genesis of hope.

Those who are dogmatic and certain that they are right don't feel vulnerable and have no desire to have conversations. They only want to convince.

Conversation is an integral part of the Indian tradition that has influenced me. Every evening, with the cows safely home and a cloud of pungent smoke from cow-dung stoves lingering over the village, men would sit on their *charpoys*, or string cots, and talk over local and national issues. Over the years I often joined in these discussions and was subjected to severe cross-questioning about the BBC reports they had heard on their transistor radios. Even now, in small towns every tea shop has a copy of a newspaper and customers linger long after drinking the last drop of the milky sweet liquid in their cup to discuss the news. In Delhi, when two strangers find themselves waiting for the same bus it is not long before they get into conversation. In government offices it often seems as though conversation is the only activity!

This love of conversation has its down side. Because Indians talk to each other so much, the bush telegraph remains a very effective media for spreading rumours, and rumours can be a powerful weapon in the hands of troublemakers. When I worked for the BBC I was sometimes a victim of the bush telegraph myself. I suppose it's a backhanded tribute to the corporation that our reputation for reliability led rumourmongers to authenticate their false information by claiming to have heard it on the BBC. For example, on the first day of Indira Gandhi's Emergency in 1975, when it was still uncertain whether all her cabinet would endorse the constitutional coup that suspended democracy, a rumour was spread that I had broadcast reports of the resignation of a senior minister and the house arrest of other members of the government. After the Emergency was over, the Information Minister at that time, Inder Gujral, told me that the rumour reached Indira Gandhi's inner circle. Apparently, Gujral was ordered to 'send for Mark Tully, pull down his trousers, give him a few lashes, and send him to jail'. Fortunately, he declined the task, saying it was the Home Minister's job to imprison people, not his, and called for the monitoring reports of the BBC's broadcasts. He found that they contained no reference to ministerial resignations and happily my backside was not bruised.

The Indian Nobel Prize-winning economist and philosopher Amartya Sen, a former Master of Trinity College, Cambridge, has demonstrated how wide, deep and relevant India's tradition of conversation and questioning is in his collection of essays called *The Argumentative Indian*. In his preface he speaks of 'India's long argumentative history' and explains:

> Discussions and arguments are critically important for democracy and public reasoning. They are central to the practice of secularism and for even-handed treatment of adherents of different religious faiths (including those who have no religious beliefs). Going beyond these basic structural priorities, the argumentative tradition, if used with deliberation and commitment, can also be extremely important in resisting social inequalities and in removing poverty and deprivation. Voice is a crucial component of the pursuit of social justice.

But in the modern Western tradition voices are all too often drowned out by the din of constant conflict – conflict that is frequently engineered by the media. Whether it be in politics, economics, religion, or any other sphere of human activity, the bandying of certainties frequently passes for discussion, and shouting from opposite corners is considered the way to conduct an argument. In India, too, the media, which takes its cue from the West, seems to think its role is to promote aggression not discussion, and conflict not conversation. One regular verbal punch-up on television is a show called *The Big Fight*. I am forever asking my friends in Indian television why, whenever there is a national religious dispute, they put members of the extremist factions into the ring to fight over it, instead of giving viewers the opportunity to hear a reasoned debate. To make matters worse, the programme's presenters often allow the extremists to claim that they speak for the entire Hindu or

Muslim community, which all electoral results so far show to be untrue.

I believe that the Indian tradition of argument and discussion provides a way forward between the rock of dogmatic modernism and the hard stone of post-modernism. This was confirmed for me by my conversations with Chaturvedi Badrinath. Badri, as he is always known, had the good fortune to be a senior civil servant in the Southern State of Tamil Nadu at the height of the movement that destroyed the Brahmin domination there. As Badri was a Brahmin himself, the politicians discriminated against him by not giving him any work to do. But the politicians couldn't take away his right to an office and a stenographer, so he spent much of his career happily pursuing his personal interest in Indian philosophy, and had someone to type out his thoughts. During our many discussions on that philosophy, it was he who gave me the clue to navigating the path between modernism and post-modernism.

Badri stressed the importance of the Sanskrit word *neti*. He pointed out that in the Hindu scriptures known as the *Upanishads* it is suggested that the Sanskrit expression *neti, neti* needs to be added after any definitive description. He translates *neti* as 'it is not this alone.' To me, the word implies that we should not go to extremes, that we can reach conclusions but we should not claim our definition is absolute or final; the door for discussion must remain open but there can be sufficient grounds for taking positions. Mahatma Gandhi once said, 'I claim to have no infallible guidance or inspiration'. At the same time he insisted, 'I want the windows of my house to be open to the winds blowing from all corners of the world, but I don't want to be blown off my feet.'

I come back to my friend Badri for an explanation of what I have come to believe should be the aim of all this discussion. He has written:

The question is one of knowing the true place of everything in the scheme of human life. To value too greatly or too little a particular human attribute in its relation to the rest is to disintegrate the natural wholeness of human personality. To value the material over the spiritual, or the spiritual over the material, the transient over the eternal, or the eternal over the transient, the body over the mind, or the mind over the body, the individual over the society or the society over the individual, the self over the other or the other over the self, is to create conflicts both within ourselves and with the rest of the world.

And so, to me, the Indian tradition has come to imply that in everything in life we should seek to be balanced, and that the quest for that balance never ends. We are like tightrope-walkers; we have to concentrate on our balance all the time.

One of the most crucial balancing acts we have to perform is between fate and free will – between acknowledging that capabilities and opportunities are given to us and exercising our free will to make the best of them. I was simply acknowledging the workings of fate when I accepted that Puri would be the place to start this book. But I also acknowledge that it has required willpower to write it. The modern cult of individualism, and the belief that competition provides the driving force for progress – that without competition we would all sink into self-satisfied sloth – makes fate appear to be a dangerous word. Anyone who speaks of fate is almost bound to be called a fatalist, to be accused of being like the man described in M.E. Hare's limerick:

> Said a philosopher – suddenly – "Damn
> It's born in upon me I am
> An engine that moves
> In pre-destinate grooves
> I'm not even a bus, but a tram."

It is particularly dangerous to speak of fate in the context of Indian culture, which is so often accused of fatalism. But that morning in the BNR hotel in Puri is by no means the only time I have been aware of fate playing a role in my life. Indeed, fate plays a role from the very beginning of all our lives because we don't choose our parents; we don't even choose to be born. If we exaggerate the role of free will in our lives we become either arrogant, attributing all our achievements to our own efforts and abilities, or depressed, attributing all our apparent failures to our weakness.

What I have learnt from India might be summed up in that old-fashioned word, 'humility'. Acknowledging the role of fate in our lives; accepting that our knowledge will always be limited; seeking to discuss rather than to dogmatise; appreciating that we need always to be examining ourselves if we are to maintain the desired balance – all these acts surely require humility. Humility, like fate, is a dangerous word in times when success is the prevalent religion and celebrities are its gods. Discussing *India's Unending Journey* with a friend, I mentioned that, all things considered, it was probably a book about humility. She replied, 'That will certainly be counter-cultural!' The copy of the *Oxford Dictionary of the Christian Church* that I bought as a theology student many years ago (and still have) seems to me to describe humility in a way that should offset any fears that I am necessarily talking about a denial of self-esteem. The dictionary says that humility represses 'inordinate ambition and self-esteem without allowing man to fall into the opposite error of exaggerated or hypocritical self-abjection'. In other words, it's a matter of balance. It would be hypocritical of me, and lacking in humility, to say that I have got that balance right in my own life; I can only say that living in India has taught me to be aware of the need to try to get it right.

One of the most moving acknowledgements of the value of humility I have ever read was written by Oscar Wilde, a poet and playwright who was anything but humble before he was found guilty and jailed on a charge of homosexuality. A letter written from jail to the man with whom he had had the homosexual relationship was later published under the title *De Profundis* (Latin for 'from the depths'). In it, Wilde writes of humility being 'hidden away in his nature', but now being:

> ... the last thing left in me and the best: the ultimate discovery at which I have arrived, the starting point for a fresh development. It has come to me right out of myself, so I know that it has come at the proper time. It could not have come before, nor later. Had anyone told me of it, I would have rejected it. Had it been brought to me, I would have refused it. As I found it, I want to keep it.

Humility came to Oscar Wilde; he did not take credit for discovering it.

What I have learnt in India seems to me relevant not only for our personal lives but also for humans as a species. If we had properly cared for balance in the first place, we would not have put nature as seriously out of balance as it is now. If we had been more humble, we would not have treated nature as inferior to us, as a resource for us to use. We would have realised sooner how dependent we are upon it. We must remember that we neither created the system that sustains us, nor do we sustain it.

It may seem contradictory to speak of humility and then write a book in which my own life features. Certainly I have never thought of writing an autobiography because I do not want to give the impression that my life is particularly important. But for the last ten years I have been presenting the Radio Four Programme *Something Understood*. The title is taken from the last line of George Herbert's poem 'Prayer'. In the programme we discuss the boundaries of our understanding . and how certain we can be in life. As a result of *Something Understood*, I have been invited to speak in many different parts of Britain. The reaction of these audiences, the conversations and correspondence I have had with listeners, and the many conversations I have had with my colleagues, who contribute so much to *Something Understood* – particularly my producer for the last ten years, Eley McAinsh – have led me to believe that there is an interest in the ideas discussed in this book. So much of what is written about the way we live our lives is in the third person, and I often want to ask how the ideas put forward have affected the author's life and how they fit into his or her own experience. By writing in the first person, I hope to answer that question and perhaps make my arguments more authentic. It would have felt wrong to me to write in any other way, since I advocate learning from personal experience.

I start with my schooldays because it was at school that I learnt much of what I later had to unlearn in India. I came to believe there was only one way, that life was all about winning and that academic ability was the only index of intelligence. Humility was not a virtue that was encouraged.

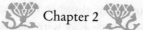 Chapter 2

MARLBOROUGH: AN EDUCATION IN ABSOLUTES

I WAS educated at Marlborough College, a traditional British public school. I returned there recently with Richard Wilkinson, a good friend who shared a study with me in my last year. I had come back to Marlborough with Richard to discuss the impact that the school had made on me. Although I had gone on to Cambridge and then to theological college, I felt sure that I had been most profoundly shaped by my school days. I also wanted Richard to help me determine whether I was justified in looking back on Marlborough in the way I did. Not only had he been very close to me during my time there, but he had ended his teaching career at Marlborough, having earlier been the headmaster of two other schools. Although he had retired from teaching full-time, he still kept in touch with Marlborough by teaching at the summer school there.

Now, the two of us stood in the spacious courtyard, or quadrangle, that lies at the heart of the school. At the far end of the courtyard stands an imposing early eighteenth-century mansion, which was built for the Duke of Somerset and later converted into a coaching inn for passengers travelling from London to Bath. The college then turned this magnificent building into a boarding house for boys and it became known as 'C House'. At the other end of the courtyard, near the gates, stands the college's other notable building, the chapel. Tall, thin and long enough to accommodate nearly nine hundred worshippers, the chapel is an inspiring example of high Victorian Gothic architecture. When I was a boy at Marlborough, we were obliged to go to chapel every day, where we regularly got down on our knees and confessed our sins in the words of the Anglican Prayer Book, begging God 'to have mercy upon us miserable offenders'.

Opposite the chapel is one of the less impressive buildings surrounding the courtyard, a late Victorian block of classrooms. Richard recalled how a scripture teacher had strutted up and down one of those classrooms, with his thumbs in the waistcoat of his tweed suit, bawling at the boys, 'I don't understand all this rot about Christian humility. I'm not humble and I don't have to be. I'm Colonel Harling and I'm a damn fine fellow!'

Marlborough was founded in 1843 for the education of the sons of the clergy, but, in spite of its ecclesiastical origins, it did little to convince me personally that the best way to live life was to 'humble myself in the sight of the Lord', or to be confident that 'He shall lift you up' (James 4.10). Rather, it taught me that life was all about striving to be 'a damn fine fellow' and lifting myself up without help from anyone else. Preposterous though Colonel Harling seems to me now, to my mind he truly represented the ethos of my school years at Marlborough, an ethos in which humility seemed to have little or no place. Success was what counted, and the only successes that really seemed to matter were those that were athletic or academic. What's more, our successes were ascribed entirely to our own efforts. The gifts we had been given at birth, the circumstances of our lives, and the advantages of our earlier education were not taken into account when our achievements were considered.

In spite of its religious tradition, Marlborough also seemed to be a place where learning was confined to the dictates of reason. I didn't come to understand until much later in life what imagination and other forms of perception could teach me. Nor did Marlborough encourage questioning in my experience. Everything was black or white. Religion appeared to be more about morality rather than experiencing God, and the school's particular brand of morality left me with a heavy burden of guilt about my burgeoning sexuality.

I realise that this description of my school days must present a very black picture indeed, and, as I have said, if there is one thing I have learnt from India, it is to appreciate how little in life is totally black or, indeed, purely white. There are many men of my generation who look back with gratitude at Marlborough, and it is certainly in part my own fault that I don't. But all I can do is describe honestly the influences that Marlborough had on me personally. Those influences stayed with me until I began to understand something about Indian philosophy, religion and culture. Indeed, it was partly as a result of the extent to which those influences had unsettled me, destroyed my self-confidence and undermined my religious beliefs that India eventually made such an impact on me. So if I was to write a truthful book about the influence of India in my life, it seemed necessary not only to discuss these earlier influences but also to authenticate them, as I am attempting to do now.

Richard and I started our visit by walking to our old House, which was tucked away in a corner of the courtyard. The Marlborough website describes 'B' house as a square building built around a court. However, I was pleasantly surprised to discover that dark green and black were no longer the dominant colours on the walls and that the ground floor had light, modern furniture. But nothing could disguise the layout of the interior, which reminded me of a prison, with high railings piled floor on floor, surrounding what we pupils had called a 'well' rather than a 'court'. It had seemed like a grim place to live, but – now I thought about it – had life there really been so grim?

Before revisiting Marlborough, I had re-read John Betjeman's long poem 'Summoned by Bells', which is about the poet's childhood and undergraduate days. Luxuriating in his bath and looking back on his days at Marlborough, Betjeman 'reflects in comfortable retrospect':

> ... 'thank God
> I'll never have to go through them again.'
> As with my toes I reach towards the tap,
> And turn it to a trickle, stealing warm
> About my tender person, comes a voice,
> An inner voice that calls, 'Be fair! Be fair!
> It was not quite as awful as you think.'

These words came back to me now as a timely warning about my own memories of my schooldays. 'I must not,' I thought, 'exaggerate their awfulness.' In fact, once I had got over the tears without which I never succeeded in leaving home, I had enjoyed school life. I had been good at being 'one of the lads', aided and abetted by my crude sense of humour. I had never been short of friends, nor had I been over-awed by senior boys. Beatings were unpleasant but – as Betjeman said – 'brought us no disgrace only a kind of glory'.

When I was there, Marlborough had a reputation for being a tough school, but I think it was probably less harsh than many other public schools of the period. When I mentioned this to Richard, he agreed with me. 'I think there is more bullying now,' he said. 'When I was teaching here not so long ago, one poor boy was accused, wrongly, of reporting a senior for coming back drunk and stuffing juniors' heads into the lavatory. He was so badly bullied, had his bed stripped every night and other things, that he left the school.' He continued, 'Sometimes senior boys were bullied too. There was also a case of a boy who was not allowed to work, as his tormentors kept on banging on his door. I put that kind of bad behaviour down to money,' he explained. 'Marlborough's a rich children's school now, but it

wasn't in our days – what with all those sons of badly paid cler-
gymen. Rich boys think they can do anything they like. They
have far less humility.'

'Isn't this part of the whole modern business of worshipping
success?' I wondered. 'Because their fathers are revered for
being rich and successful, the boys think they have the right to
do whatever they like?'

'You know,' Richard sighed, 'I think it also comes back to
what we have often talked about in the past – competition and
the school going in for this encouragement of success.'

Success in our days had always seemed to be very narrowly
defined, such as coming top of the class or being on the first
team. But what about those poor unfortunates who weren't
going to achieve either academic or sporting honours? Richard
agreed with me, reminding me of the lists of marks and places
in classes that used to be read out at the end of term in front
of the whole school. In the case of the lower forms, the
bottom place could be as low as 120th. A friend of ours
often used to come near the bottom of the lists, and Richard
believed that the repeated humiliation of this experience
had gradually destroyed his self-confidence. But Richard
was not criticising healthy competition, nor was he of the
view that results aren't important. He firmly believes that
teachers should encourage children to get the best results
possible.

I had not been in the top flight at Marlborough, even though I
passed the entrance exam well and had initially been put in the
same stream as those who, like Richard, had won scholarships.
Surrounded by my new companions, I was at first ambitious to
win the accolade that was the highest mark of success at
Marlborough: a scholarship in classics at Oxford or Cambridge.
But I was soon told I wasn't up to that. After our first term
specialising in classics, my year was divided into sheep and goats

– fast stream and slow stream. Demoted to the slow stream, I felt that my peers and I had been condemned to failure, and there seemed little point in doing more than the bare minimum of work. In this attitude I was certainly not alone, as our class of goats became renowned for being a bolshy lot. Being bolshy and rebellious became the means through which I established my identity and attempted to satisfy my need to stand out, to have other boys take note of me. I didn't realise that this behaviour was a form of egotism, that finding myself and my own sense of destiny was what should have mattered, not worrying about being judged by others

Richard had timed our visit to coincide with one of the rare compulsory chapel services. The pews run parallel with the nave down the length of the chapel, and we sat in the back row, which was reserved for masters. Above us were plaques displaying the names of those men of whom Marlborough was proud. One of them had been a hero to both Richard and me: Sir Nigel Gresley, Chief Mechanical Engineer of the London–North Eastern Railway. He had designed the streamlined locomotives that pulled the London–Edinburgh expresses, one of which still holds the world speed record for a steam engine.

Pre-Raphaelite paintings of biblical scenes ran along both walls of the chapel. Opposite me, a particularly ferocious Abraham was depicted, his hand raised and his dagger poised over his son Isaac, who was strapped to an altar. A nervous angel fluttered above them. When I was a boy, this picture had added to my confusion about the nature of Christianity. I couldn't understand why God would have wanted Abraham to be so afraid of Him that he was prepared to offer his son as a sacrifice. How could this version of the Almighty tally with a God of love? It already seemed to me then that love and fear did not go together. However, the chapel was nevertheless a place in which

I found a lasting meaning in life. It gave me a faith I have never lost (although I have come near to it) and an abiding love of the Anglican Church and its liturgy.

To me, the liturgy is like poetry. It inspires rather than explains. It is like a mantra too, a permanent and always reliable source of comfort and strength. It was at voluntary evensong on Sundays, the most peaceful service of the week, with a small congregation and a full choir, that I started to understand the strange paradox of liturgy. It is familiar yet awakens a sense of a mystery that is beyond all understanding. In a school where the emphasis was mostly on rational thought, evensong was the one time when it seemed to me that there might be some level of comprehension beyond reason.

In later life, John Betjeman also came to appreciate the liturgy he had absorbed at Marlborough. For him, it was an antidote to a form of religion that was too rational and which put all its emphasis on understanding rather than experiencing. 'With age,' he confided,

> ... I find myself enjoying more and more the words and rhythms of the Book of Common Prayer. Apart from their meaning, they sound right and they are not talking down by being 'matey', and where they are a bit vague and archaic, that makes them grand and historic. The words give me time to meditate and pray; they are so familiar, they are like my birthplace, and I don't want them pulled down.

Seated in the back row with Richard, I was disappointed that this service was not liturgical. I had hoped to hear the familiar words sung, but they were not. There was also something about this particular service that Betjeman might have described as 'matey'. For instance, when I was a pupil, the chaplains used to wait in the vestry until the organist pressed a bell to tell them that everyone was seated and silent. Then they would emerge and process solemnly to their pews. In contrast, this Sunday the chaplains busied themselves in the body of the church, doing I know not what, as the boys and girls straggled in, chattering. The preacher didn't mount the pulpit to preach, but walked up and down the nave, as if he were in conversation with the congregation. The chancel was filled with students seated on ugly red chairs that detracted from its sanctity and the majesty of its golden reredos. But for all this 'mateyness', the boys and girls didn't seem to sing the hymns with the same vigour and assurance as we had done. I thought this was perhaps just an old man's nostalgia, but Richard agreed, saying, 'They don't sing like we did because they think it's not "cool". What's more, they don't have the congregational practices that we had.'

One of the chaplains later explained to me that a liturgical service would have no meaning for those children who only went to chapel when it was compulsory. But then, were those same children were not being given any opportunity to learn to love the liturgy, to acquire a treasure that they might not appreciate at the time but which they would perhaps find valuable in later life? It seemed to me that Marlborough had retreated in the face of the secular onslaught. I couldn't help regretting that a school with such a strong religious tradition did not appear to be putting up a robust fight to save its Anglican inheritance.

When I was young, my understanding of Christianity led me to believe that it was immoral not be a socialist. So when we used to sing the popular hymn 'All Things Bright and Beautiful' in chapel, I was offended by the suggestion that 'the rich man in his castle, the poor man at his gate, God made them, high or lowly and ordered their estate'. Surely it was the rich man's greed that had made the poor man poor, and it was our duty as Christians to ensure that the poor man would no longer have to sit around outside his gate waiting for the crumbs from his table.

My socialism was also, I admit, another rebellion against

what I felt was the dominant ethos of the school, and as such it became something that gave me an identity and made me stand out from most of the other boys, who were Conservatives. During the 1950 general election, the school held a mock election and we socialists barely got into double figures. I took my socialism home with me, telling my father it was unjust that I went to an expensive boarding school while most of the boys where we lived had to go to the village school. He was not amused and would tell me angrily, 'You don't appreciate the sacrifice I've made to send all of you children to good schools!' As there were six of us, my father's sacrifice was considerable, but I am afraid I didn't take that into account.

On leaving school I was conscripted into the army for two years' National Service, during which I was commissioned, much to my surprise. But that achievement did not remove my sense of inadequacy and I remained a rebel. My socialism gave me the doctrine to justify my actions, and the privileges of an officer gave me yet another cause to rebel against. I defied the tradition of drinking fine wines on mess nights and made a point of ordering beer, which was regarded as the working man's drink. There were very many other minor and, in retrospect, rather stupid rebellions, but the Adjutant only gave up on me when I wrote an essay claiming that the morale problems of the army would be solved if the distinction between soldiers and officers was abolished. The Adjutant returned my essay with 'The red flag flies ...' scrawled in red ink at the bottom of the page.

But for all my socialist arguments, it never occurred to me to rebel against going to public school during the time that I was there, nor later to refuse my commission on the grounds that there shouldn't be any officers. I took my privileges as my destiny. I had been born the son of a man who had become comparatively rich through hard work. I therefore took it for granted that a private education and army commissions were what happened to boys like me. At Marlborough we were not taught to be grateful for our privileges; instead, most boys simply accepted without question that they had a right to their education and the social status that went with it. We were not taught to be grateful for our talents, either. We were not reminded that we had been given those talents, nor that, although we may have nurtured them, we hadn't created them. The competition and the emphasis on success bolstered our belief that our achievements were all our own doing. However, the tragic reverse of this was that many boys felt that their lack of success was all their own fault and gave up trying, as I had in classics.

I now think of life as a hand of cards that we are dealt. We can't change our hand but we can play it either well or badly. Knowing how misunderstood the concept of fate is, I asked Richard whether he thought this idea was nonsense. 'Not nonsense at all,' he said. 'It's profoundly true. The old Calvinist doctrine of pre-destination has a lot of truth in it. What we get from our birth and our parents we have no right to be proud about or indeed feel any guilt about.' He quoted a Methodist scholar who had come to speak to one of his classes and told them that ninety-five per cent of life was predestined and only five per cent influenced by free will, but that five per cent was 'jolly important'.

Richard's personal views on destiny had been reinforced by his experiences as a visitor to a young offenders' prison, 'I see boys there,' he explained, 'banged up for committing crimes that are sometimes really deplorable – violence, sex, a lot of drugs. They come from homes where, almost invariably, there has never been a father. Many of them have never had a home at all. Many of them are not very bright. Part of my job is to write letters for them because they are illiterate. I find it very helpful, and I hope I get this right when I reflect on what an appalling deal they have had. I don't condone their actions, but compared to my good fortune, they've had a miserable deal. When you reflect on why they are that way it makes you realise the extent to which we are all victims of our fate.'

Although Marlborough was a religious foundation, it was also a school of the Enlightenment. All the emphasis in the teaching was on reason. When it came to religion, the arguments for the existence of God were emphasised. It was a given that anything that could not be supported by reason had to be taken on trust. We were told that faith bridged the gap. But that faith was primarily a faith in the authority of the Church, accepting what it taught – a faith imposed from outside, not the faith that grows within. There was little or no mention of experiencing God personally, which later in life I was to appreciate as being so important. However, while at school I was inspired by the palpable goodness of the Chaplain, John Miller, and comforted by the kindness he showed me. He allowed me to see him whenever I liked and helped me to wrestle with my confusion and self-doubt. But I don't remember talking to him about experiencing God.

We were told to accept the authority of the Church in chapel, and in the classroom we were told to accept the teacher as the absolute authority. Marlborough was, as I have said, a school of the Enlightenment, but we were not encouraged to reason or to work things out for ourselves. We were instructed rather than taught. Almost all my teachers gave me the impression that there was only one answer to every question, and that was the answer they gave. All I had to do was to learn that answer and reproduce it correctly when tested.

In that same block of classrooms in which Richard had been taught scripture, the suave Frank Shaw had dictated notes on ancient history to our class, notes which we had to learn by heart. He kept a gym shoe in the drawer of his desk for beating anyone whose Latin or Greek prose contained a careless mistake. In the room above his classroom sat one of Marlborough's great eccentrics, Geoff Chilton, who seemed to revel in being a caricature of a school master. He taught Homer, but the teaching was all about the great poet's grammar. The beauty of Homer's poetry barely got a mention. When Chilton gave us a grammar test there was always what he called 'a face-slap question', which would be a trap. If a boy got the answer wrong, the bulky Geoff Chilton would squeeze onto the bench beside him and administer a sharp face slap or pinch his bottom. Year after year Chilton set the same test each week, until our lack-lustre class stupidly put up such a remarkable performance that he realised we must have asked the previous year what the test for the week was going to be. 'Oh, you are a lot of sods!' he sobbed.

Richard's own teaching experience has shown him that it is the teachers whose lessons children enjoy that get the good results. There were, indeed, masters at Marlborough whose classes I did enjoy, but unfortunately I was only taught by them briefly. For the most part I had teachers such as Frank Shaw and Geoff Chilton, who did not encourage straying beyond the text book or reading for ourselves. Therefore I didn't learn to take my own notes. I always crammed for exams, which fortunately I had a knack of passing. That was how I got into Cambridge, which was much easier in those days. But when I went up to my college I found myself wholly unprepared for the essays that my supervisors asked me to write. For the first time, I had to read for myself, take my own notes and balance arguments rather than repeat facts.

Although Richard had won a scholarship to Marlborough, he too felt that he had not been particularly well prepared at school for using his powers of reasoning, which was what was required at Cambridge. But now, looking back on his career, he doesn't think Marlborough was worse than many other schools. 'The fine line between instructing rather than teaching is a perpetual problem for teachers,' he said. 'After all, good teachers know what they are talking about and children are there to learn, so in a sense it's a bit like Christ preaching to the disciples in the Sermon on the Mount. But on the whole instructing is inefficient teaching and, what's worse, it discourages any form of disagreement.'

Since in our school there was only one answer to every question, it is probably not surprising that I never considered there might be other ways to God than Christianity. Yet I couldn't understand how, if Jesus was right in saying, 'I am the way, the truth, and the life. No man cometh unto the Father but by me', that way was not always clear and that truth not certain. I had been educated to believe in facts, in certainties, in a sharp divide between truth and untruth. However, in the 1950s scientists, historians and theologians themselves were casting more and more doubt upon the story of Jesus as told in the Gospels and its interpretation in the Epistles. Science particularly worried me. I thought of it as entirely factual, based on certainties, and I dreaded the possibility, as I saw it, that scientists would prove Christianity was untrue and there was no God.

It was only when I went to Cambridge and was taught by the Dean of Trinity College, Harry Williams, one of the most influential spiritual writers of the twentieth century, that I began to understand that it was experience, rather than learning, and the heart, rather than the head, that deepened trust in God. In her introduction to the recent edition of Harry Williams' collection of sermons called *The True Wilderness*, the novelist Susan Howatch writes: 'He could only preach what he had personally experienced.' In his own introduction, Harry Williams wrote: 'Christian truth, in other words, must be in the blood as well as the brain. If it is only in the brain, it is without life, and powerless to save.' Marlborough was all about brain, and so it's not surprising that my early Christianity lacked blood.

*

My blood added to my confusion about Christianity at Marlborough. We were told that all sexual activity outside marriage was a sin. One evening the headmaster went round every house to announce that he had expelled a boy for homosexuality, as though homosexuality were the cardinal of the cardinal sins. The only education we were given in sexuality that Richard can remember was when the headmaster told leavers, 'It's not clever to go to brothels.' I was acutely aware that Jesus had warned, 'Whosoever looks on a woman to lust after her hath committed adultery already with her in his heart.' But nevertheless I committed adultery in my heart many times a day when I looked at girls. I suppose that, although an Anglican, I suffered from what is often called 'Catholic neurosis'. I was told that Jesus had died to save sinners but I was obsessed with my sin.

It would be unfair to Marlborough today to suggest that it is the same school now as it was fifty years ago. These days, Marlborough accepts girls, which must make a great difference. It is less sexually repressive. Richard said any teacher who suggested, as we were taught, that people should remain virgins until they marry would be treated with contempt by the class. And, although in the old days beatings could bring glory, it can't be argued that their disappearance is regrettable. But Richard said Marlborough was just as competitive and less tolerant of eccentricity than it had been. There was more pressure to conform.

I first went to boarding school at the age of five, and remained incarcerated until I was eighteen. From school I went into the army, which was not so very different. So it was not until I reached Cambridge that, for the first time, I began to live a life that was not institutionalised. Just as I had to begin to read and reason for myself at Cambridge, so I had to learn to make my own decisions. A boarding-school education is said to make children independent. In my case it didn't because so many decisions were taken for me. Perhaps it is not surprising then, that I was swept off my feet by that first experience of freedom as an undergraduate. Looking back on it, maybe my behaviour was no more outrageous than that of many other young men who feel that they have been let loose at last when they reach university.

At college I was torn between wanting to appear outrageous and wanting to prepare myself for a career in the Church. In spite of my upset at being grouped among the goats for my classics lessons, Marlborough's competitive spirit had imbued in me an urge to shine and to be a success. I still measured success at university in academic terms, but my failure to be in the top class at school had already destroyed my self-confidence and I didn't believe I had any chance of getting a first class degree. At Cambridge, my supervisor's reaction to my first essay persuaded me yet again that I had no idea how to achieve academic success. So I reverted to the role that had at least got me noticed at Marlborough, the role of a rebel.

This time, my rebellion took the form of establishing a reputation for myself as a drinker. This reputation was enhanced when I came back late one night after a heavy session at our regular haunt, Morley's Wine Bar, also renowned for its beer. Finding myself locked out of the college, I got stuck on a spike while trying to climb over the college walls and tore the flesh off my calf. The accident got me admitted to hospital and featured in the university newspaper.

But I still believed I had a calling to be an Anglican Priest and attended the college chapel regularly. I also experimented with the many other traditions of Anglicanism available in Cambridge. I rejected the call to be saved at an evangelical service and came down on the High Church side of the fence. So there I was – a notorious drinker yet a regular churchgoer, a recipe for inner conflict.

The conflict was deepened by my religious doubts. Marlborough's rationalism had left me with the need to be convinced that God existed but tormented by the thought that no proof was available. The 1950s was a time when it was widely believed that science disproved not only the existence of God. Metaphysics was also still reeling under the attack of the 'logical positivists', who insisted on empirical evidence before verifying a statement. Moreover, Don Cupitt, an Anglican priest and Cambridge theologian, had founded a school of theology known as 'The Sea of Faith', which seemed to write off God too. I remember my tutor, Robert Runcie, who went on to be Archbishop of Canterbury, saying that some priests thought being the Dean of a college was a cushy number, but they didn't realise how lonely a Cambridge Common Room could be for a Christian at that time.

To add to my confusion, Cambridge was the first opportunity I had to acquire a girl friend, but I was afraid of women. Marlborough had left me with the feeling that my sexual urge was evil and that women would be disgusted by my desires. So I was tormented by the frustration of that urge, compounded by a sense of guilt which was deepened by the drinking. Yet the ambition to become a priest and my love of the Church would not go away. I became like the Indian philosopher-poet Bhatrihari, popularly believed to have been a king, who is said to have renounced the world seven times in order to enter a monastery, only to return to his wife and his pleasures six times. He wrote one hundred poems in praise of erotic love, one hundred poems in praise of a prudent worldly life and one hundred poems on renunciation.

Like Bhatrihari, I too finally entered a monastic institution. Although the battle between the Bible and bottle had not yet been decided in my life, Bob Runcie supported me through Cambridge in spite of all my rebelliousness, and agreed that I should go to Lincoln Theological College after I graduated.

There were a few married students in Lincoln Theological College but the majority of us lived what was essentially a monastic life. The days passed in work and regular worship, and we had little freedom. I did, however, lead the party that found time to visit the Adam and Eve pub most evenings, but that didn't particularly strain my conscience. What did was my sense of sexual conflict, which was heightened by the conviction that real priests did not marry.

Although at Lincoln it was sex rather than drink that caused me to doubt my ability to lead the life of a priest, those doubts were finally resolved by a spectacular drinking accident. I had met one of my closest Cambridge drinking friends, Victor Forrington, in a Lincoln pub at lunchtime. Vic merrily assured me that there was no danger of my getting legless because the pubs had to close at two o'clock. But I think he had deliberately chosen the Market Pub as our venue, because it was market day, which meant that the pub was allowed to stay open all afternoon. The result was that I arrived back in time for evensong, if not legless, then distinctly the worse for wear. After this episode, the Bishop of Lincoln told me he thought I would be more at home in a public house than a pulpit. So I ended my academic career with a sense of failure and, like that other old Marlburian John Betjeman, turned to the last resort of young men with indifferent degrees and no career plans: Gabbitas, Thring and Company's scholastic agency. Like Betjeman, I too became a temporary schoolmaster.

Nearly fifty years after leaving university and theological college I naturally regret that I didn't experience the excitement of learning there. After all, I would be much more learned now if I had. But, strangely, I am now grateful for the confusion in my mind as a young man and my sense of failure. Without them I might have been content with myself and perhaps not so open to new influences. I might have spent my time in India as a foreigner, as an expatriate, instead of developing an interest in the country that has become a lifelong passion, keeping me there long after my retirement from the BBC.

Richard's difficulties at Marlborough and Cambridge were less acute than mine, but, I wonder, if he had been a prefect at Marlborough as he had wanted to be, or got the first he was certainly worthy of at Cambridge, would he have had such sympathy with the children he taught later, particularly the less obviously gifted ones? The writer-priest Harry Williams was able to preach only from experience – rather than repeat what he had been taught – after he had passed through his personal wilderness, which took the form of a nervous breakdown that was so devastating he couldn't preach in his college chapel at all for two years. Only then did he realise that he had been using religion 'as an attempted escape from the ambiguities and anxieties which belong inevitably to being human'.

The immediate result of my education was a sense of failure and a closed mind. I still prized academic achievement above all else and I had not achieved it. I still believed in the utter supremacy of reason but feared that it would disprove the existence of God and so destroy the Church, and its liturgy, which I loved.

It was India that truly opened my mind, that led me to value experience as well as reason, and that taught me the experience of God is so widespread I need not fear the death of religion. But above all it was India that taught me to see my failures and achievements in context, to value humility, to suspect certainties and to seek for the middle path. So how might the lessons India has taught me be relevant to the way we all live? That is what I am going to discuss next.

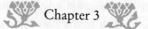 Chapter 3

DELHI: AN INDIAN UNDERSTANDING

WE who live in the Indian capital are always being scornfully told that Delhi isn't India. It certainly isn't, but then nowhere *is* India. India is far too large and diverse a nation for any city or region to claim that privilege. The vast Indian metropolitan cities all vary enormously. Mumbai is all about money; Kolkata, which was once all about making money too, is not really a commercial city anymore but a strange amalgam of Marxist influences and the last vestiges of the British Raj. Chennai, or Madras as it used to be known, has a sober south Indian culture which is less concerned with moneymaking than with the old-fashioned virtues of manufacturing. Bangalore is the IT capital of India.

But what to say about Delhi? When a sordid political coup ended the veteran Gandhian Morarji Desai's s brief Premiership and he finally gave up politics, he said, 'I will never come back to Delhi again. It's a city of thieves and thugs.' There is some truth in those words – Delhi is indeed a city of politicians, bureaucrats and *dalals*, or agents, who broker deals with the former, and their dealings are often unsavoury. But Delhi is much more than that. It has a history stretching back, we are told, almost 3,500 years to the days of the great Hindu epic, the *Mahabharata*. Compared with that past, the other metropolitan cities are all upstarts. But, as far as I am concerned, the most important thing about Delhi is that it's been my home for nearly forty years now, the home in which I discovered the India that has changed me. I know that Mahatma Gandhi said village India is the real India – and that is one reason why I have travelled far and wide – but I have always returned to Delhi, so I suppose Delhi is my India.

What a vast difference there is between the Delhi I first came to know in 1965 and Delhi today. There has been a population explosion. Whereas about three million people used to live in Delhi when I first came there, now it has some 13 million citizens – and probably many more than that if you include the new towns that have sprung up adjacent to the capital. In the sixties Delhi was still an old-fashioned city, a city of cyclists, horse-drawn transport and carts pulled by bullocks that plodded sedately along the streets, oblivious to all the noisy protests from speedier traffic. There was only one permanent bridge across the river Yamuna, an old double-decker iron construction with clanking trains on the top and traffic jams underneath. One of the first traffic jams I experienced on that bridge was caused by a cart so overloaded that it had tipped backwards, lifting the horse off his front legs. There wasn't a department store in the city, let alone a shopping mall. The central shopping area, Connaught Circus (now renamed Rajiv Chowk), was still surrounded by bungalows. The government's Ashoka Hotel, a sprawling, red sandstone building in the heart of diplomatic Delhi, was the only hotel that could be called five star. Today, the animals have almost entirely disappeared from the streets of Delhi, except for stray dogs and the occasional cow wandering in the middle of the road in search of newspaper to chew, or the odd elephant padding to a hotel, a wedding, a temple festival or anywhere else she will be welcome and earn money for her *mahout*. Connaught Circus is now surrounded by high-rise buildings and Delhi is a modern city with plenty of five star hotels and highways, shopping malls, headquarters of multinational companies and – at last – the beginnings of a metro railway. Delhi has changed and I have inevitably changed with it.

In 1965, I arrived in Delhi feeling insecure both within myself and in my career. The discovery that I didn't have a vocation to be a priest had left a vacuum in my life that had not yet been filled. I was still floundering around, trying to discover an alternative vocation. The chip that my academic career had bequeathed me still sat firmly on my shoulder. I hadn't discovered any other talent that could compensate me for my feelings of inadequacy. I still clung to the religious certainties I had learnt during my education, regarding them as absolutes and being unwilling to yield an inch, and I felt threatened when they were challenged. The merest suggestion of a chink in my intellectual armour threatened my whole position.

One of the friends I have remained closest to since leaving Cambridge remains Victor Forrington, who once persuaded me to spend an afternoon drinking in Lincoln. Yet in our college days and for years afterwards we used to have quite bitter arguments about the existence of God. Vic was a mathematician and maintained that it was scientifically impossible to believe in God, whereas I desperately wanted to adhere to my belief. But in my heart of hearts I feared his arguments were much stronger because he understood science and I did not. The more shaky I felt, the angrier I got.

Now that India has taught me the uncertainty of certainty, I no longer feel threatened when my beliefs are challenged, because I don't believe science, theology, philosophy or any other discipline has the final answers to questions about the meaning of life and the existence of God. I realise that we have to discuss with those who have other points of view, not block our ears as I used to do in those arguments with Vic. I learnt this open-mindedness in Delhi.

When I landed in Delhi all those years ago, I was driven to Claridges Hotel. I had been warned not to expect the luxury of the famous London hotel of that name, but I was agreeably surprised to find that for the first time in my life I was staying in a room with my own bathroom. My room had a small balcony, or verandah, too. When I went out onto the verandah I breathed in the smoke from a cow-dung stove on which the gardeners were cooking their lunch. This smell was mingled with the strong scent of marigolds and the whole of my Kolkata childhood flashed through my mind. Afterwards I could only think of describing the experience as akin to watching an express train shoot through a station at full speed. Smell is the most powerful of the senses when it comes to reviving memories, and standing there on the verandah had revived my memories of our garden in Kolkata and the servants' cow-dung stoves there. I suddenly felt I had come home. After some years, I came to realise that this incident was the first sign that India was meant to play a special role in my life.

A few weeks later, it was Christmas and I went to midnight mass in the Anglican Cathedral. After Independence in 1947 the Anglicans in South India united with the Methodists and some other Protestant Churches to form the Church of South India. By that Christmas of 1965 negotiations for a similar union in North India were well under way. These unions were based on a compromise reached through the Indian tradition of dialogue and discussion, of listening and learning from each other, and it's now some sixty years since they were agreed. In contrast, Anglicans and Methodists in England have still not come together.

The yellow sandstone cathedral was constructed in the dying days of the Raj, after the capital had been moved to Delhi from Kolkata. The building owes a lot to Lord Irwin, the Viceroy between 1926 and 1931, who has been described as a man of 'singular and exemplary piety'. He not only raised funds for the cathedral but often came to check on the progress of the builders and to discuss the plans with the architect. As the Viceroy was an Anglo-Catholic, he was particularly pleased that the cathedral was designed for the High Church tradition of worship. Judging by the building's gloomy interior, its lofty roof and its altar distanced from the congregation by a long chancel, the architect clearly intended that the emphasis of worship in it would be on mystery, on the transcendental, and with particular reverence for the sacrament.

Although the Church of North India was on the verge of a merger which Anglo-Catholics in Britain criticised for sacrificing certain basic Catholic principles to reach a compromise with the Protestants, I think that Lord Irwin would still have found much that was familiar in that midnight mass of 1965. The sense of mystery was preserved, with the priest celebrating the mass in sparkling white and gold vestments, and clouds of fragrant incense pouring from the censer vigorously swung by an acolyte. However, I was surprised to see turban-wearing Sikhs, as well as Hindus, among the congregation packed into the cathedral. I had come from a Britain where my Roman Catholic friends would never attend a service with me, and I had rarely been to any service that was not Anglican. It was obvious that not only were Christians of different denominations welcome in Delhi's cathedral but also those who were not Christians at all. Rather than the consecrated wafer and wine, these individuals were given a blessing when they came up to the altar rails. But that did not always satisfy them. A priest told me later that he had had a prayer book thrown at him once when he refused communion to a non-Christian. And on another occasion that same priest gave in when a Hindu came to the altar rails for a second time and begged for a wafer, saying, 'I need it, I need it, I must have it!' It is understandable that Hindus and Sikhs should expect to receive the Christian sacraments when they visit churches and cathedrals, as everyone who visits their temples and *gurudwaras* is offered *prasad*, or food that has been blessed, and it would be an insult not to accept it.

The multi-faith congregation at that midnight mass was my first indication of India's religious pluralism and enthusiasm for the festivals of all faiths. But where did that tradition come from? To find out I was advised to read a short book by Dr Sarvepalli Radhakrishnan, who was then President of India. As an undergraduate he had studied at Madras Christian College where, even though he knew that Christian priests would be among his examiners, he had written a thesis refuting the claim that Christ was unique. Radhakrishnan had gone on to enjoy a distinguished university career, which had included holding the Chair of Eastern Religions and Ethics at Oxford. He was a formidable academic and, although academics are not always known for accessible writing, I found his short book, *The Hindu View of Life*, easy to read. Indeed, it subsequently had a profound impact on me, helping me to overcome my early prejudices.

When I was a child in Kolkata, my parents had always told us that Muslims were like us because they believed in one God, yet Hindus were 'beyond the pale'. Not only did they believe in many gods but they worshipped idols. Idolatry is, of course, a practice that is specifically forbidden in the Ten Commandments. So I was bought up to believe that Hinduism was a contemptible religion. Sometimes I saw the processions at the end of the great Durga Puja festival winding through the streets of Kolkata on their way to immerse the goddess in the river Hooghly. To my young eyes, the multi-coloured images of the goddess Durga riding on her tiger appeared gaudy, garish and terrifying. The shouting and the bands, a chaotic cacophony, alarmed me, and I was intimidated by the ecstatic devotees. Fear of Hinduism lodged itself in my mind.

When I came back to India I brought my childhood prejudices against Hinduism with me. However, as I quickly made Hindu friends, I realised there was nothing to be afraid of in Hinduism and that the religion could not be contemptible if so many good and intelligent people subscribed to it. But Hinduism still seemed so diverse and so different from Semitic religions – and in particular from those precise Christian certainties I had been taught – that I thought I would never be able to get my head round it. Radhakrishnan's *The Hindu View of Life* first persuaded me it was worth having a try, so I regard the book with a particular affection and always recommend it to anyone who comes to India wanting to learn more about Hinduism.

In his book, Radhakrishnan explains that Hinduism does not demand the kind of certainty that had always troubled me so much about Christianity, as I understood it. He says there has never been 'a uniform, stationary, unalterable Hinduism whether in belief or in practice' and he describes Hinduism as 'a movement, not a position; a process not a result; a growing tradition, not a fixed revelation'. Because it was not fixed there could be no certainty and the possibility of further development must always be allowed. But, even so, Radhakrishnan warns against thinking that 'Hindus doubted the reality of a supreme universal spirit'. Rather, Hindus accept that there can be many descriptions of this spirit and that none is complete. That is why in the *Brhad-ananyaka Upanishad* those two words *neti, neti*, which I mentioned in Chapter 1, are repeatedly added after a description of the supreme spirit or reality. Radhakrishnan translates *neti* as meaning 'not this'. But, as I have mentioned, my friend the Sanskrit scholar Chaturvedi Badrinath always insists it should be translated as 'not yet complete', 'not this alone', because the word *neti* implies that we can never come to a final and complete definition of God, the ultimate reality or the supreme universal spirit – call it what you will.

But here I have to be careful. When I was discussing this chapter with another Sanskrit scholar, Chakravarthi Ram-Prasad, he said, 'I don't really agree with your concept of Hinduism's suspicion of certainty. Hindus are often very certain they are right and others are wrong. What they do say, however, is that their certainty is not necessarily the only certainty.

Although, of course, even then, with the variety of Hindusim, there are some who would insist that their certainty is a better explanation than any other.'

I replied, 'But saying yours is not the only certainty is so far removed from the certainty of the Semitic religions, from the "Jesus is the only way" form of Christianity I was taught, that it seems to me to be – if not a suspicion of certainty – a denial of it.'

'Well, I can see your argument,' Ram conceded, 'and I can certainly see where you are coming from. However, I'd be more cautious than you are when you talk of Hindu suspicion of certainty. But I agree that Hindu pluralism does require a degree of humility and that is one of the themes of your book.'

Hinduism doesn't have a monopoly on pluralism. It is part of the general Indian tradition of questioning, discussion, dissent and indeed scepticism that Amartya Sen describes in his book *The Argumentative Indian*. Pluralism is a characteristic of all the major religions born in India, but it was through my interest in Mahatma Gandhi, and through reading Radhakrishnan's work, that I first came to be aware of it. Since then, Hinduism has been the Indian religion I have read and talked most about. Without wanting to venture into arguments about what exactly constitutes Hinduism or to what extent the foundational culture of India is Hindu, because eighty per cent of the people living in India today are classified as Hindus, and culturally it is the dominant religion in India today, *India's Unending Journey* is inevitably a book in which Hinduism takes centre stage.

To my mind, pluralism involves humility. It means acknowledging that you don't have the complete or final answer, that what you know may *seem* right, but there are other points of view. That is where the controversial word 'compromise' comes in. I was taught to believe that compromise was a dirty word, smacking of cowardice, but that was not Mahatma Gandhi's point of view. While I was making a radio programme about the Mahatma in South Africa, more than one South African told me with pride, 'Indians say we gave you Gandhi, and we say we gave you back a Mahatma.' When Gandhi arrived in South Africa he was an unsuccessful lawyer. When he left twenty-one years later, the prominent South African Boer politician Jan Christian Smuts said: 'The saint has left our shores. I sincerely hope forever.'

Gandhi's road to sainthood started with his first case in South Africa, which was resolved by a compromise. From then on Gandhi came to believe that the purpose of a lawyer was not to defeat an opponent, not to score a victory, but to make peace between two factions at war with each other. He later said, 'The very insistence on truth has taught me to appreciate the beauty of compromise. I saw in later life that this spirit was an essential part of *satyagraha* [non-violent resistance].'

Early on in my own career I believed I was fighting for principles and didn't even consider the possibility of compromise. For four happy years I promoted the work of the Abbeyfield Society, which was a new organisation that pioneered housing for old people by integrating them into their neighbourhoods to prevent loneliness. But there was tension between the director of the charity, who wanted the society to expand as fast as possible, and the founder, Richard Carr-Gomm. Richard was afraid that the unique principles he had laid down for Abbeyfield were being sacrificed in the hurry to provide more and more housing. The director complained to the committee that Richard was preventing him running the society in a business-like manner. The committee supported him and sacked Richard. I and the two other regional directors for England resigned in protest. At the time, taking this course of action seemed to me to be a matter of principle. Nowadays I am much more suspicious when people start talking about 'matters of principle'. Had my colleagues and I been less certain that right was entirely on one side we might have been able to act as brokers and persuade Richard and the director to reach a compromise.

I see my journalistic career as an example of another lesson India has taught me about humility and accepting uncertainty – the importance of acknowledging the role of fate in our lives. I am often told, not asked, in India: 'You must have always wanted to be a journalist.' But I have to acknowledge that I never intended to become one. I am also told: 'You must have come back to India because you wanted to return to the land of your birth', and I have to admit that I never thought of returning until there seemed no alternative. If, after my experience on the verandah that first day when I returned to the country, I had not somehow stuck to the belief that my destiny lay in India, I might not have had a career at all.

It was fate rather than any deliberate effort on my part that had brought me back to India. I managed to move from the Abbeyfield to the BBC because of a chance vacancy in the personnel department. The tattered remnant of my vocation to the priesthood led me to think that personnel might involve caring for people and would prove to be the career for me. But it soon became clear that the job was more to do with files and application forms and was not the career for me at all. So when the assistant representative in the Delhi office fell ill and had to be flown home, I applied for his post. In spite of my knowledge of Hindi being limited to nursery rhymes, I got the job.

It soon became apparent that yet again my career had gone down a dead end. I found that the job of assistant representative was a non-job. One of my few responsibilities was supervising the office accounts. But they were always prepared for me by Harbans Lal, who had already been working as the office accountant for years and had no need of my help. When my father left Kolkata and joined a company in Britain he would often say, 'My *babus* in India did the work of six people here and did it much better!' Lal Sahib possessed all the qualities that my father had admired in his juniors, and all I had to do was to sign off the paperwork.

My boss, Mark Dodd, encouraged me to fill my time by learning about broadcasting and to make my first broadcast. It was a radio feature on the annual vintage car rally in Delhi. The feature included a champagne breakfast with the Maharaja of Bharatpur – which was probably what sold it to the audience. The Maharajas have always fascinated Indians and Westerners. From then on, I gradually expanded my broadcasting activities and moved into journalism.

Accepting the role of fate in life can, of course, lead to fatalism, and needs to be balanced by accepting the role of free will as well. I was not encouraged to find that balance by the competitive, individualistic culture I was brought up in. Maintaining that balance also requires an understanding of the importance of experience, something I was not taught to develop by my rationalist education.

The importance of experience was brought home to me by Radhakrishnan, who wrote: 'In Hinduism, intellect is subordinated to intuition, dogma to experience, outer expression to inner reality.' Radhakrishnan's stress on experience sent me back to the Christian theologian Harry Williams, who taught me at Cambridge. I re-read his collection of sermons, *The True Wilderness*, in which he said he could only preach what he had experienced and warned that 'Christian truth must be in the blood as well as the brain'. In the first sermon, Harry Williams describes two sorts of truth, an outer truth and an inner truth. The outer truth is 'all that knowledge we acquire, our intellectual capital. It's our property over which we have complete control'. The inner truth 'has a life of its own and can therefore sweep in upon us in ways we can not control'. Harry Williams gave an example of the difference between the two.

Take for instance something of superlative beauty – music, painting or what you will. We can indeed study and master its outside truth - how it is constructed - how it is related to what has gone before and so forth. But its reality eludes us altogether unless it penetrates us and evokes from us a response we can't help giving.

For me the most superlative beauty has always been the beauty of nature. The awesome Himalayas; even in bustling, worldly Mumbai, the sight of the sun setting over the Arabian sea; the wild moorland country of Yorkshire – all sometimes overpower me. Their magnificence makes me feel infinitely small. Such beauty diminishes all human achievement, yet at the same time it affords me a sense of being part of something very real, though way beyond my comprehension. At times I feel certain it's the grandeur of God that has overcome me.

I have talked to many other people who have been overcome at one time or another by the magnificence of nature. All have felt profoundly humbled by the experience. Of course, by no means do all of them believe they are experiencing the grandeur of God, and some say I only believe that because I want to have my faith in God confirmed. That may be true, but unlike some modern theologians I don't think wanting to believe in God necessarily means God is merely a figment of my imagination. All I can say is that these experiences stay with me and confirm my belief in someone or something that I can only describe as God. The Jesuit poet Gerard Manley Hopkins was a keen observer of nature. These first lines of his poem 'The Grandeur of God' indicate that nature inspired in him if not necessarily an experience of God's glory, certainly a sense of it:

> The world is charged with the grandeur of God.
> It will flame out, like the shining of shook foil.
> It gathers to a greatness, like the ooze of oil
> Crushed. Why do men then now not reck his rod?

Hopkins goes on to speak of the damage that men have inflicted on nature by not 'recking God's rod', by not respecting Him and nature. He ends with the confident assertion that for all this damage 'nature is never spent'. And why?

> Because the Holy Ghost over the bent
> World broods with warm breast and with ah! bright wings.

Sacred buildings saturated with the devotion – with the worship, the prayers, and petitions – of centuries also bring me a sense of the presence of God. I have felt that presence in Britain's great cathedrals, with what a priest once described to me as 'their prayer-soaked walls', and in sacred buildings of other religions in India.

To me, the most evocative sacred place in India is the Golden Temple in Amritsar, the Sikh's holy city. I experience a particular serenity there, with the singing of Sikh hymns floating across the lake in which the Golden Temple stands, the steady stream of pilgrims flowing around the marble pavement that surrounds the lake, the elderly Sikh priests, with their long white beards, reading the Sikh scriptures, and the shining white marble of the Akal Takht, the shrine opposite the Golden Temple. Pilgrims form an orderly queue – a rare occurrence in India – to cross the causeway to the Golden Temple itself. Inside, there is none of the pushing, shoving and incessant chatter that are a common feature of many other Indian shrines.

I was therefore appalled by what I saw as a member of the first press party to be escorted into the Golden Temple after 'Operation Blue Star' in the summer of 1984. The Indian army had stormed the shrine's precincts and killed the Sikh separatist leader Sant Jarnail Singh Bhindranwale, who had taken control of all the buildings and turned the Akal Takht into a fortress. The hymn singing had been silenced and there wasn't a Sikh priest or a pilgrim in sight. Instead, the whole complex was in the hands of the army. There were blood stains on the marble pavements, and the white walls were peppered with bullet holes. The library, containing invaluable manuscripts including copies of the Sikh scriptures, the *Guru Granth Sahib,* handwritten by some of the Gurus themselves, was a charred ruin. But most shocking of all was the state of the Akal Takht. The army had brought tanks into the precincts, crushing the marble pavement and pounding the shrine with squash-head shells. The whole frontage of the building had been blasted; every room seemed to be blackened by fire; and marble inlay and other precious decorations had been destroyed. The army hadn't even cleared away the empty shells that carpeted the rooms where Bhindranwale and his colleagues had put up their last stand. Only the Golden Temple itself seemed to have been saved from the devastation. But India has a great capacity for absorbing catastrophe, and the Golden Temple has since regained its sanctity, as any sensitive visitor will discover.

I personally find it comforting to sense the presence of God in sacred places such as the Golden Temple, or in the awesome beauty of nature. But Harry Williams makes it clear that this presence is not necessarily comforting. Opening ourselves up to the experience of God can involve confronting unsettling elements of ourselves or, as Harry Williams phrased it, make 'me meet sides of myself I prefer to ignore'. The experience can also make demands on us that we don't readily want to accept. In the Christian tradition, Jesus did not want to be crucified; he wasn't a sort of superman for whom even that terrible form of punishment held no fear. During one period of my life, I resolutely refused to meet sides of myself I preferred to ignore, or to meet demands I knew I should meet. But those experiences of God still occurred and kept the embers of my faith glowing.

But I have to be careful not to let my own belief in the importance of personally experiencing God run away with me. I don't want to give the impression that mystical experience is all that counts and that reason has no relevance to religion. I feel it is important to be able to offer some rational arguments to counter the widespread belief that religion is irrational and therefore incredible, that it should be able to stand up to scientific scrutiny but that it cannot.

Mind you, I have often found that those using such arguments forget that science itself does not make discoveries purely by means of scientists exercising their powers of reasoning. Science makes progress through uncertain steps; it doesn't proceed from certainty to certainty but out of hypotheses that spring from intuition and which are then explored through experiments. (And even when those experiments appear to confirm the original hypotheses, this by no means necessarily means that definite conclusions can be drawn from them.) Einstein once wrote: 'The fairest thing we can experience is the mysterious. It is the fundamental emotion which stands at the cradle of true art and true science.' Of course, Einstein was not denying the importance of reason, and nor would I suggest that reason was unimportant to him, but it would appear that for him there was more to the workings of science than pure reason. Although I hesitate to interpret Einstein's thought, to my mind he seems to be acknowledging that we can all experience the mysterious, that which is beyond reason.

Reason is not only an important tool that enables religious people to have discussions with non-believers; we should also be prepared to use reason as a test of the continuing validity of religious traditions. Doctrine has to develop in the light of new knowledge and the changing norms of society. If it flies in the face of reason it deteriorates into obscurantism, and nothing gives religion more of a bad name than that. Perhaps one way to put it would be to say there has to be a balance between reason and revelation. We have to accept the limitations of both by saying, 'Neti, neti'.

It is not always easy to find that balance. I once gave a talk in Hereford Cathedral about the need to examine our certainties. In it, I suggested that the Church needed to examine the exclusive claims it has made for its revelation and for the certainties of its moral code. After my talk, the Bishop of Hereford indicated that he would like to ask a question and I thought, 'I'm going to get a roasting now!' But the Bishop said, 'I agree with a great deal of what you have said. But if I were to say as much, I would be accused by the press of lacking resolution, of watering down Christianity and of being a woolly-minded liberal.'

As if to prove his point, a woman stood up at the back of the cathedral and asked me in an aggressive tone, 'So, Mr Tully, what have you got to say about Jesus' words "I am the way, the truth and the light"?' I didn't know what to say that would resonate with her and I also didn't know what I could say to the Bishop, who had to minister to people who – in complete sincerity – held such absolute views as that.

It is a common tendency among followers of Semitic religions to believe that all doctrine is set in stone. They therefore see no need to balance reason and revelation, because, in their opinion, the one is a human activity while the other is a gift of God and as such cannot be challenged by us humans. Biblical fundamentalism is one of the manifestations of this mind set. Keith Ward, formerly the Regius Professor of Divinity at Oxford, is a born-again Christian and is able to remember the exact day Christ entered his life. While many born-again Christians tend to resist reasoned arguments and learning from new knowledge, in his book *What the Bible Really Teaches*, Keith Ward says that: 'Discussion, debate, reflection and exploration should be an essential part of church life, always looking for new disclosures of the unfailing love of God in new contexts, and looking to the Bible as a model and inspiration for such creative exploration, rather than as an unchangeable barrier to any new thought.' And for Keith Ward, science should be one of the sources of that new thought. He believes that 'the anthropomorphic imagery which the Bible often – not always – seems to suggest needs to be sublated by a greater knowledge of the extent and diversity of the universe, which only post-sixteenth century science could give'. By 'sublated' Keith Ward means 'cancelling an obvious or literal meaning by discovering a deeper spiritual meaning that can be seen to be the fulfilment to which the literal meaning points'.

Unlike the modern secular world, which I once heard a priest describe as 'drunk on change', Semitic religions usually come down too heavily on the side of tradition. Hinduism, I have often been told, is a process; in the modern jargon, it is 'on-going', so in theory it can readily accept change. But the grip that caste still holds on India would appear to contradict this position. I know from experience that many people are obsessed by caste and that this is not a positive obsession as far as Hinduism and, indeed, India are concerned. Every time I talk in Britain about India, no matter what aspect of it – past, present or future, secular or religious, economic or political – when it comes to question time, I am inevitably asked about caste

After I had spoken about what we might learn from Hinduism in the town hall of Marlborough, where I went to school, a man in the audience sprang up and declared, 'I regard Hinduism as an evil religion! I was in the army and I saw the dreadful fate of untouchables.' On another occasion, because I had tried to give a balanced description of caste in my book *No Full Stops in India*, I was subjected to a television inquisition that lasted an entire programme. In it, no matter what I said, the inquisitor came back at me with the accusation, 'So you defend slavery?' I repeatedly tried to explain that caste did not imply ownership of one social group by another. I pointed out that I had condemned the excesses of the caste system, and I also attempted to convince my inquisitor that the caste system had some merits. But all to no avail, as before I could finish speaking the allegation was hurled back at me, 'So you defend slavery!'

Even though I am well aware of the danger that I will be misunderstood, as *India's Unending Journey* charts a quest for balance, drawing upon the Indian tradition of reasoned discussion, I can hardly avoid discussing an institution that raises people's hackles. But first it is important to emphasise that untouchability is roundly condemned by many Hindus too. Dr Karan Singh, a scholar-politician whose father was the last Maharaja of Kashmir, has written in his book *Hinduism*: 'There were certain categories beyond the pale of the caste system which were known as the outcastes and whose treatment over the centuries is a standing disgrace to the remarkable achievements of Hinduism.' By the time I arrived in India, untouchability had become officially unacceptable, and independent India had legislated against the practice. But of course condemnation and legislation do not automatically lead to the complete disappearance of a practice and so I would still read reports in the papers about atrocities committed against Dalits, as the former untouchables like to be known, and hear stories about Dalits who were not being allowed to drink from village wells, sit in tea shops or worship in the same temples as other villagers. Shortly after I settled in Delhi, a female guest asked me, 'What caste is your cook?' I didn't need to ask her why she wanted to know. It was obvious that she wanted to make sure he was not from a caste she would regard as polluting.

Although I have never been asked that question again, when I started investigating Hinduism through Dr Radhakrishnan's book *The Hindu View of Life*, I couldn't see how he could do anything but condemn the entire institution of caste. However, Radhakrishnan maintained that caste had a value because it made society cohesive, with everyone playing their allotted role rather than competing with each other. It represented an organic view of society rather than an individualistic one. This argument led me to think about the British society that I had grown up in. It had not been a very individualistic society. An individualistic society requires social mobility, and it was only in the second part of the twentieth century that British society really opened up, making it no longer rare for people to break free from the circumstances into which they had been born. I am sure I would never have been commissioned in the army if I had not been to a public school that identified me as upper-middle-class, or in other words the officer class. I am not sure I would have got into the BBC without any professional qualifications if I hadn't followed my army commission by going to Cambridge, where it was still relatively easy for a public school boy to get admission.

Even in today's much more individualistic Western society, only a free will fundamentalist would deny that a parent's circumstances – education, job, position in society – all have an impact on his or her child. In a mobile society that impact might well be a strong urge in the child to 'better' him- or herself, to achieve a higher social standing or greater prosperity than the parent, and that urge might well be fulfilled. In a society that was not mobile, in which climbing up the social ladder or becoming substantially wealthier was rarely possible, caste held out hope for those who were disadvantaged by the circumstances of their birth. The hope was provided by the Hindu belief in reincarnation, according to which those who don't get off to a good start this time round may, depending on their actions in this life-time, have a better opportunity when they come to be born again. As Radhakrishnan pointed out, 'However lowly a man may be, he can raise himself sooner or later by the normal process of evolution to the highest level.' Those lines from the hymn 'All Things Bright and Beautiful', which I quoted in Chapter 2, show that Christianity accepted society was static and hierarchical until relatively recently. The

Christian hope held out for the disadvantaged in Jesus' promise that 'the kingdom of heaven is theirs' is not necessarily of any greater comfort to them than the Hindu hope of a more privileged reincarnation in the future.

Christians such as Mother Teresa, who see Jesus in the poor, lay themselves open to the criticism that they are sanctifying poverty. This is where suggestions that there is hope for the disadvantaged in God's kingdom, or in another life on this earth, become dangerous. If they tip the balance in favour of fatalism they allow society to accept inequality. But I believe it would be equally misguided to tip the scales the other way and unquestioningly advocate an equal opportunities society. Seeking to provide equal opportunities for everyone is clearly to be commended, but the danger is that from here it's only one all-too-short step to believing that society should be a meritocracy. Meritocracy is a cruel concept because success becomes the goal of life and we can never all be given equal opportunities from birth onwards in order to succeed and become a meritocrat. Those who do not succeed in a meritocracy often suffer mentally because the social ethos implies that it is their fault that they have failed. Put in other words, such societies tend to turn into a rat race, with those who lose being regarded, and regarding themselves, as failures. What we need is a society which, while trying to remove disadvantages, at the same time recognises that we can never all be equal and respects every sort of achievement. That would mean respecting the person who does the least glamorous job as much as the person who does the most glamorous. Today's Western societies, with their worship of celebrities, do the opposite.

Going back to caste, the system does have a certain social value. Each of the main divisions of caste is divided into hundreds of *jati* and these are the key to the social system. Each individual should marry within his or her own *jati*, and it is the members of a person's *jati* who form that person's *biradari* or community. That community can form a rudimentary social security system.

For many years I had a Dalit cook, Ram Chandra, or Chandre as he was always known (and, incidentally, even though he was a Dalit no guest ever hesitated to eat his food). Because he had become the head of a household instead of the sweeper, which had been the customary position for a Dalit, he became an important man in the eyes of his own community. Anyone coming to Delhi from his home village would call on him, and he would spend hours sitting outside the kitchen, sharing a hookah with his visitors, discussing the news from home or that he'd heard on his radio.

Chandre always wanted to know about any weddings that might be coming up within the community. When my partner, Gilly, and I went to his own daughter's wedding in his village, we discovered that members of his *biradari* had contributed to the wedding expenses. 'Mind you,' Chandre reminded us, 'I have to contribute to their weddings too!' We watched the contributions being noted down carefully after a lengthy discussion about who had contributed what to other weddings and how much they should therefore contribute to this one. All contributions were officially loans, but sorting out the repayments would have been beyond the ability of any bank manager.

I nevertheless have to admit that sometimes, when I have attempted to explain that caste is not entirely negative, I have failed to acknowledge the pain and suffering it can inflict. Dr Radhakant Nayak, a former senior civil servant and now a member of the Upper House of Parliament in India, is a friend whose opinion I value greatly. R.K. (as he is fondly known) is a Dalit who was converted to Christianity as a young man by a catechist who visited his village in Orissa, one of the poorest states of India. When I showed him the first draft of this chapter he wrote a lengthy critique in which he suggested that I had been too generous to Hinduism and he criticised the caste system ruthlessly. With his direct experience of what it feels like to be discriminated against and to be at the bottom of the social heap, he decried the caste system as:

> ... the chain of social hierarchy, reflecting an ascending scale of reverence and descending order of contempt that cannot be allowed to be broken in this life. If you are an 'untouchable' you are told you should remain so and you are warned that if you deviate and do not discharge the duties of an untouchable and a scavenger you will not get to a higher position after death.

R.K. also maintained that caste had no conscience and compared Christian beliefs about society with the caste system, saying:

> The Church teaches that Christ came for the poor. The rich man is made to feel responsible for the poor and is warned that it's easier for a camel to go through the eye of a needle than it is going to be for him to go to heaven. In the caste system the rich man's conscience is not pricked. He tells the poor: 'What can I do about your problem? You are suffering for your past life.'

When I sent a reply to his critique suggesting that the suffering of the poor might serve to warn the rich that they will pay for their selfishness in their next lives, R.K. replied succinctly, 'In my experience it doesn't!'

While I cannot but respect my friend's position, especially as I have lived a highly privileged life, it seems to me worth noting that protest movements have arisen in Indian society when the caste system has become too rigid. Buddhism was one of these. Within Hinduism there was also the powerful *Bhakti*, or devotional, movement in the middle ages, which produced the Hindu mystical poets known as saint-singers. The west Indian *Bhakti* saint Jnanadeva had a group of devotees that included an untouchable. The most prominent north Indian saint was Ramananda, and he opened his sect to all comers. One of his followers, Sant Ravi Das, is still widely revered by *Dalits*. In the south, Basavanna, a devotee of Shiva, created an influential sect based on a rejection of inequality of every kind. He did something revolutionary for his time by allowing two of his followers, a boy born an untouchable and a girl from a Brahmin family, to marry. The Sikh movement, which opposed caste, emerged in the Punjab in the sixteenth century. The nineteenth century saw the rise to influence of Bengali reformer Ramohan Roy, who was the first of several prominent Hindus who sought to reinvigorate their religion and remove the divisiveness of caste. In the twentieth century, a high caste Hindu, Mahatma Gandhi, led a movement against the excesses of the caste system, and another movement was led by Dr Bhim Rao Ambedkar. Unlike Gandhi, Bhim Rao Ambedkar was a *Dalit* himself, one of the very few who managed to get a good education in those days, becoming a brilliant lawyer and playing a major role in drawing up India's new constitution after Independence. Today it is Ambedkar who is the hero of the *Dalits*, not the Mahatma.

The caste system is shifting now, in a typically Indian way. Changes are taking place, although not necessarily fast enough, but there is no talk of revolution, or of a violent swing against this progress. Paradoxically, caste is also enabling Dalits to stand together in the fight for their rights, and as a result they have become a powerful political force. India's most populous state, Uttar Pradesh, or UP as it's always known, has had a Dalit Chief Minister who, moreover, is also a woman. She remains one of the most powerful politicians in UP. In eastern UP, in the village of Jakrauli, near the River Ganga beyond Varanasi, I came to know a Dalit called Budh Ram, an agricultural labourer. The British television network Channel Four had commissioned me and the television producer Jonathan Steadall to make a series of television portraits of Indians to mark the fiftieth anniversary of India's Independence. These portraits ranged from a Maharaja to a Dalit, and that Dalit was Budh Ram.

We learned that Budh Ram's *biradari* had decided that they didn't want to worship in the same temple as the upper castes but wanted to have their own temple in which to pray to their own saint, Sant Ravi Das. The upper castes had put up stiff resistance to this, and also objected to the Dalits' annual festival celebrating the birthday of Sant Ravi Das. Because the Dalit *biradari* had stood together and the local legislator had backed them, by the time we arrived to film they had built their temple, and we filmed Budh Ram worshipping in it. The Dalits were less confident about the future of the festival, but later I discovered that it continued to take place each year.

Because the Indian way, as I understand it, is the middle way – a gradual process of balanced progress – I have found that I must strive to change my own way of looking at things accordingly or become out of balance myself. But the search for balance can also be taken too far. It can lead to woolly-mindedness or indifference. Once I came to believe that it was unbalanced to claim that Jesus was the one way, the one truth and the one light, following that way seemed less important and I gradually stopped being a practising Anglican.

In my early fifties I was brought up with a jolt when I nearly died from measles. The period of recovering from a serious illness is often a time of introspection, and for me it also proved to be another of those significant moments in my life in which free will played no part. The British High Commissioner of the time, Sir Robert Wade Gearey, came to visit me and gave me a copy of the Jesuit Gerard Hughes' book *The God of Surprises*. I don't know why he chose that book, because I had never discussed religion with him before, but it proved an inspired choice.

Gerald Priestland, a great religious affairs correspondent of the BBC, had also recommended *God of Surprises*, saying it might be particularly useful for those 'who find it hard to forgive themselves: the stumblers and agnostics who hardly dare believe that God is in them'. He was right. At that stage in my life I was little more than an agnostic who had stumbled very often. I found the book more than useful: it made me realise how agnostic I had become and what a loss that was. In the directions Gerard Hughes gave for beginners seeking the God he said was in all of us, he seemed to me to be talking of the God of experience, the God of inner reality that Sarvepalli Radhakrishnan has also written about.

But at the same time, the Jesuit also warned against 'go it alone' religion, saying, 'Because we are liable to self-deception and tend to use God and Christ to justify and support our narrow ways of thinking and acting, we need the institutional and the critical elements of the Church as a check to our self-deception.' I realised that I also needed the Church's worship, liturgy, and sacraments, which had first awakened in me that sense of the transcendent I believe is latent in all of us. So I returned to the Anglican tradition, and although I have found it difficult to commit myself fully, I believe that if I ever come as close as Gerard Hughes has done to the God within me it will be within the tradition of my Church. I have certainly conceived a love for that Church's tradition that I never felt before.

That said, it's impossible to live in India for long without taking an interest in yoga, which is not a normal Anglican practice, although it too is concerned with spiritual awareness. In its many different forms yoga is much more than a mere keep-fit technique or an alternative to the ubiquitous gyms which are one of the latest Western imports to India. Gyms seem to me to be little more than torture chambers and one of the first things my yoga teacher taught me was that you should never torture your body; you should make gradual progress. She told me,

'You have a saying – "a healthy mind in a healthy body" – and that is what yoga is about. It teaches that the mental and the physical have to be kept in balance.' Of course, physical exercises are just one part of yoga and even they, properly understood, have a goal beyond physical and mental welfare.

I once made a radio programme about one of the great yoga teachers of our time, B.K.S. Iyengar, whose centres are now found throughout the world. We started the programme with Guruji, as he is known to his followers, talking to me while standing on his head. At the age of eighty he was still amazingly fit and able to do the most advanced yoga exercises, but he stressed that these were not just bodily exercises. 'Why develop like a racehorse, as is the case with so many wrestlers, athletes, and gymnasts? In time the racehorse becomes a cart horse,' he said. 'Instead, realise that the body and the mind have to be integrated and spiritual awareness has to flow with each movement.'

The aim of all forms of yoga is to achieve spiritual fulfilment. But does practising yoga mean that we can dispense with organised religion, as so many in the West seem to think? I had never thought that yoga conflicted with my Anglicanism, but when I decided to write this book I felt I should discuss this issue. So Gilly and I caught the misnamed Mussourie Express from Delhi, travelling overnight at an average speed of about twenty-five miles an hour, to arrive at Haridwar, a historic pilgrimage place on the Ganga, just after dawn. There, we took a taxi up to Rishikesh, another site sacred to Hindus.

When I first visited Rishikesh more than forty years ago, it was a small pilgrimage centre for those who wanted to worship the Ganga as she emerges from the Himalayas to begin her long journey across the north Indian plain. Pilgrimage has now become an essential part of India's leisure industry, to the extent that one bank of the Ganga is scarred by the ramshackle urban sprawl that is standard throughout Indian towns that have developed too rapidly.

A walk across the suspension bridge named the Laxman Jhula, or 'swing of Laxman', after the god Rama's brother, leads to the garish temples, the ashrams and the dharamsalas where pilgrims stay. We were headed for an ashram some distance away from the centre of Rishikesh to discuss the relationship between yoga and organised religion with Swami Veda Bharati, one of the leading teachers of yoga meditation. Before setting out I had read his book, which has the bold and some might consider presumptuous title, *God*. In the book he says:

> God, for me, is truth, and truth is that which exists in all times – the past, present and future. It is self-existent; it was never born, so it never dies. It is the fountainhead of light and love ... That truth is both within and without, so one can directly attain it by realizing the truth within himself. It is possible to do this.

The truth, Swami Veda Bharati believes, can be experienced through yoga meditation, but he would never suggest this is the only way to experience it.

Swamiji's master, Swami Rama, was a renowned teacher who had spent long years in the Himalayas learning from the ascetics who lived in caves there. He had many strange experiences, which he recorded in his autobiography. These included witnessing a Swami decide the day he should die – and did die – only to return to life again because he was so disgusted by the Hindus, Muslims and Christians squabbling among themselves over who should perform his last rites. Stories like this are difficult for most of us to accept, but they did nothing to damage Swami Rama's credibility among his followers.

His own powers, his magnetic personality and his spirituality attracted disciples of all religions and from all parts of the globe; and they were not necessarily unworldly credulous people. They raised the money to buy an old monastery in the United States to convert into a meditation centre, and during the last years of Swami Rama's life they enabled him to build a large modern hospital and medical school near Rishikesh. I was shown around the hospital by a doctor who had returned from an eminent career in America – so eminent that a kidney complaint was named after him. He wasn't a man to accept lightly that there could be a return to life after someone had been declared clinically dead, yet it was Swami Rama who had inspired him to give up his career in America and to come to this hospital in a remote part of India.

Before he died, Swami Rama appointed Veda Bharati as his successor. Veda Bharati had already taken the vows of a Swami in a long ceremony during which he had to state that he had risen above the desire 'for sex and family, for wealth and comfort, for fame and honour'. He was also asked whether he would abandon his 'previous name, previous life and previous relations', and performed the ceremony for honouring the memory of the dead as an acknowledgement that 'everything of I and mine is dead'. After the ceremony, the only possessions Veda Bharati would be allowed were a water vessel, a loin cloth for underwear, upper garments, lower garments and wooden slippers. At the end of the ritual he was presented with robes the colour of 'the light of the rising sun' and told: 'Wherever you walk you bring peace of the morning, of the light of dawn, the light of the rising sun ... From now you are a being of light.'

The last time I had met Swami Veda Bharati was at the greatest of all Hindu festivals, the Maha Kumbh Mela, at Allahabad in 2002. On the most auspicious bathing day of the Mela, he had taken part in the procession of one of the *Akharas*, or Hindu monastic orders, down to the confluence of the sacred rivers Ganga and Yamuna. The procession had been led by naked ascetics dancing, jumping and shouting like children in their excitement. Then came a long line of more sober monks robed in garments the colour of the rising sun. Swami Veda Bharati had been among the few who were enthroned on chariots pulled by a tractor. At one time they might well have ridden on elephants, but elephants had been banned from the Mela for fear that they might run amuck. The chariots were reserved for the men and women who had been awarded the title of *Mahamandaleshwar*, the most senior honour bestowed by the *Akharas* on scholars. It had been awarded to Swami Veda Bharati in recognition of his knowledge and his understanding of the *Vedas* and yogic texts.

However, Swami Veda Bharati's elevated status has not gone to his head. He remains warm-hearted and welcoming. When I e-mailed him about this book, he immediately suggested that I come to his ashram in Rishikesh. His book *God* had aroused doubts in me about reconciling yoga with Anglicanism, or indeed any form of organised religion. Swami Veda Bharati said, 'In yoga one simply practises the methods and waits for the doctrine to emerge out of the experience.' To my mind, that seemed like putting the cart before the horse, as doctrine had come first in my life. The doctrines of organised religion seemed to be very much a secondary concern in yoga. According to Swamiji: 'The yogi ministers to people of all faiths, lets them see the ever-present God in their own church, temple, mosque, or pagoda, but first see him in the temple which is the human personality.' While I wanted to find the God in my human personality, I also wanted to stand in the Anglican tradition as a check to the sort of self-deception Gerard Hughes warned against.

It was a busy time at the ashram because a fifty-day *yajna* (a Vedic sacrificial rite) was coming to an end, and one of the *Shankaracharyas* – the holder of an important, historic Hindu office – had come to take part in the final rituals. Gilly and I were allotted a small cottage opposite Swami Veda Bharati's, but it wasn't until the evening that he was able to spare us some time.

The Swami is quite small and appears to be almost swamped by his robes, which are the colour of the rising sun. But unlike many Hindu holy men, he has quite neatly cut grey hair and is clean-shaven. He speaks with a slight North American twang.

The Swami travels a great deal in North America and so we talked about the individualism of American culture. When I suggested that America had got this out of balance, he replied, 'I've found that every weakness is a weakening of a strength. American pioneers had two strengths: one was their individualism – you can't be a pioneer without that. The other was their interdependence: they couldn't have constructed America without working together. Now their interdependence has weakened.'

We discussed the lack of a religious sensitivity in the West today and the lack of humility in a culture that exalts itself above nature. Eventually coming to the subject that had brought me to Rishikesh, I said to Swami Veda Bharati, 'I get the impression from your book *God* that yoga doesn't have much time for religious traditions, their scriptures, liturgies, rituals and teachings.'

Swami Veda Bharati smiled. 'Surely I must have some time for organised religion or why would I be a member of an order of Hindu monks and why would I have accepted the title of *Mahamandaleshwar*?'

'But how do you reconcile your practice of orthodox Hinduism with your belief that personal experience must come first?' I wondered.

'There are two parts to everything, from outside in and inside out,' he said. 'The great prophets and founders of religion – did they have any doctrine to develop their religion from? No, they had their experience and they translated that into language. For a large number of people, however, religion is the path to God. It's only the other way round with the ground-breakers: God gives them the religion.'

'Well, I'm certainly not a ground-breaker,' I admitted. 'It was my love of liturgy and worship which formed my path to God, and I still seem to have a long way to go before I get there!'

The Swami laughed. 'Well, you really must come here for a longer time and learn to meditate. But seriously – we are not too far apart. I enjoy all the liturgies, but if it stops there and doesn't give a person the aspiration to personally experience God then it becomes dogma.'

To reinforce his point, Swami Veda Bharati went on to maintain that religions are based on the experience of their founders. 'The scriptures point you towards God by telling you what Jesus experienced or what the Buddha experienced,' he said. 'Their experiences were so powerful, so peaceful, so life-changing that those around them had no option but to believe, and their belief became a religion.'

'So where does yoga come in?'

'It was Swami Rama who told me I must verify the scriptures I read by experience gained through yoga meditation. I find many Roman Catholics who have verified their scriptures through yoga meditation, experience a deep meaning in their religion for the first time. Even those who are absolutely atheistic discover there is something beyond "physical being" and some go on to join churches or other religious organisations.'

The next day I witnessed the Swami's commitment to his religious tradition with my own eyes. Two ceremonies ended the fifty-day Vedic sacrifice. The first was a final *Yajna* in the ashram's temple. The ritual was celebrated by more than twenty Brahmin priests. Swami Veda Bharati and the *Shankaracharya* sat cross-legged in front of the sacred fire. The Brahmins invoked Agni, the god of fire who carries the offerings and messages of us humans to the other deities and brings back their messages. The flames crackled as tins of *ghee*, or clarified butter, were poured on them. They rose so high that Swamiji had to stand back and hold a long hollow bamboo through which one of the Brahmins poured more ghee onto the fire. The Brahmins also threw handfuls of *samagree,* a mixture of more than thirty barks, roots, herbs, and leaves, onto the fire. Each time they chanted words to the effect of: 'Not mine, not mine – I offer all the claims of my ego as an offering of worshipful surrender. I burn all my desires and claims in the fire.'

In the second ceremony, Swami Veda Bharati sat in front of a line of nine young girls and one young boy, while texts glorifying the Divine Mother were recited and sacred mantras repeated time and time again. The Swami then prostrated himself before the children, washed their feet and made offerings to them. He explained to me later, 'I find great fulfilment in feeling that I know myself to be smaller than a little girl and prostrate myself before the deity in their form. Having invoked the presence of the divinity, the girl becomes a manifestation of the divine presence.' Swami Veda Bharati told me that the experience he had gained through meditation had verified the rituals he performed and given them a deeper meaning.

My experiences in India forced me to think again about the faith I had been taught because I felt that I couldn't just ignore what was right before my eyes: the existence of many ways to God. I did get lost, but my gradual acceptance of these many ways enabled me to return to my tradition with my faith strengthened. When I came to understand that, for thousands of years, in changing historical circumstances, in different countries and cultures and climates, people had experienced the existence of what appears to be the same reality, although describing that reality differently, I saw that a universal God made far more sense rationally than one who limited his activities to Christians.

The descriptions of the divine may be different, but the experience seems to me to be fundamentally the same, and this has strengthened my conviction that God or the Ultimate Reality does exist. Of course, many will argue that this experience is merely an illusion and a response to the desire to believe that life has a purpose and doesn't end with death. If that is so, it is an extraordinarily powerful, persistent, and prevalent illusion. Maybe it's the arrogance that can accompany rationalism that prevents many people from acknowledging that there could be a God, or a reality, far more powerful than we mortals and our powers of reasoning can comprehend. It is the arrogance that can accompany religious certainty that prevents many from acknowledging the validity of other experiences of God than their own. My feeling is that we have to be humble enough about our religion to recognise that it will never be certain; there has to be an element of questioning and doubt. But Tennyson's Ancient Sage was surely right when he advised us to 'cleave ever to the sunnier side of doubt'.

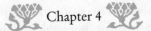 Chapter 4

RAIPUR: A GOD TOO SMALL

RAIPUR was just a district headquarters, not a very significant town, until it became the capital of the new state of Chattisgarh, carved out of the vast Madhya Pradesh that sprawls across central India. Dr Praveen Togadia, a cancer surgeon and evangelist of a version of Hinduism that runs contrary to all that I been saying in the previous chapter, had arrived there one Sunday to denounce Islam and Christianity as enemies of Hindus and of India. I had come to film and interview Dr Togadia.

During the interview, I asked the balding, middle-aged doctor why he was so intolerant of other religions. He pointed his finger at me aggressively and said, 'Let me tell you, Mr Tully, it has nothing to do with religion! We are all from the same ethnic stock, our ancestors are the same. Religion doesn't matter.' Needless to say, Togadia maintained that that original ethnic stock was Hindu, and those ancestors were Hindus. Although he said religion didn't matter, he saw every reason why the missionaries of his World Hindu Council, known as the Vishva Hindu Parishad or VHP, should proselytise forcefully to convince Indian Muslims and Christians to 'come home' to Hinduism.

At the VHP meeting that evening, Dr Togadia was preaching to the converted. However, the audience was divided in two. The middle-class and the middle-aged sat sedately in neat orderly rows, appearing for all the world as though this gathering was just another Sunday outing for them – a weekend diversion for the family perhaps. But behind their orderly rows, the young men of Raipur roamed around the park with the saffron bandanas of the VHP tied around their heads, exploding crackers, yelling '*Jai Shri Ram!*' ('Victory to Rama!', the Hindu god) and wielding tridents, which are the symbol of the god Shiva. Inevitably, they surrounded us as we started to film, yelling even more loudly and waving their tridents in our faces.

Those tridents were lethally sharp, and their use had been banned in some states. When I asked the youths why they were carrying them, they replied, 'Because they are the symbol of Lord Shiva.'

'Is that the only reason?' I wondered.

One young man blurted out, 'No, it's to kill *Pathans*!'

'You mean Muslims?'

'Yes!' they all roared.

Togadia's arrival was greeted with another round of crackers and even more frenzied yelling. He mounted the dais, acknowledged the welcome, and began to rant against Muslims and Christians. He punctuated his speech in true demagogic style by raising his voice in crescendos, followed by pauses to allow his words to sink in and the crowd to yell their applause.

'Muslims,' he bawled, 'invaded India and streams of Hindu blood flowed, and yet Hindus have remained tolerant. But now we are expected to protect Muslims. This is a perverted way of thinking, the result of a thousand years of oppression.' He went on to warn Muslims to accept *Bharat*, a code word in his language for a Hindu India, or else 'face what will happen when 800 million Hindus become Praveen Togadias'. No Muslim would want to live in a country full of Hindus as hostile as Togadia. Yet Togadia maintained that, far from being threatened by his brand of Hinduism, Muslims themselves were threatening India. There was, he claimed, a threat of terrorism sponsored from outside India, as well as a threat within India itself because

Islam did not allow birth control and so the Muslim population in India was continuing to increase. As for Christians, they had converted innocent Hindus with bribes of bread and money and now they wanted to convert the whole of Chattisgarh!

'Doesn't the Pope claim the right to convert the whole world?' Togadia bellowed. 'So how can the Church claim it doesn't want to convert the whole of your state? Will the Pope allow Hindus to preach in the Vatican? Why then should we allow Christians to make conversions in our country? I warn you: the Church is training an army of missionaries and nuns to convert Hindus!'

Although under Indian law anyone who insults the religious feeling of another person is liable to imprisonment, the police were silent spectators of the insults being heaped on Muslims and Christians at this rally. Which brings me to the question: if middle-class Hindus can spend a Sunday evening listening with approval to Praveen Togadia, doesn't this suggest that, no matter how ancient India's tradition of pluralism is, it is dead now? To this, I would reply that while Togadia and his ilk are certainly a threat to that tradition, and as such should not be ignored, I believe it is still intact.

In 1992 the international press was full of dire foreboding when followers of Togadia's brand of Hinduism defied the government and tore down the medieval mosque in Ayodhya, which they claimed stood on the birth site of Rama. The media wondered if India would 'fall to the zealots'. The apprehensive atmosphere became graver when riots broke out in many parts of India, and in particular when the police joined in attacks on Muslims in Mumbai. But whenever my opinion about events was canvassed by BBC interviewers, I held to my belief that the storm would pass, saying, 'In my experience tempers in India flare up very rapidly but cool down quickly too.' And so they did.

I believe the reason that tempers did eventually cool down, as

I had expected they would, is because the Indian tradition of religions living side by side in comparative harmony eventually reasserted itself. In the sixty years since Independence, India has demonstrated the resilience of that tradition time and time again. At Independence, India's greatest leader, Mahatma Gandhi, didn't take part in the celebrations because he disapproved of the division of the country on the basis of religion. In fact, Nehru and other leaders of the Congress party had only acceded to the demand for a Muslim homeland, the new nation of Pakistan, when they became convinced there was no other way of reaching an agreement with the Muslim League leader, Mohammad Ali Jinnah. The more extreme Hindu organisations regarded Mother India as sacred and her division as sacrilegious. When partition came, it led to a massive two-way migration and to appalling bloodshed. To this day, the debate continues about exactly how many people were butchered and how many fled their homes. This bitter legacy might have been expected to result in the new Muslim Pakistan being matched by an India which was a Hindu nation instead of a secular democracy. If India had been declared a Hindu nation, hatred and irreconcilable differences might have arisen between Hindus and the millions of Muslims left behind in the country after partition. India could have become another Northern Ireland or another Lebanon – a country torn apart by sectarian strife.

Since Independence, India has faced a number of crises between communities, the nature of which would have destabilised many other countries. Probably the most dangerous of these was sparked off by the attack on the Golden Temple, described in Chapter 3. When news broke of the damage to the shrine, Sikh soldiers mutinied in several different places. Sikhs have always been prominent in the Indian army and this was the first time the integrity of the institution – which was the final guarantor of India's security and the last resort when riots broke out – had been threatened.

That was followed by the assassination of Indira Gandhi on 31 October 1984 by two of her bodyguards, who were Sikhs. I was halfway up a mountain, more than 200 miles from Delhi, trying to keep up with the entourage of Princess Anne, who was visiting schools for Tibetan refugee children, when I overheard two policemen discussing the news that Indira Gandhi had been shot. Her son, Rajiv Gandhi, who was in eastern India, rushed back to Delhi after hearing my colleague Satish Jacob's report on BBC World Service radio. The sudden death of such a dominant leader left a dangerous power vacuum. Indira Gandhi had ensured that no one anywhere near her stature had emerged in the Congress party, so now the senior ministers fell back on Rajiv. As he had been in politics for only about four years, it is perhaps not surprising that he floundered dangerously at first.

When I attempted to hurry back to Delhi from the Himalayas, my car was surrounded by an ugly mob in the town of Muzaffanagar. The crowd was shouting slogans against America – in those days always assumed to be the villain – and I only managed to pass through it unharmed by frantically shouting, 'English, English, BBC!' This was the first I saw of the violence that subsequently erupted across India.

For two days the police lost control of the capital. Gangs roamed the streets with lists of houses where Sikhs lived. They attacked the houses, killed their occupants and looted their property, and it wasn't until Rajiv Gandhi called out the army that the violence in Delhi started to subside. Sikhs were attacked in many other places as well. The government admits that in this violence nearly 3,000 people were slaughtered, 2,000 of them in Delhi.

Although the Sikhs are a comparatively small community, they play a very important role not only within the army but also in all the security forces. They have a large presence in the capital, and their home state, Punjab, is on the border with Pakistan. So if Amritsar and the violence after Indira Gandhi's death had alienated them permanently, there would have been a dangerous wound festering at the heart of India. But that wound didn't fester; it healed.

Sikhs were not alienated because India's pluralist tradition reasserted itself. India is like a great ocean liner, which is hit from time to time by storms and giant waves that would capsize most ships. She pitches and rolls dangerously but sails on. However, sailing through such stormy waters and surviving can lead to dangerous complacency, a sense that India will always muddle through somehow and so there is no need to worry. The fact that Togadia and his ilk have not succeeded in setting India on fire is no reason for failing to try to understand why he does appeal to a significant number of Hindus. It is impossible to say exactly how significant because, with a campaign of hatred against Muslims, buttressed by all the paranoia of the war on terrorism, there may well be many Hindus who don't come out in public but who secretly have some sympathy for Togadia's views. Since I believe that pluralism is the only way India can survive, and the only way the world can solve not only the religious but also the ethnic and linguistic conflicts that plague us, I am aware that I too must examine the Togadia phenomenon.

There is one obvious reason for the rise of Hindu nationalism and that reason is politics. Nationalism is a cause around which some Hindus will inevitably rally and it therefore gives the Bharatiya Janata party, or BJP, which comes from the same family as the VHP, a constituency. It also provides an enemy – an essential requirement in ethnic, linguistic or religious politics. For the VHP, the minority communities are the enemy, especially the Muslims, who are identified as the community standing in the way of a Hindu India. Any suggestion that Muslims are being privileged in the name of secularism is leapt on by the Hindu nationalists. Their whole strategy is designed to create a constituency of Hindus who reject India's pluralist tradition and want their religion to have a dominant role.

Togadia also plays on a religious grievance. The population of Chattisgarh is dominated by tribes who used to live in the forests and who were outside the mainstream of Indian life, as well as the mainstream of Hinduism. They had a vibrant art and culture of their own but were easily influenced and exploited by more sophisticated people. One wall of my flat is covered with paintings by a tribal artist friend of mine, Jangarh Singh Shyam. His death was a cruel example of how tribal peoples can be exploited. A Japanese art dealer regarded Jangarh as a commercial prospect and lured him to his country. There he sat him down to paint. Jangarh became more and more lonely but he was not allowed to return home. He sent despairing letters to his family but they could do nothing to help him, and in the end he committed suicide.

During the Raj, some Christian missionaries also exploited the tribals. They persuaded them that their animism was superstition and that only Jesus could save them, using the added lure of food and sometimes money to convert them. The missionaries created a class known as 'rice Christians' who were not treated with respect by the better educated members of the Church. These were almost always Christians who had been converted from higher castes and were far fewer in number than the rice Christians. Reporting on a flood in central India, I came across some tribal Christians who had taken refuge in the large compound of the parish priest's house. Instead of caring for them as members of his flock, the priest pointed to them and said to me, 'You see the state we are in. I have to put up with these sort of people in my house!' On another occasion, a Roman Catholic headmaster from south India said to me, 'I wouldn't take communion from the hands of a Dalit priest.' The Dalit converts were also known as rice Christians.

It was this tradition of mass conversion that gave Togadia the ammunition he needed against the Christians in Raipur. The same tradition gave rise to the Hindu sect, the Arya Samaj, that provides his theology for him. In the nineteenth century a scholarly and persuasive Swami, Dayanand Sarasvati, became a bitter critic of the Christian missionaries and their tactics. Commenting on Jesus' promise to make his followers 'fishers of men', the Swami argued, 'Jesus founded his religion in order to entrap people. He set out to accomplish his object by ensnaring others into his net like a fisherman. Is there any wonder, then, that Christian missionaries follow their master in ensnaring other men into their religion?' Dayanand Sarasvati admired the missionaries' zeal and decided that the only way to beat them was to play them at their own game. Realising that the cohesion of the missionaries' message depended on their having an authoritative scripture – the Bible – to work with, he declared the *Vedas* to be 'the supreme authority in the ascertainment of true religion' and said, 'Whatever is enjoined by the *Vedas* we hold to be right; whilst whatever is condemned by them we believe to be wrong.' Swami Dayanand also accepted Christian criticism both of idol worship as superstition and of caste, which he realised was dividing Hindu society, although he still advocated a social hierarchy. He encouraged conversion, establishing a new ritual to welcome converts, because traditionally it was believed that you had to be born a Hindu – you couldn't become one. Modelled closely on the Western dogmatic religious tradition, the Arya Samaj became what the respected French scholar Christophe Jaffrelot has described as 'one of the first crucibles of Hindu nationalism'.

Partly because of the attack mounted by the Hindu nationalists, the main denominations of the Church today have realised that the only way to ensure that Christianity will survive in India is to support pluralism. This means avoiding the old missionary tactic of claiming that other religions are in some way inferior to Christianity, and being very cautious about conversions. When I asked an Indian Jesuit whether the Church still had a mission in India to convert, he said, 'The Church does not convert; God does, and God does not seem to regard this as a high priority...'

A leading Dalit priest put it a little more positively, saying, 'Conversion is not our priority, but if people want to come, what can we do? The truth is that there is much more sheep stealing going on than conversion.' The 'sheep stealers' in question are Protestant sects outside the mainstream Churches, such as the Apostolic Christian Assembly, which declared on its web site recently, 'Heartening and praiseworthy, demanding special thanks given to the Lord, is the ever increasing number of persons being baptised and added to each of our branch churches, the proof of the Lord's continuing work and presence in the Branch ministries.' Unfortunately, this kind of activity is grist to Dr Togadia's mill.

It is because the main denominations have come to accept India's pluralist tradition that they are reluctant to make converts. But this presents an obvious problem for any Christian organisation, as Christians believe that Jesus was not only an incarnation of God but the *only* incarnation, and as such the one way to God and to salvation. That is why it has been the mission of the Church to convert since its foundation. This dilemma is particularly difficult for Roman Catholics in India to deal with, as they have traditionally claimed there can be no salvation outside the Church.

The Jesuits were in the forefront of the Church's conversion drive in the colonial days, and established the Inquisition in Goa, one of whose tasks was to prevent any Hindu practices seeping into Catholicism. Now they are spearheading the move for the Roman Catholic Church to accept pluralism, to shed its Western identity and to become recognisably Indian.

I have long been intrigued by the Jesuits; when I was at Cambridge a Jesuit Father by the name of Joe Christie made an indelible impression on me when he wiped the floor with his opponent during a debate about the existence of God. A friend who had been educated by the Jesuits told me stories about their long and arduous training, their discipline and the discipline they enforced in their schools. So quite early in my time in India I was fascinated to be introduced to a Jesuit priest in the Jesuit Formation Centre at Kurseong, which lay halfway up the mountain road to Darjeeling. At the time I was still naïve about Indian religions myself, but even so I was taken aback by his contempt for Hinduism and his insistence on the Church's mission to convert India, which seemed rather ambitious to me. But perhaps he was an exception, as some years later I met a very different Jesuit, the elderly Father Van Exim, who had advised Mother Teresa in all her negotiations with the Vatican when she was establishing her new order.

When I met him, Father Van Exim was living in one small room in the Jesuit college in Kolkata. He was rather frail because he could not throw off the effects of having been poisoned by a rat bite when he was working in the slums of Howrah, across the river from Kolkata. He certainly came from a harsh tradition: when his order sent him to India as a young man he was told he would never be allowed to go back home to Belgium to visit his family. However, he was anything but a harsh man himself and was in no way dogmatic. He had spent his time in India studying Islam and trying to establish a dialogue with Indian Muslims. When I talked to him about Mother Teresa he would say, 'You have to understand that she is a very orthodox Catholic.' The latent implication from the smile on the elderly priest's face was that he himself was not so orthodox.

Now the Jesuits have moved from remote Kurseong to Delhi, where it's all happening, and there is no question of any of their number showing contempt for Hinduism. I was once asked to organise a gathering of representatives of all the major faiths in India to meet Prince Charles. If I remember correctly there were at least eight faiths represented. The Jesuit scholar Father Samuel Ryan explained how his Church was now adapting itself to the Indian plural tradition. He also maintained that it was because of Indian theology that the Vatican no longer claimed there could be no salvation outside the Church.

I had first met Father Samuel when attending the daily Mass in the Jesuit Formation Centre in Delhi. I remembered a Catholic diplomat friend of mine who had also gone to Mass there saying, 'I hope I am a reasonably progressive Catholic but that was too much for me.' So I was not surprised to find that the Mass had a distinctly Hindu flavour to it. All the teachers and students sat cross-legged on the floor. The altar was a small, low table reminiscent of those on which the image of the deity is placed when a Hindu *pandit* performs a *puja*, or ritual, for a family. Like a Hindu *pandit*, the priest celebrating the Mass sat by the table wearing a simple shawl instead of a vestment.

Acceptance of pluralism and what is called the 'inculturalisation' of Indian Catholicism, demonstrating that Christianity can be as Indian as any other religion, requires a major theological rethink. Two Roman Catholic theologians who have pioneered the search for a theology of pluralism have both spent many years in India. Like Father Van Exim, Jacques Dupuis was a Belgian Jesuit. He was also a renowned scholar, who after teaching in India for twenty-four years, went on to become Professor of Theology at the Gregorian University in Rome. There, he wrote a book called *Towards a Christian Theology of Religious Pluralism*. The difficulty of the task he set himself became apparent when the Vatican Congregation, headed by Cardinal Ratzinger, declared that his book contained 'serious errors against essential elements of divine and Catholic faith'. After two years of uncertainty, which did nothing for Dupuis' health (he was suffering from a severe kidney complaint), he was allowed to defend himself before a hearing attended by Ratzinger. The strictures on his book were softened. Although he was warned that serious confusion and misunderstanding could result from reading his book, the Vatican recognised that it represented 'an attempt to remain within the limit of orthodoxy in his study of questions hitherto unexplored'.

Dupuis, who was considered too liberal by the Vatican, was regarded as too conservative by his colleagues when he taught in India. Father Rudi Heredia, the Jesuit who told me as much, once warned his fellow Indian Jesuits in their theological journal that if Indian Christianity did not engage with the country's religious pluralism it would certainly end as 'a nihilistic relativism, if it does not collapse in annihilating chaos'.

The questions Dupuis raised had been largely unexplored in the past because there had been a lack of dialogue between the Roman Catholic Church and other religions. Dupuis commented, 'Until recently, theology often seemed in Christian circles to belong to Christianity as its exclusive property; worse still, in Western Christianity First World theology seemed to have the monopoly.' Dupuis recognised that pluralism must be part of God's intention for us and warned that Christianity had to discover what the place for other historical religious traditions was in God's plan for mankind. He suggested that this plan was a 'marvellous convergence' of these traditions, a coming together of them. That coming together could not merely be determined on the basis of a single religion's theology and tradition. It couldn't come about because Christianity, or any other religion, had proved itself right and the others wrong. That said, Dupuis maintained that it seemed possible to speak of 'a general convergence of religions upon a Universal Christ who fundamentally satisfies them all'. But he said that the convergence would have to respect the differences between religions fully and create a 'mutual enrichment and cross-fertilization' between them all. 'Dialogue,' Dupuis noted, was 'the necessary foundation of a theology of religions'.

Dupuis' book is detailed and in places quite dense reading,

but I got the impression of a scholar doing his utmost to pay respect to the various religions he had encountered in India, and hence to stand in the country's tradition of religious pluralism and dialogue. I was particularly impressed by his insistence that dialogue between religions should not be merely an attempt to find the lowest common multiple or, indeed, the highest common factor; rather, it should involve a willingness to learn from each other. At one point in his book, Dupuis acknowledged that 'contact with Hindu *advaita* mysticism may help Christians to purify and deepen their faith in the divine mystery'.

Another prominent Western Roman Catholic theologian who believed there ought to be an understanding between his own tradition and the Indian religious tradition of pluralism was Bede Griffiths. He was a Welsh Roman Catholic monk of the order founded in the sixth century by Saint Benedict, who is often called 'the patriarch of Western monasticism'. Bede lived the latter part of his life in India, where he attempted to marry the faith he had been taught with the insights that country had given him. His best known book is called *The Marriage of East and West*.

Bede Griffiths came to India because he had begun to feel that there was something lacking in the Western Church, and indeed in the Western world as a whole. 'We were,' he said, 'living from one half of our soul, from the conscious, rational level and we needed to discover the other half, the unconscious intuitive dimension.' He sought to re-establish balance between the two, which is the traditional search that Sarvepalli Radhakrishnan writes about in his book *The Hindu View of Life*.

I regret never having met Bede Griffiths, who died in 1993 at the small ashram in south India where he had lived for the last twenty-five years of his life. However, after his death I went to his ashram, where I met Father Christadas, one of his disciples. Father Christadas looked more like a Hindu holy man than a Christian monk; he was bare-chested, with a straggling beard and unkempt hair, and wore a plain saffron *lungi* wrapped around his waist and extending to his ankles, and beads around his neck. I remember asking him why, when he was a Christian monk, he should want to look like a *sadhu*. He replied, 'Since I am an Indian I don't want to lose my identity, and the Christian heritage doesn't exclude me from practising my rich Indian heritage.' This, I thought, was an answer that would have pleased Bede Griffiths.

The ashram itself was a celebration of Bede's marriage of East and West. The chapel was known as the temple, and its bright technicolored dome was surrounded by Hindu iconography, with Jesus in the centre, also clad like a Hindu holy man. Like the Jesuits in Delhi, Bede Griffiths used to celebrate Mass by sitting on the floor in front of a small low table for an altar in the manner of a Hindu priest. In the garden there was a statue of Jesus meditating and enfolded by a lotus, a flower sacred to Hindus. Bede Griffiths also used to meditate in front of that statue.

Bede Griffiths' marriage of East and West was a partnership of equals, with both giving and receiving. He wanted to find a meeting point between the West's emphasis on reason and the East's emphasis on imagination. He was not blind to the faults of either side, saying once that:

The tragedy of the modern world is that reason has taken charge and driven imagination underground…. The East must learn the use of reason, in science, in industry, in politics, and I would say above all in moral life…. But the West has to recover its lost imagination, not only in art, but in economic and social life, not least in sex.

How did this translate into traditional Christian terms? For Bede Griffiths, the Bible had to be interpreted as myth, and that required imagination, because he saw myth as the 'symbolic expression of reality in terms of the human imagination'. Jesus was a person who went beyond imagination to the realisation that he was at one with that reality. Bede Griffiths inevitably accepted that knowledge of this reality was not limited to Roman Catholics or even to Christians. To get around this issue, he suggested that the Church should embrace all those who sincerely seek God, 'because there is no limit to the grace of God revealed in Christ. Christ died for all men from the beginning to the end of time, to bring all men to that state of communion with God, with the eternal truth and reality for which they were created'. But this didn't mean that the Church should dispense with its own particular doctrines and sacraments. What's more, Bede Griffiths did not offer comfort to those who believe that they can do without organised religion. He insisted that he had not rejected anything he had learnt of God, Christ or the Church. He saw the Church's doctrines and sacraments as 'human expressions or signs of the divine reality'. His ambition was to go beyond those signs to reach what they signified – the ultimate reality. But he argued, 'As long as we remain in this world we need these signs and the world today cannot survive unless it rediscovers the "signs" of faith, "the Myth", the Symbol in which the knowledge of reality is enshrined.'

When I was a young man, rationalism was so firmly drummed into my head that I couldn't see there was any difference between a myth and a lie. Either it had to be true that Jesus was the one and only son of God, or it had to be untrue. My faith diminished and my doubts grew when Anglican bishops and clergy cast doubt on some of the miraculous stories about Jesus' life, such as the virgin birth and the resurrection. But the more I came to understand the importance of experience in religion, the more I came to realise that what mattered was the impact these stories had on me. As Bede Griffiths might have said, it was what they were signifying and the reality they were symbolising that mattered.

I remember attending a Mass in Old St Paul's Church in Edinburgh a few years ago that preserved the High Anglican tradition of mystery and was accompanied by beautiful music. As I was kneeling at the altar rails to take communion, I said to myself, 'I don't know exactly what this means, but I do know it means an awful lot to me.' That feeling could be dismissed as mere emotion, even nostalgia, induced by an inspiring service. Obviously it was not a rational thought. But, to my mind at least, it was a sign of the deeper reality enshrined in the sacrament.

I recently came across a passage in Karen Armstrong's book *A Short History of Myth* that helped me to understand why that Mass had meant so much to me. Comparing the medieval Catholic Mass with the communion service of the sixteenth-century Protestant reformers she says, 'Like any pre-modern rite, the Mass had re-enacted Christ's sacrificial death, which because it was mystical was timeless, and made it a present reality. For the reformers it was simply a memorial of a bygone event.' Because the Mass in Edinburgh had been celebrated in the Anglo-Catholic tradition and because it was celebrated with such reverence for the mystery of the sacrament, it had become a present reality for me. But I have nevertheless found that myth can be seductive. The concept of a meaning that can't be expressed in words has sometimes lured me into forgetting the importance of expressing in words whatever we can.

Like Christianity, Islam is a Semitic religion, and it is as difficult for Muslim theologians to accept pluralism as it is for many Christians. Nevertheless, there are Islamic scholars in India who have taken a public stand in favour of pluralism. One of them is Maulana Wahiduddin, who lives on the other side of the main road from my flat in Delhi. The Maulana was one of the religious leaders who met Prince Charles at the gathering I organised. In a brief presentation he said, 'I am a Muslim; Islam is my religion but I honour other religions.'

When I set out to write this chapter, I went to see Maulana Wahiduddin again. He was quite elderly now and, with his long beard and untidy hair held down by a traditional turban, no one could have mistaken him for anything but a Muslim scholar. I was anxious to get the Maulana, who is an orthodox Sunni scholar, to expand on what he had said at the meeting with Prince Charles.

'I can put it quite simply,' he explained. 'There is this quotation from the Holy Koran: "For you your religion, for me mine." So the only logical formula is mutual respect.' He went on to tell me a traditional story from the life of the Prophet. One day when the Prophet was living in Medina, he saw a funeral procession passing by and stood up as a mark of respect. One of his companions asked him why he had paid respect when it was the funeral of a Jew, not a Muslim. The prophet replied, 'Was he not a human being?'

I asked the Maulana what he would say to those who dismissed non-Muslims as *kafirs*, an abusive word for non-believers. He explained that this was a specific term that was relevant only to those who were contemporaries of the Prophet and had heard him preach for twenty years but who still did not accept what he taught. It was a word that had had no relevance since the Prophet's life time. 'According to my studies,' he said, 'everyone is a human and no one is a *kafir*. If you say a Hindu is a *kafir* that is a heresy.'

The Maulana rejoiced in India's religious pluralism and believed that Muslims enjoyed 'far better conditions' in India than in any Islamic country, saying, 'In Islamic countries they either have peace or freedom; in India they have both.'

'Why is that?' I wondered.

'Because India has respect for all religions,' he replied. 'The credit goes to Hinduism. It is a very special kind of religion, which believes all religions are true. No other religion on earth believes that.'

Sadly, Maulana Wahihuddin and Muslims like him don't only have to face provocation from extreme Hindu nationalists such as Dr Togadia. In 2006, BJP Members of Parliament refused to accept a sensible compromise in a row which blew up when the government unwisely announced that the centenary of the nationalist song *Vande Mataram* should be celebrated by being sung in all schools. *Vande Mataram* might well have become India's national anthem if Muslims had not objected to the song, which calls on Indians to worship the motherland. Islam, being strictly monotheistic, allows only the worship of Allah. When some Muslims reminded the education minister of the difficulties they had with the song, he agreed that only those children who wanted to sing it need do so. However, instead of accepting this suggestion, the BJP Members of Parliament attempted to provoke a Muslim backlash by charging onto the floor of the Upper House of Parliament chanting *Vande Mataram* and shouting slogans such as 'Traitors, leave India!', impugning the loyalty of the Muslim community.

To suggest that anyone can be a traitor to India merely because of their religion plays right into the hands of those Muslims who are not as open-minded as Maulana Wahiduddin, and who do not want their followers to believe that they are equal citizens of the secular democracy that has been guaranteed by India's long tradition of pluralism. When I was working with the BBC, the Shahi, or Royal Imam, of the Jama Masjid, the principal mosque in Old Delhi, was a political prelate who attempted to build up a constituency by highlighting Muslim grievances. His was an important position. As Imam of perhaps the largest mosque in India – which was built by the architect of the Taj, the Mughal Emperor Shah Jahan, to outdo in splendour any other mosque – the Imam regularly addressed large congregations and didn't hesitate to preach politics from the pulpit.

The Imam became a big-time player in the confused political scene that followed the defeat of Indira Gandhi at the end of the Emergency in 1977. He was wooed by warring politicians, who believed he could influence the Muslim vote, and was much given to confusing them by issuing enigmatic statements from his office in a corner of the mosque.

I particularly remember one occasion when I struggled to the Jama Masjid, having received a call from the Imam saying, 'Tully Sahib, you have to come today! I have a very important announcement to make.' At the time, controversy raged over who should become the Prime Minister after the fractious Janata party had won the post-Emergency election. After a lengthy discussion about the political scene, I eventually asked, 'Imam Sahib, where do you stand in all this?'

A bulky man of impressive appearance, the Imam sat back, paused, looked at his watch and eventually said slowly, in his deep sonorous voice, 'Today, at two o'clock, I have reached this conclusion – that I am not yet in favour of anyone nor against anyone.'

Eventually the Imam came down on the side of a politician opposed to Morarji Desai, the Gandhian who eventually emerged from all the bickering as the Prime Minister. Being on the losing side, the Imam aroused Muslim anger against the government. Desai wrote to one of his senior colleagues, 'It is quite clear to me that wherever he goes, [the Imam] is indulging in propaganda which is likely to create further communal hatred and pose problems for us. His approach to the problems is blatantly prejudiced.'

In India, maintaining the tradition of pluralism is essential for the unity of the nation. In a country where the majority of people are devout, religion cannot be ignored, while the wide range of religions within the nation means that each one must respect the others' beliefs.

In a country such as Britain, the growing number of Hindus, Muslims and Buddhists has brought the issue of creating mutual understanding between religions into the spotlight. The troubled history of Ireland, and in particular the recent history of Northern Ireland and the sectarianism in Scotland, with its attendant rivalry between Catholics and Protestants, shows that there was always a need for pluralism, for more understanding between Christians of different denominations in the British isles. Now in Britain, Christians face the same challenge as Indian Christians – the challenge of accepting that other religions can lead to God.

Pluralism involves acknowledging the uncertainty of certainties. Unlike in India, where there is no sign of a weakening in any religion, surveys indicate that Christianity has been on the decline in Britain for many years now. If that decline is to be reversed, it seems to me that the Churches still have to be more willing to accept uncertainty about some of their moral teachings, to acknowledge that the ways in which people live their lives have changed and that therefore the Churches must change too if they are to remain relevant. Just as the Catholic Church in India is trying to integrate itself more into the life of the nation, so must the British Churches become more integrated into modern life in Britain, and that process means shedding some of their previously held certainties.

The Churches must, for instance, come to terms with science when its findings suggest that changes need to be made to their moral codes. The Anglican Community continues to be torn apart by the dispute between liberals, who accept scientific research showing that homosexuality is not a disorder, and those who insist on the traditional condemnation of all homosexual activity. Significantly, both sides insist on unconditional surrender. They are certain they are right and are not willing to consider compromise.

The dispute about homosexuality is particularly damaging to the Anglican Church because, as I remember from my younger days, it all too often gives the impression that morality is all about sex. Even today I meet people who ask me, 'Why is the Church so concerned about what we do in bed? Why doesn't it care more about what we do when we are out of bed?' If the Anglican Church were to find a way of accommodating the modern research that shows that homosexuality is not a disorder, it would help to dispel the image of an institution obsessed by sex. It would also surely bring the Church more in line with the message of a loving God that it preaches. Similarly, the Roman Catholic Church must also question its certainty about birth-control and about celibacy of the clergy.

The Churches are still very reluctant to admit to any doubts about their moral codes, and so at a time when people are seeking a religion of experience they all too often give the impression that morality remains Christianity's prime concern. Jesus, the teacher who inspired his followers with a Gospel of love, becomes instead the poet Swinburn's 'pale Galilean' 'from whose breath the world grew grey'. Of course, the Churches have to be concerned with morality, but they should surely be concentrating on teaching Christians how to experience God so deeply that they are inspired to live moral lives, rather than imposing an inflexible code on them. It is not as though moral doctrine hasn't changed and developed in the past. If it hadn't, the Churches for instance would not be able to practise usury by accepting interest on their investments – and where would that leave their finances? They would have to advocate abolishing the entire financial system on which the global economy is built.

*

When my tutor at Cambridge, Robert Runcie, became Archbishop of Canterbury he had to deal with various controversies that threatened to tear the Church of England apart. These principally concerned the ordination of women, who until then had not been allowed to become priests, and of homosexual men. He saw it as his job to prevent irreparable divisions in the Church. Although the Archbishop was personally in favour of the ordination of women, he urged the General Synod to proceed carefully, saying, 'We need to encourage some interplay between the various points of view.' He was attacked by his own colleague, the Bishop of London, as well as a Labour MP who was a member of Synod. They dismissed him as 'someone usually to be found nailing his colours to the fence', implying that he was a coward.

Those who implied that Robert Runcie was a coward had got him totally wrong. As a young officer in the Second World War, he was decorated for gallantry.

As Archbishop, he stood up to the imperious Prime Minister Margaret Thatcher throughout the controversy over the Church's critical report on the state of Britain's inner cities. When he preached at the service to celebrate Britain's victory in the Falklands War in 1982, he knew that Margaret Thatcher, her entourage and the powerful Conservative press were expecting a triumphant sermon. What they got was very different. The leader of the Conservatives' Backbench 1982 Committee said, 'I was sad and disappointed that there was no mention during the service that the Falklands crisis was an example of Britain standing alone for international law, freedom and democracy.' Robert Runcie had described war as a 'sign of human failure'. He had also said it was right to pray for the relatives of Argentine soldiers killed in the war as well as those who were bereaved in Britain.

In my view, the key to Robert Runcie and the reason I admire him so much is his insistence on the Church giving 'positive witness to the fact that integrity is a more fundamental virtue than orthodoxy ... A man of unimpeachable orthodoxy and questionable integrity is a far greater threat to Christian truth than the man of questionable orthodoxy but undeniable integrity.' Although he was the leader of the Anglican Communion, there were times when he too had doubts about his faith, and he had the integrity to admit that.

While the Churches are declining in Britain there is evidence that interest in spirituality is increasing. The heaving shelves of the Body, Mind and Spirit sections in the bookshops testify to this, as does the response my colleagues and I get to the radio programme *Something Understood*, which explores spiritual matters. The Australian academic David Tacey has written a book called *The Spiritual Revolution* about this phenomenon. He describes the revolution as:

> ... a spontaneous movement in society, a new interest in the reality of the spirit and its healing effects on life, health, community and well-being. It is our secular society realising that it has been running on empty, and has to restore itself at a deep primal source, a source which is beyond humanity and yet paradoxically at the very core of our experience.

When I was in the BBC in India there were occasions when I found myself acting as the guardian of various spiritual seekers who had some sort of connection with the corporation. Once, I was telephoned by two young men who had been arrested at a religious festival for not having their passports. They said this was the only call the police were allowing them, so I must do something to help them. Through friends in the Rajasthan police I managed to get them back to Delhi, where they could pick up their passports from the hostel in which they had left them, but I was not able to prevent the young men being brought to the city in chains.

Young people who come to India nowadays in search of spirituality still stop by to have a drink or a cup of tea at my home – not, I hasten to say, because they think I am likely to be the guru they are looking for. Some are the children of friends; some I have met on my visits to Britain; some have listened to broadcasts, and some have read Gilly's and my books. Whoever they are, it is always interesting to talk to them, although these days the spiritual seekers I encounter are rarely Christians. Often they seem to be confused, thinking that there is a divide between organised religion as they know it and spirituality.

Why are these spiritual seekers so seldom Christian? When I ask them about this, the explanations I get include variations on the following themes: 'The Churches are not relevant any longer', 'the Churches do nothing but preach about morality', 'Christianity is not a spiritual religion'. The Churches must bear some of the blame for this. As the Irish poet Diarmuid O'Muyrchu says in his book *Religion in Exile*: 'the prevailing culture, especially within the formal Church or religion, tends to protect the old values and can be quite harsh in its treatment of those whose spiritual growth leads them in other directions'.

The Anglican priest and philosopher Giles Fraser provides an example of how harsh the Church can be on spiritual seekers. In an article in the Anglican newspaper the *Church Times*, he describes spirituality as religion that has been mugged by 'capitalism's only moral value; choice'. Giles Fraser accuses private and inner religion of 'the moral failing of being easily conscripted by self regard' and goes on to explain that:

> ... the moral and philosophical objections to 'spirituality' coalesce on the insistence that religion can never be a conversation of one. Religion, and religious experience as a part of it, is properly a conversation with others. It's always part of a tradition.

But he nevertheless admits that spirituality-shopping reflects a failure of the Church.

And Giles Fraser has a point: spirituality should be part of a tradition, otherwise it can all too easily become self-indulgent and concerned with how we feel and not how others do.

The Dalai Lama is the much-loved spiritual superstar of our times, although he would never accept that description of himself. He is so widely loved because of his simplicity and because he does not take himself too seriously, qualities all too rarely found in superstars. I once interviewed him in connection with a concert of music of all religions that he was promoting. When I asked what music meant to him I expected to be told about the spirituality of music, but instead the answer I received was wonderfully honest: 'I'm not very good at telling tunes,' the Tibetan secular and spiritual leader confessed, and paused for one of his inimitable giggles. 'I prefer silent meditation.' Another giggle – 'Helps you go to sleep, you know!' – by which point I was also in fits of laughter.

I once heard the Dalai Lama asked why there were different schools of Tibetan Buddhism. With a broad smile he replied, 'Because there are different sorts of people.' But while being open-minded, and accepting the role of the individual in choosing which faith to practise, the Dalai Lama does not support those who take individuality so far as to refuse all involvement in organised religion. He is the heir of a religious tradition that began in India 2,500 years ago, and, as such, he believes that his tradition and the traditions of others have a common purpose. This is: 'the betterment of humanity, to bring about a more compassionate and harmonious humanity'.

While the Dalai Lama has played a major role in the growth of interest in Eastern spirituality in the West, so inadvertently have the Western Churches, by giving the impression that they don't always welcome spirituality. Yet Christianity itself has a long tradition of spirituality, which is still alive today. Beginning with the Bible, who would say that some of the psalms, St John's Gospel and passages from St Paul's Epistles are not spiritual? Then, in the early days of the Christian Church, there were the Desert Fathers, who lived extraordinarily ascetic lives. The middle ages saw the creation of such spiritual classics as *The Sixteen Revelations of Divine Love*, written by the fourteenth-century mystic Julian of Norwich, and the anonymous work *The Cloud of Unknowing*. These works were followed by the writings of metaphysical poets such as George Herbert, Henry Vaughan and John Donne in the late fifteenth and sixteenth centuries. And so the Church's history of spirituality continues, until we come in my own life time to the works of writers such as my teacher Harry Williams and poets such as the Welsh R.S. Thomas, also an Anglican priest. Thomas described poetry as 'that which arrives at the intellect by way of the heart'.

But I must not be too hard on the Churches. They still provide for spiritual seekers. When I read the Roman Catholic magazine the *Tablet*, I am struck by the advertisements for Christian retreats; renewal programmes; mind, body, spirit courses; spirituality centres and other places in which to read, pray and reflect.

The modern Christian Meditation Movement provides a particular link with the East, as its founder, John Main, first learnt to meditate from a Hindu monk. When he himself became a Benedictine monk, he was discouraged from meditating by his novice master, who did not regard meditation as a Christian practice, but eventually he overcame that traditionalist attitude. Now John Main's successor – another Benedictine monk, Lawrence Freeman – travels the world, teaching Christian meditation. (He landed up in my flat on a recent visit to India.) So the marriage of East and West appears to be flourishing.

Yet, for all that they do offer, it seems to me that the Churches in Britain will not attract the sort of spiritual seekers I meet in India if they don't become more Indian themselves; that is to say, more tolerant of plurality and more willing to question their certainties. But the Indian tradition must not be understood to mean that Christianity should forfeit all claims to certainty merely in order to avoid conflict with others, or that it should come to feel it should avoid all moral judgements.

Sarvepalli Radhakrishnan describes the Hindu attitude to the *Vedas* as 'trust tempered by criticism' – tempered, he says, 'by the recognition of the truth that God has never finished the revelation of his wisdom and love'. This comes close to the thinking of Richard Clarke, an Anglican bishop I once met in Ireland. In his book *And Is It True*, the Bishop criticises the Western Church for being 'awash with certainties for centuries'. But this does not mean he gives up on Christianity. He uses the metaphor of no man's land in the First World War – the trenches that soldiers had to move into if they were to advance – as a metaphor for where Christians should stand today. He describes it as 'a place of acute vulnerability, a place where one is exposed, almost defenceless, often floundering, probably wounded, and very likely caught in continuing crossfire from the trenches on both sides'. No man's land may be an uncomfortable place, but Richard Clarke assures his readers, 'I am certain that we should not expect to find truth or God in the safety of our personal custom-built trenches.' According to the Bishop, 'to be afraid of truth is to be afraid to change one's ideas and is, in the poet Blake's phrase, "to breed reptiles in the mind".'

When I read those words, I took Bishop Clarke's no man's land metaphor as a personal warning. I sometimes find that, by accepting uncertainty, I am standing safely in a trench, protected from any attack on my beliefs because I believe there is no ultimate truth that can undermine them. So I need to remember that the Indian tradition does not say there is no truth, no ultimate reality. What it does say is that the ultimate reality cannot be fully and finally defined – there is always that *neti, neti*. And we have to keep on searching in order to get closer and closer to it.

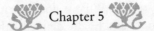

Chapter 5

CAMBRIDGE: LESSONS IN HUMILITY

CAMBRIDGE is a beautiful city at any time but, with my tendency to nostalgia, I like it best in the autumn. My old college, Trinity Hall, is one of those on the banks of the River Cam, overlooking the famous meadows known as 'the Backs'. Autumn is a season of change. The trees are bare and the Backs are carpeted with golden leaves. It was in autumn that I started my first term at Trinity Hall, a time of great change in my life. At last, after all those years in boarding school and then the army, I felt free.

I went back to Cambridge in the autumn of 2006, exactly fifty years after the beginning of my first year there. I had returned to take part in a special weekend of events organised by the University for its alumni. The amazing variety of activities included the opportunity to sing in a performance of Mozart's *Requiem*, which was to be conducted by one of Britain's best known modern composers, John Rutter. Not trusting my musical ear sufficiently, it was an opportunity that I didn't intend to take up.

However, another of the activities was to be a discussion on religion and secularism, which I was to lead and in which some of the University's outstanding scholars were to take part. The publicity for Alumni Day stated that we would be talking about 'the growing tension between religious belief and the outside world, and trying to address the very topical question: which came first – aggressive secularism or religious fanaticism?'

The panel was chaired by the Regius Professor of Theology, David Ford, and one of the other participants was the atheist Simon Blackburn, Professor of Philosophy at Cambridge. Not surprisingly, wide differences emerged among the panel, but these were discussed calmly and rationally. Inevitably, I was nervous that I would be intellectually mauled by scholars who had studied this subject much more deeply than I had, but I need not have worried. We all treated each other's views with respect.

In my introduction to the discussion, I suggested that the Indian tradition of accepting that there can be many different ways to God, and thereby respecting the followers of all religions, as well as those who didn't believe in any religion, could prevent conflict arising between the opposing factions of aggressive secularism and religious fundamentalism. I described a day when I had woken up in Delhi and switched on the BBC World Service broadcast as usual only to hear a debate about Christmas cards. It was suggested that the cards were no longer appropriate because they were not 'secular' – that much abused word again – and might offend believers of other religions. The cards, it was proposed, should simply say 'Happy holiday' instead of 'Happy Christmas'. Yet that same morning over breakfast, when I picked up my copy of the *Hindu*, an Indian daily, I found that the picture on the front page showed the Governor of West Bengal, a Hindu, throwing a Christmas party for children, the vast majority of whom were not Christians.

After the discussion was over, a member of the audience who came from Bradford (a city in the north of England with a large Muslim population) approached me and said she thought cutting Christmas out of the December holiday would be justified in order to avoid offending Muslims. So I told her about the way that religious holidays are celebrated in India.

There, we have public holidays to mark the births of the Prophet Muhammad, the Hindu god Rama, the Sikh Guru Nanak, the Buddha and Mahavira (the patriarch of the Jains), as well as the birth and the death of Jesus Christ.

At Eid, men and boys dressed in sparkling white new clothes, with prayer caps on their heads, hurry to mosques scattered all over Delhi to pray. Little girls, decked out in bright new *shalwar* suits and looking like tiny dolls, hold tightly to their fathers' and brothers' hands. The congregation at one of Asia's largest mosques, Delhi's Jama Masjid, overflows into the surrounding streets. The rows of the faithful bow almost as one man in the ordered worship presided over by the *Shahi*, or Royal Imam. Every Eid that we are in Delhi, Gilly and I are invited by Muslim friends living near the Jama Masjid to their family feast of home-made shami kebab, korma and biryani.

On other occasions, I have stood alongside Hindus and Muslims in the small north Indian town of Mustafabad to watch young Shia men walking bare-foot over smouldering coals and then see them process through the streets, pounding their chests and lashing their backs with knives attached to chains. They identify with the agony of Imam Husain, the Prophet's grandson, whose martyrdom in a conflict over the leadership of the Muslim community in the early years is remembered on the tenth day of the Muslim month of Muharram.

Crowds of all faiths watch Sikh warriors ride their prancing horses (which are clearly overfed with oats) and joust with eight-foot long spears to celebrate the martial tradition of their religion during the spring festival of Hola Mahalla. As for Christmas – then every bazaar is as brightly illuminated as London's Regent Street and no one would dream of questioning the theme of the decorations, which is, of course, 'Happy Christmas'.

All these and many other religious festivals are observed in India without any questioning. Yet India describes itself in its constitution as a 'sovereign, socialist, secular, democratic republic'.

There is, however, a form of secularism that I sense is hostile. While I certainly don't wish to suggest that I am opposed to secularism in as far as it implies the separation of state and Church, I am uneasy about a form of secularism which goes beyond that. This form of secularism argues that religion should be entirely confined to private life, and doesn't accept the right of public figures to express their religious convictions. It is an extreme, unbalanced, but nevertheless highly influential secularism that tends to regard religion with scorn and often portrays it as disreputable. This secularism claims to advocate freedom as its highest value, but doesn't always seem to accept that people should be free to practise their own religion. The ban in France on Muslim school children wearing headscarves is an obvious example of a legal constraint on freedom of religion. Britons interpreting secularism as meaning that there should be no public celebration of Christmas, provide an example of a social pressure that impinges on religious freedom. Perhaps because believers in this type of secularism have no time for religion themselves, they see no need to provide a place in society for those who do.

As I understand it, there are four main causes for the rise of the sort of illiberal secularism that sets up a shouting match with religion. Those reasons are fear of religion, hostility to religion, a misunderstanding of science and indifference to the issues central to religion.

It is easy to understand the fear generated by Islamic terrorism, by the Christian terrorism that used to plague Northern Ireland, or by the Sikh terrorism in India during the eighties. But time and again I am told that religion is evil because it *causes* terrorism – as though it were the only cause. There are many other causes of terrorism in the world. For example, disputes between different ethnic groups can cause terrorism, such as the campaign of the Tamil Tigers in Sri Lanka. There are also instances of linguistic and regional terrorism, but do we say that we should all speak one language because differences of tongue provoke terrorism, or that taking pride in our ethnicity, our place of birth or culture is wrong because this too can provoke terrorism?

And what about state terrorism? The two most appalling perpetrators of state terrorism in the twentieth century were Hitler and Stalin. Hitler massacred Jews in the name of racial, not religious, purity. And Stalin was enforcing an atheistic creed. While the Spanish Civil War has gone down in history as a righteous war against Fascism – and I would agree that Fascism should have been challenged, and that in this instance the Church was on the wrong side – the republicans turned the civil war into a battle between atheism and Catholicism, a war in which they burnt churches, and killed bishops, priests and monks. Even nuns were not spared. The writer Hugh Thomas describes horrific incidents in which priests' ears were cut off, rosary beads were shoved into monks' ears to perforate their eardrums, the mother of two Jesuit priests had a rosary forced down her throat, and 800 people were thrown down a mine-shaft. There were certainly atrocities on the other side as well, but – as Hitler, Stalin and the Spanish republicans show – religion does not have a monopoly on terrorism.

Whenever there is violence in the name of religion it is important to set this violence in a broader context, to look for the political and economic issues that may well be involved, and to discover whether the violence is spontaneous or engineered. Since the sixties, Ahmedabad, the main city of the western state of Gujarat and the city in which Mahatma Gandhi established his first Indian ashram, has earned for itself an unenviable reputation for what is called in India 'communal violence'. This term almost always refers to violence between Hindus and Muslims.

The worst outbreak of communal violence during my first spell in India occurred in Ahmedabad in 1969. The official figure for people killed in six violent days when people were hacked to death, speared and burnt alive, was 1,200. This is bad enough, but some say the figure should be 2,500. When it was all over, sober political analysts reckoned that the riots had been caused by the widening rift between the Prime Minister, Indira Gandhi, and her rival within the Congress, the veteran Gujarati politician Morarji Desai. There was indeed evidence to suggest that the riots had been engineered by members of the Indira Gandhi faction in order to discredit the Chief Minister of Gujarat, who was a supporter of Morarji.

After the riots in Ahmedabad in 1990, which broke out in the middle of Ramazan, the Muslim month of fasting, I interviewed a group of Muslim women who earned a living by hand-printing cloth. Muslims had, as is more often than not the case, come off worst in the riots. But the consensus among these women was summed up by Hasina, the most vocal member of the group, who said, 'These riots are nothing to do with Hindus or Muslims. It's all about politicians. When the Congress comes to power the BJP does it, and when the BJP comes to power the Congress does it. It's just to give the new government a bad name!'

Raoof Valiullah, a Muslim Congress member of the Upper House of Parliament whose ancestral home was in the heart of the old city, said to me, 'Communal strife arises because a communal riot is the only thing which can bring down a government.' Ela Bhatt founded in Ahmedabad one of the most admired Indian NGOs, the Self Employed Women's Association, or SEWA. When I asked her about Valiullah's view, she said, 'I agree with those who say that riots are used to change the politics of the state.'

The opposite was true of the outbreak of communal violence in Ahmedabad and other parts of Gujarat in 2002. In that instance, the Chief Minister, Narendra Modi, a hawkish member of the BJP, clearly thought that riots would strengthen his own position. It was reported that Muslims had attacked a train just outside a station in north Gujarat. Many of the passengers on the train were members of Hindu organisations who were returning from a rally in Ayodhya, where they had been to protest against the failure to build the controversial temple I mentioned in Chapter 4. A fire broke out in which many of the passengers died. Although it's still not clear exactly what happened on that train, it's all too clear what happened afterwards: three days of rioting followed, in which the police totally failed in their duty to maintain law and order, allowing Hindu mobs to roam freely around Ahmedabad and other towns in Gujarat attacking Muslims and their property. Then, instead of apologising for the riots, Narendra Modi went on to mount a distinctly communal campaign to fight the next election to the state assembly.

I find that those who suggest we should try to understand why some young men were so hostile to America that they were prepared to kill themselves on 9/11, are all too often dismissed as being soft on terrorism. However, President Bush's call for a 'war on terrorism' is subconsciously, and often consciously, interpreted by Muslims as American imperialism's call for a war on Islam. If Muslims are to be convinced that this is not the case, then the United States and other Western countries have to open a dialogue with Islam. This will involve challenging the West's certainties and discovering what it is that Muslims find disturbing about Western culture.

When I have asked Islamic clerics in India, Afghanistan, Pakistan, and Bangladesh why Muslim fundamentalism is spreading, they have almost all replied, 'Because Muslims are afraid of your culture, which they regard as godless and obscene.'

Fundamentalism feeds on fear. An Anglican Bishop in Ireland recently said to me, 'When people are frightened, they rush to nanny and the security of the nursery – and fundamentalism is the nursery, where all your thinking is done for you.' In *The Battle for God*, her study of how and why religious fundamentalist thinking arises, Karen Armstrong writes: 'Fundamentalism exists in a symbiotic relationship with an aggressive liberalism or secularism and, under attack, increasingly becomes more bitter, extreme, and excessive.' Shouldn't the United States and Europe take the time to consider whether their culture might appear to be aggressive to Muslims, just as Islam appears to be aggressive to them?

I have been told so often by Islamic clerics that Western culture is obscene that when Kabul was captured from the Taliban I was struck by a thought that may appear strange to many. At the time, it was virtually impossible to open a newspaper or turn on a radio without hearing about Afghan women throwing off their *burqas*. But I wondered whether we shouldn't also be taking this opportunity to discuss the possibility that our Western attitudes to nudity and our explicit sex scenes in films and books might unintentionally have strengthened the hands of those who forced their women to cover themselves from top to toe in the first place. Our attitudes may have given them the grounds upon which to insist that the *burqa* is essential to protect women from the culture propagated in the West.

Given recent demands to ban not only the *burqa* but also headscarves in some European countries, I can't help feeling that the Indian Muslim writer M.J. Akbar is right to question which is the more civilised – the headscarf or the thong. If it is illiberal to attack near-nudity, why is it not illiberal to attack wearing certain clothes? The British playwright David Edgar ends an article called 'We can't just pick and choose what to tolerate' with this statement:

> Yes, the veil can be alienating to people trying to communicate with the person wearing it. But if we want to have a leg to stand on when we stand up for *The Satanic Verses*, or *Behzti*, or *Jerry Springer*, we must defend to the death the right to wear it.

In Western eyes the *burqa* has become a symbol of Islam as a repressive religion and, as such, it is impossible for many of us to conceive that there might be women who prefer to wear it. In 1993 I made a programme for BBC Radio 4 called *Fundamentally Wrong*, which argued that Islam took many different shapes in Pakistan and that by no means all Muslims supported fundamentalism. My partner Gilly, who was the programme researcher, spoke to women belonging to two different families in Lahore. She discovered that the women of one family liked wearing *burqas* whenever they went out because they felt safer in them, as they were protected from men staring at them and from the sexual harassment sometimes suffered by those women who didn't wear *burqas*. In the other family, the women went even further. They said they were quite happy to be obliged to stay at home. One said, 'Women basically are everything. Men are only good for working outside the home. But there is no home without us, no family, no society.'

In a village outside Lahore, we came across women who envied those living in *purdah*, the practice of shielding women from the eyes of male strangers, even in the home. One of the village women said, 'Those who eat well can afford *purdah*. We who are poor, even by hard work we can't get enough to eat, so we can't afford *purdah*. But if we get a chance we'll do it. Mind you,' she added, 'we are used to roaming around the place, so we might find it a little suffocating.'

Of course, we also found women who did not want to be

in *purdah*, but even they resented what they saw as Western society telling them what to wear and how to live. A woman psychiatrist felt this resentment was inevitable as long as the West remained rich and so many Islamic countries poor. She told me, 'As the gap between developed and under-developed countries increases, the people who are poor are going to feel more and more threatened, and we are going to stick to our customs and our religions in order to have some security, some self-esteem.'

So if we in the West routinely criticise Muslim customs because they offend our concept of secularism, and thereby give the impression that we are hostile to Islam, we may well only be strengthening the fundamentalist form of the religion that we fear.

Hostility to religion, which I hold to be the second of the four contributing factors to illiberal secularism, is stirred up by secular fundamentalists who are often quite as aggressive as any religious fundamentalist. When we were talking about this at the Alumni Weekend discussion in Cambridge, Simon Blackburn, the Professor of Philosophy, argued that atheism couldn't be aggressive or dominant by itself because you couldn't be aggressive about something you didn't believe in. 'We just tiptoe past,' he said. The Roman Catholic Eamon Duffy, one of Britain's leading historians of the Church, disagreed, saying that he was a reader of the *Independent*, a British national newspaper, and was 'more or less daily deeply offended by some of the journalism'. He quoted a recent article in which the journalist had said, 'We should hate Pope Benedict'.

Polly Toynbee is one of the prominent secular fundamentalist journalists. Her attacks on Christianity include a virulent review of the film made in 2005 about the much loved *Narnia* stories by Christian apologist C.S. Lewis. She warned non-believers watching it to 'keep their sick-bags handy'. Her piece also described Aslan the Lion, who is clearly a representation of Christ, as 'an emblem of everything an atheist objects to in religion. His divine presence is a way to avoid humans taking responsibility for everything here and now on earth'. But surely humans have shown time and time again that they are not capable of taking responsibility for everything and that it's precisely when they take upon themselves too much responsibility – when they play God – that they bring about disasters.

Similarly, instead of encouraging the growth of a genuinely secular society in which everyone's faith or lack of faith is respected, the National Secular Society of Britain promotes hostility to religion. It claims that secularism should be supported by those who want to be 'on the side of all humanity, the side of intelligence, rationality, and decency'. The Society is certainly 'vigorous in its opposition to the forces of superstition, obscurantism, and illiberalism'. However, the view that any cause that is not secular is illiberal, seems to me to be illiberal itself.

There are many in India who speak of the form of secularism established by Nehru as if it involved being opposed to religion. But although Nehru himself was not religious, he had a great respect for Indian culture and understood that the new nation must provide space for its ancient tradition of religious pluralism. He had many opponents who believed there were only two alternatives – a secular state that did not have any time for religion, or a theocratic state. Yet Nehru was quite clear that there was a middle way, that secularism should and could involve respect for religion. He said, 'When we talk about a secular state, this does not mean simply some negative idea, but a positive approach on the basis of equality of opportunity for everyone, man or woman, of any religion or caste.'

Purshottam Das Tandon, who mounted a serious challenge to Nehru in the early days of independence by putting himself forward as a candidate in the election for the President of the Congress party, called on Indian Muslims to adopt 'Hindu culture'. In reply to this, Nehru said scathingly, 'It is only those who lack all understanding of culture who talk so much about it.' It often seems to be the case that it is those who talk most about secularism that understand it the least; and the same goes for those who talk most about religion. In India, it's certainly true that those who chant secularism like a mantra fail to understand that secularism does not imply hostility to religion. It is equally true those Hindus who talk most about Hinduism often fail to understand the pluralism of their religion. The Hindu politician Dr Praveen Togadia (whom we met in Chapter 3) speaks incessantly about religion, but many Hindus would venture to say that he knows little about his own faith.

As for the Indian secular fundamentalists, they regard anyone who speaks about religion at all as being a religious fundamentalist. Some years ago a secularist organisation asked me to be one of the judges of a competition for students who had been asked to draw posters advocating secularism. The one chosen as the winner depicted a Muslim cleric, a Hindu priest and a Christian clergyman, with a slogan underneath that ran, 'Would you trust any of these?' The obvious implication was that all religious teachers were dangerous fundamentalists.

In 2003 I made a film about Mahatma Gandhi's view on the place of religion in India which I mentioned in Chapter 1. I interviewed Gurcharan Das, the former head of a multinational's Indian operation. To illustrate an Indian secularist attitude to religion, he told me about a friend who had asked him how he was spending his retirement. Gurcharan Das said, 'Looking at the *Vedas* among other things.'

His friend replied, 'Oh, so you have become one of them!' By 'them', he meant the followers of Hindu extremists such as Togadia.

*

Those scientists who oppose religion on the grounds that it is not scientific, and who claim that science disproves the existence of God, form my third contributing factor to illiberal secularism. Of course, it would be illiberally religious to deny that there are many arguments that can be made against the existence of God. In India as well as in the West, atheist and materialist schools of thought have enquired profoundly into many of the same questions about the meaning of life that religions have tackled. Some would argue that by accepting that death is final, in which case life might be held to be meaningless, atheists show more courage than theologians. But scientists who argue that God doesn't exist because his existence can't be proved scientifically are often fundamentalists in that they believe that science alone holds the answers to every question.

That said, it's hardly surprising that many people do put their faith in science and technology. The achievements of both are amazing and their progress apparently never-ending. Science and technology are forever unveiling new discoveries about our world. Through them, we are able to travel into space, improve our chances of longevity and invent more and more ways of communicating with each other.

There have been tremendous advances in my own lifetime. When I was a child, we had to travel to and from India by ship, as air transport was still in its infancy. When my uncle was sent to India to become a tea planter in the plains below Darjeeling, he was only granted his first home leave after seven years, whereas now I am able to fly back to Britain at least twice a year.

When I first came to India, we still often sent despatches by telegram. When we did try to send them in voice, we had to go through an incredibly cumbersome process that involved sitting in a studio while engineers pushed leads into sockets and pulled them out again, shouting, 'Can you hear me, can you hear me?!' It took a long time for the answer 'yes' to come back from the London end of the line. Even when we had progressed to using telephones, after three or four attempts at getting my despatch across in good quality sound, the traffic manager receiving my call would all too often complain, 'I'm awfully sorry, Mark, but it's still not broadcastable.' Then I would wake up the next day and switch on the radio to hear the deathly words after my report: 'That despatch was read in the studio.' So much for my attempts to phone it through. Nowadays reporters can easily send top-quality despatches and pictures from any part of the world by using a satellite telephone.

However, no comparable scientific progress has been made towards making our communications with God clearer, so perhaps it's natural that many people – especially those seduced by the success of science – believe that therefore God cannot exist. These same individuals then become contemptuous of religion. But, as Ravi Ravindra, Professor Emeritus of Canada's Dalhousie University (where he held the Chair of Comparative Religion and was also Professor of Physics), has said: 'The relationship between science and religion is best understood as one of constructive dialogue rather than the popular idea of a conflict that science is winning.' And the Indian thinker Ananda K. Coomeraswamy comments: 'A real conflict between science and religion is impossible: the actual conflicts are always of certain scientists ignorant of spiritual philosophy with fundamentalists who maintain that the truth of their myth is historical.'

Those scientists are the high priests of scientism, a creed that upholds the primacy of science over all other interpretations of life and regards reason and empirical experiments as the only valid source for truthfully addressing questions about the world. This is an unbalanced creed because it allows little or no validity to other means of perception. Ravi Ravindra warns:

The search for truth – when it becomes more and more mental and divorced from deeper and higher feelings such as compassion, a sense of the oneness and the like – leads to feelings of isolation and accompanying anxiety ... Then one wants to control others and conquer nature. Much of our predicament arises from this very dedication to truth in an exclusively mental manner.

The Oxford biologist Richard Dawkins is, in my view, one of the most pugnacious and best known preachers of scientism. He is as zealous in his attempts to root out religion as were the Christian missionaries who preached the gospel and tried to eradicate beliefs they classified as pagan. For him, religious believers appear to be like the heathen described by the second Bishop of Kolkata, Reginald Heber, in his hymn 'From Greenland's Icy Mountains to India's Coral Strand'. Heber's heathen 'bow down to stick and stone' and need 'to be delivered from error's chain'.

Dawkins once asked: 'What has theology ever said that is of the smallest use to anyone? When has theology ever said anything that is demonstrably true and is not obvious?' He misses no opportunity to challenge religious people. His latest book has the confrontational title *The God Delusion*. In it he asks questions I need to ask myself, and reminds me that atheism is not just credible but honourable too. Discussing God's role in consoling us in the face of death and offering us an alternative to the prospect of annihilation, Dawkins quotes Bertrand Russell's declaration in his essay of 1925:

I believe that when I die I shall rot, and nothing of my ego will survive. I am not young and I love life. But I should scorn to shiver with terror at the thought of annihilation. Happiness is none the less true happiness because it must come to an end, nor do thought and love lose their value because they are not everlasting. Many a man has born himself proudly on the scaffold; surely the same pride should teach us to think truly about man's place in the world. Even if the open windows of science at first make us shiver after the cosy indoor warmth of traditional humanizing myths, in the end the fresh air brings vigour, and the great spaces have a splendour of their own.

Reading this, I have to wonder how much my religion is a hangover from cosy beliefs that comforted me as a child.

However, it's not the validity of Dawkins' arguments that I would question so much as the absolute way that he puts them across. I was surprised to find that, according to his book, Dawkins doesn't 'by nature thrive on confrontation' and doesn't think that 'the adversarial format is well designed to get at the truth'. Be that as it may, to my mind, one of the main problems with his arguments lies in the antagonistic format he adopts and his intention to confront religious believers.

Dawkins doesn't appear to be particularly open to dialogue and discussion when, on the first page of his book, he writes: 'Imagine, with John Lennon, a world with no religion. Imagine no suicide bombers, no 9/11, no 7/7, no Crusades, no witch-hunts, no Gunpowder Plot, no Indian partition ...' and the discussion continues in that vein. Isn't this opening gambit a misleading over-simplification of those tragic events, designed to confront religious believers? And doesn't it imply that if there were no religion there would be no persecution, no terrorism and no war? Then, in a chapter called 'Childhood, Abuse and the Escape from Religion', Dawkins provocatively relates an incident in Dublin when, after a lecture, he was asked about sexual abuse by the Catholic clergy. To which he replied that 'horrible as sexual abuse no doubt was, the damage was arguably less than the long-term psychological damage inflicted by bringing the child up a Catholic in the first place.'

Dawkins maintains that biology has shown that natural selection explains the development of the universe and this means there cannot be an intelligent creator. He also says that the concept of a creator is so improbable that it can't be accepted as a solution. Keith Ward's book *God, Chance and Necessity* rebuts Dawkins' arguments. He points out: 'Any assertion that the hypothesis of natural selection can account for all the facts is a remarkably bold claim, when so many facts still remain unaccounted for, even in the realm of evolutionary biology.' In other words, Dawkins takes his theory too far. Ward also argues that Dawkins constructs his own God in order easily to knock that image down. According to him, Dawkins' God is a 'naively imagined, anthropomorphic God, who is unreasonably, irrationally, and blindly flattered and obeyed'. Atheists might well argue that this description tallies with the God of some religious people, and indeed this version of God may also emerge from an over-literal reading of scriptures. But this is not the concept of God embodied in the Christian God of Love, nor Allah the All-Merciful of Islam, nor the Ultimate Reality of Hinduism.

I suppose we all make our own God to some extent. I know that, over the years, I have adapted the image of God that I was taught to believe in when young into a far more tolerant deity, and that this is probably because I don't want to be as obsessed by sin as I used to be. Maybe I should be less lax about sin and revere a less tolerant God. On the other hand, Dawkins seems to replace God with an image that reduces us to nothing more than machines. He has said that we are 'survival machines – robot vehicles blindly programmed to preserve the selfish molecules known as genes'. He would, I am sure, hate to believe that his non-God and his barren mechanical human beings are his own creations. He believes that his version is scientific. But surely his rejection of God is influenced by his enthusiasm and his talent for science? Some have also suggested that Dawkins is influenced by the prevalent competitive capitalist, dog-eat-dog culture of Western secularism. That suggestion certainly fits with his interpretation of the evolutionary theory of the survival of the fittest.

However, scientists such as Dawkins do raise the difficult and crucial question of evil. He himself has made a television series called the *Root of All Evil*, referring inevitably to religion. Later he admitted that he regretted the title because 'no one thing is the root of all anything'. But he certainly didn't appear to regret attributing a great deal of evil to religion.

I realise that the issue of evil presents an insurmountable obstacle for many of those people who would otherwise be prepared to keep an open mind about religion. Religious leaders have to accept that God does not only appear malign to committed atheists such as Richard Dawkins. They also have to tread carefully when speaking of an omnipotent and loving God from the security of their pulpits when television brings into the homes of their congregations pictures of every natural disaster and the voices of survivors who have lost everything.

Discussion of the problem of evil becomes obscured when we fail to differentiate between man-made and natural disasters. I happened to be in London in September 2004, the day after the appalling tragedy at the Russian school in Beslan, North Ossetia. There, more than 340 people were killed when commandos stormed the building to release children held hostage by Chechnyan militants. To my mind, this was clearly an example of moral evil at work; and, when I heard one of the presenters of the BBC's combative breakfast show, *Today*, open his interview with the Archbishop of Canterbury by asking, 'So where was God yesterday?', I thought to myself, 'Where was *humanity*?' We humans were responsible for that terrible event. We can't take pride in our achievements, rejoice in our free will and then not accept responsibility for our failures.

Many disasters that are classified as natural have been caused or compounded by our human failures. In the aftermath of Bangladeshi cyclones, I have flown over uprooted villages and flooded fields littered with bodies – some floating in the water, some lying twisted in grotesque shapes, naked, their scant clothing torn away by the sea and the wind. And I've wondered about the economic system that forces people to scratch a living from islands that are below sea level. Can we really blame God for that economic system? Do we humans have no responsibility for it at all?

Diseases are often cited as proof that there can't be an omnipotent loving God. But God can't be blamed for all diseases. A few years ago I drove from the capital of the central Indian state of Chattisgarh to a hospital in a remote area run by a volunteer team of some of the country's best doctors. On the way we passed a government granary, which was so full that sacks stuffed with grain were piled in mountains outside as well as in. However, the doctors at the hospital told me that half of the patients they treated would not be ill if they had an adequate, balanced diet. Leprosy was one of the diseases that continued to afflict those weakened by malnutrition.

It would nevertheless be inhuman to deny that there are many disasters and diseases that are entirely beyond human agency. Although some cancer patients may have contributed to their illness by smoking and there are human-created environmental factors for some cancers, the majority of sufferers have done nothing to make themselves ill. Similarly, neither children nor their parents can be blamed for congenital illnesses. And, even if it was our economic system that put those Bangladeshi farmers at risk, why should there be a cyclone at all? Why should there be earthquakes? Why should there be droughts? Do they not prove that God is not all powerful – or, worse, that God is malign?

According to the Buddha, the world is suffering but we can end our suffering if we eliminate our desire. Some Hindu teachers maintain that suffering creates the longing to seek the realisation of God. Some Christians see the cross as a symbol of the need to suffer. They talk of 'redemptive suffering', meaning that suffering can lead us to reassess our lives and to realise that we need to find a deeper meaning than materialism alone can provide. It seems to have been almost obligatory for the great Christian mystics to suffer those long dark nights of the soul in which they were separated from God. But then why should a loving God make it necessary for us to suffer?

I can't pretend to have the answers to these profound questions, but I do know from personal experience that a belief in God and in the grace of God can provide comfort, hope and meaning in times of suffering. To explain suffering I have to fall back on the mysterious nature of God and on the realisation that He, and the suffering he apparently tolerates and perhaps even creates, cannot be entirely understood through reason alone. I am aware that those who think that the problem of suffering means we can dismiss God rationally would regard my views as a cop-out. But do they have a better explanation for suffering? Perhaps they would argue that we just have to accept its existence as a fact, and grin and bear it when there is nothing that can be done to alleviate or eliminate it.

In the modern classic *The Hitchhiker's Guide to the Galaxy* by Douglas Adams, there is a sound warning to all scientists, philosophers and theologians who claim too much certainty for their answers to the great questions about life. In *The Guide*, two philosophers threaten to call a strike of the Amalgamated Union of Philosophers, Sages, Luminaries and Other Thinking Persons because scientists have asked a 'stupendous, super computer' the answer to 'life, the universe and everything'. The philosophers realise that if the computer comes up with the answer they will be out of a job. However, when the computer is asked how long it will take to find the answer, it replies, 'Seven and a half million years', and it goes on to tell the philosophers that running a programme to answer the great question is bound to generate huge public interest, and therefore they'll be much in demand on the media. The scientists abandon all thoughts of a strike and walk out of the room 'into a lifestyle beyond their wildest dreams' ...

The fourth reason I gave for the rise of illiberal secularism was indifference. When people are indifferent to the questions that religion raises, they tend to be scornful of those who have a religious faith.

The ethos of Western society is materialist. As the Christian philosopher John Haldane has said, 'Growing material affluence has shifted consciousness away from questions about the objective meaning and value of life towards choices about which tangible goods to acquire and which lifestyle to cultivate.' It was put rather more bluntly to me by an Irish priest who noted that, 'We seem to be happy being cows in clover or pigs wallowing in plenty.' In an age in which it's possible to talk sincerely about the benefits of 'retail therapy', perhaps my priest friend is right. Serious questions about the meaning of life don't tend to arise when all is comfortable and pleasures abound.

The media has a powerful impact on the ethos of a society and in the West it tends to be indifferent to religion and often positively hostile. The British media has lost no opportunity to misrepresent Tony Blair's Christianity during his time as Prime Minister. There was, for instance, the controversy fuelled by the media in 2006 when, speaking of his decision to go to war with Saddam Hussein, Blair said, 'The only way you can take a decision like that is to try to do the right thing according to your conscience. I think if you have faith about these things then you realise judgement is made by other people ... and, if you believe in God, it is made by God.' The Prime Minister was accused of using God to justify his actions and thereby escape the consequences of the Iraq war. Yet he wasn't saying that God would necessarily justify his decision. Rather, he implied that God would be the judge of him, which is of course a Christian belief.

But that distinction was too subtle for the secular British press. The mere mention of God was enough to set off a Pavlovian response. Poor Mr Blair would have been better to remember the dictum of his former spin doctor Alistair Campbell who, when asked about his boss's religious views, said, 'We don't do God here.'

When the Western media is not overtly hostile to religion, it tends to be indifferent towards it. The Director General of the BBC at the time of writing, Mark Thompson, is a Roman Catholic himself and he has to tread carefully in order to avoid handing the secularists a weapon to use against him. Nevertheless, he admitted to the editor of the Roman Catholic weekly, the *Tablet*, that religion had been the poor relation of the BBC's programming and that he was trying to encourage 'more of a spirit of adventure' in the Corporation's output. He talked about 'looking at the more interesting aspects of religion' and attempting to 'reinvent' the BBC's approach. But in the following week's edition of the *Tablet*, the Director General was warned that his ambitions might get bogged down in a swamp of indifference. In a letter to the editor, Patricia Maxwell Lewis, a BBC television producer, said the problem with religious broadcasting lay not at the top of the Corporation but on the shop floor. She pointed out that individual producers had their own agendas and world views, which she said might be 'disturbingly narrow and invariably secular in nature'. The television producer claimed that she had only succeeded in getting religious items aired by stealth and was 'consistently dismayed by the dismissive way in which religious proposals were generally regarded'.

The message the media puts across is not limited to the news it reports, the articles and columns it publishes, or the programmes it broadcasts. There is also the message of the advertisements that the media depends on for its revenues. Advertisers probably make a more powerful contribution to the social ethos than journalists do. Their message is simple and stark: it's what you buy that matters, not what you believe. The subtext of their message is that God won't work miracles for you, but another holiday, a make-over of your house, a new car or fridge, the latest fashion in shoes or clothes might.

In India, religion continues to hold its own on television. There are channels that broadcast non-stop guru-speak. Some of the Hindu preachers who sit in front of cameras for hours on end to put across their message, have become hugely popular. The BJP politicians who fancy themselves as crowd-pullers were very put out when a sit-in they staged, in protest at the arrest of a prominent Hindu priest, didn't attract much attention until they asked a TV guru to join them. Then the crowds turned out in force.

But consumerism – with its message that the body, not the soul, is what counts – is mounting a formidable challenge to the god-men and -women. There are even more advertisements on Indian television than there are on the British independent channels. Taking advantage of India's cricket mania, advertisers have invented the five-ball over, with advertisements often being shown before the sixth ball has been bowled. I don't know why Indians don't rise in revolt against the crass commercials that interrupt their national game – I know that it drives me mad to see the batting genius Sachin Tendulkar holding his bat one moment and clutching a fizzy drink bottle the next!

Living in India, I can almost physically sense the enormous pressure that the nation is under to conform to the Western secular, materialist way of life. Many of the influential elite in India can't see that there is any alternative to this development and so don't think it's worth trying to find a middle way that would combine increasing the country's wealth with the preservation of its culture. In their eyes, you are either in favour of economic development and therefore of today's Western culture, or you are some antediluvian romantic.

I have fallen foul of such criticism myself in the past, perhaps most notably when I wrote a book called *No Full Stops in India* whose theme could be summed up in this saying of Mahatma Gandhi, which I quoted in the introduction:

> My *swaraj* (self rule or independence) is to keep intact the genius of our civilisation. I want to write many new things but they must all be written on the Indian slate. I would gladly borrow from the West when I can return the amount with decent interest.

A reviewer in the *Hindu* described the book as shameful. And then one of India's most pugnacious television interviewers accused me of trying to take the country back to a golden age of spirituality that had never existed and to rob Indians of the chance of enjoying the prosperity that the West enjoys. I replied to him, 'Do you want a poor imitation of America or an India true to itself?'

Modern Western secularism is a product of a particular form of materialism which can't conceive of striking a balance that finds a place for the spiritual as well as the material. It's not surprising, therefore, that this form of secularism has tended to write off traditional Indian culture as irrational, unscientific and unrealistic, and to ignore the heritage of Indian rationalism. Amartya Sen points out in his book *The Argumentative Indian* that the Western perspective has not always taken adequate notice of India's immense contributions to rational subjects such as mathematics, astronomy, grammar and linguistics. Those contributions date back to the early centuries of the first millennium, and the tradition continues today. What's more, Amartya Sen stresses the historical importance of what he calls 'the interactive openness' of Indian work in different fields. He notes that in those early centuries of the first millennium, Indian scientists and mathematicians learnt from work being done in Babylon, Greece and Rome. In their turn, Indian mathematics and astronomy contributed to the flowering of Arabian maths. Amartya

Sen suggests that this interactive openness is the result of India's tradition of scepticism and questioning. In the past, India was prepared to learn from developments in other parts of the world and, in turn, influenced those developments itself because its culture wasn't seduced by certainties and its mind remained open to the ideas of others. Of course all that is a long time ago, but, turning to India today, could a culture imbued with spirituality to the extent that it had no place for rationalism ever have given birth to the technological revolution that has made India such a major player in the global IT market?

According to Chakravarthi Ram-Prasad, who teaches in the department of religious studies at Lancaster University, Western philosophers nevertheless continue to ignore Indian philosophy. He gives several reasons for this. The first is that Eastern philosophy is different; it has risen from its own tradition of intellectual practice. Moreover, it is not usually taught in departments of philosophy, but in departments of religion – which inevitably gives the impression that it is indeed irrational – or in departments concerned with studying India as an area, which gives the impression it is peculiarly Indian and so irrelevant to Western thinking. According to Chakravarthi Ram-Prasad, Indian philosophers haven't helped to improve matters, as many of them spend their time trying to identify the points at which their philosophy meets Western philosophy rather than promoting an understanding of it on its own terms.

If secularists were to take the Indian philosophical tradition seriously, then they might be more humble about humanity and less certain of their opinions about life and the great questions it asks. They might be a little more like Indian philosophers who, as Chakravarthi Ram-Prasad puts it, 'agree that our ordinary life is defective; our experience is marked by suffering, our understanding is marked by severe limits to knowledge, our conduct falls short of its ethical requirements, and we live in fear of our mortality'.

And what might the humility to appreciate the limits of our knowledge achieve? A society in which reason and intuition are kept in balance. A society that has a place for the sacred, and which understands the difference between a myth and a lie. A society that is not drunk on change. A society that recognises that technology does not have answers to everything and that science has its limits. A society that appreciates the limits of rationalism and acknowledges the wisdom of these words written by Tolstoy: 'If you describe the world just as it is there will be in your words nothing but lies and no truth.'

Humility is also a quality that many religious leaders might benefit from as greatly as the secularists. Only those religions that acknowledge that there must be a balance between tradition and the need to move on, and that welcome questioning, rejoicing in the variety of experiences of God and the traditions these have given rise to, can have any hope of remaining relevant and intellectually respectable in a secular era.

Religious leaders also need to appreciate the successes of science and to encourage an open dialogue with scientists if they are to play their part in achieving the crucial balance between reason and intuition – the balance described by Prince Charles in his Reith lecture when he said:

> I am not suggesting that information gained through scientific investigation is anything but essential. Far from it. But I believe we need to restore the balance between the heartfelt reason of instinctive wisdom and the rational insights of scientific analysis. Neither I believe is much use on its own. So it's only by employing both the intuitive and the rational halves of our own nature – our hearts and minds – that we will live up to the sacred trust that has been placed in us by our creator – or our 'sustainer' as ancient wisdom referred to the creator.

According to Indian thought, we have to practise *ahimsa*, or non-violence, if we are to live up to that sacred trust. Because we hold everything in trust, we should not do violence to ourselves, to others or to nature. In his commentary on the *Mahabharata*, Chaturvedi Badrinath writes: 'There has hardly been anything in human history that has produced greater violence and killing than conflicting perceptions of what truth is.' It is when those perceptions leave no room for doubt or questioning, when they are held too firmly, that violence follows. Of course, that does not mean only physical violence. In this chapter we have, for instance, seen examples of verbal violence.

I was once accused of verbal violence myself when I spoke to a London dining club and a member leapt up, exclaiming, 'This is the most disgraceful rant against secularism I have ever heard!' In case any reader should think I am violently prejudiced against secularlism, in the next chapter I am going to discuss Ireland, a country which, it might be argued, was once not nearly secular enough.

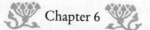# Chapter 6

MAYNOOTH:
LOSING FAITH

IN 1979, one-third of the population turned out to see Pope John Paul the Second during his visit to Ireland, the most Catholic country in western Europe. However, a little over twenty years later the Irish theologian Vincent Twomey published a book with the title *The End of Irish Catholicism?*. That a theologian should feel it necessary to address such a question indicates the rapid decline in the Irish Church's influence at the end of the twentieth century and the attendant rise of secularism. The speed with which this change has taken place is a unique example of Western culture's tendency to discard one certainty only to replace it with another, which is the opposite of the Indian tendency I advocate in this book. Moreover, the new secular culture of Ireland represents many aspects of the Western materialism that I fear may swamp Indian culture. For these reasons, and also because I was inspired by an article I had read by the Irish Poet and philosopher John O'Donohue, I decided to go to Ireland to discuss my ideas and learn from the changes there. I wanted to find out why the Church, once arrogant in the certainty of its authority, had been humbled, and what the country had lost, and gained, in the onrush of secularism.

Writing in the *Irish Times*, John O'Donohue had described the decline in the Church's influence as 'a free-fall away from religion'. He went on to say that 'the dominant thought-frame is now the economic one. The demise of religion means that there is nothing to counter or critique the awakening of such avarice.' O'Donohue called for 'prophetic reflection' to understand the depth of what was happening in Ireland, and for 'quest and question'. I too believe in the role of quest and question, and in particular in the need to question the role of economics – the new 'dominant thought-frame', the new Irish certainty.

My own memories of the heyday of Catholic Ireland date back to 1960, when I spent my honeymoon there with my wife Margaret, from whom I am now separated. As an Anglican alarmed by the decline of my own Church (which was underway even before the onset of the secular revolution of the sixties), I had been fascinated by the Roman Catholic Church's power in Ireland, the prevalence of worship and the prominence of the clergy there. However, when the proprietress of the Butler Arms Hotel showed us to a table at which two black-suited priests were already sitting, I thought to myself, 'I know I'm interested in the Church and theology, but it's going a bit far to have to spend a holiday with priests!' But the proprietress was a formidable lady and her dinner guests sat where they were told. Anyhow, it would have been difficult to find a table at which there were no priests. In those days priests had to say Mass every day, and there were so many priests dining in the hotel that the proprietress went from table to table allocating different times for each one to say Mass next day in the local church.

As it happened, we were in luck – Father Delaney and Father Kelly turned out to be excellent company. Father Kelly was a Benedictine monk from a monastery in Scotland, while Father Delaney's career was typical of many of the Diocesan clergy who served in Irish parishes in those days. He had studied at the most famous Irish seminary in Maynooth, near Dublin, for six years, with as many as 600 other future priests, and had been ordained in the Dublin Diocese. Although Father Delaney was in his fifties, there were so many priests in the Dublin diocese that he still didn't have a parish of his own but was only the

Senior Curate, or assistant priest, in a church that was a land-mark for passengers arriving in Dublin by the short sea route. (In fact, Ireland produced such a large number of priests that the Church couldn't find jobs for all of them and many were sent overseas.)

As we kept them company, Father Delaney teased his friend about the vow of poverty he had taken as a monk, saying, 'Father Kelly doesn't have any money so his mother pays for his holiday, including a car. As a parish priest I have to pay for my own holiday and I can't afford a car.'

The discipline of the Church in those days was so strict that Father Delaney wasn't even allowed to take off his clerical collar and black suit on holiday. But his uniform commanded great respect. Several times while I was with him elderly women knelt before him and asked for a blessing.

Nevertheless, Father Delaney didn't take himself too seri-ously and delighted in telling jokes about the Church. He was a big, slow-moving man, with a face and figure that spoke of his enjoyment of good food and a glass or two of whisky rather than any inclination for physical exercise, and so he took a particular delight in telling me a joke about an elderly priest in a remote country parish who was surprised to find that his new curate was commended in his seminary report for gymnastics: '"What's this gymnastics?" he asked irritably. "We never had such a thing in my days at Maynooth." So to explain gymnastics the curate did a series of somersaults down the aisle. In the middle of this demonstration of his skill two elderly ladies entered the church. Horrified, they crossed themselves fervently and one said to the other, "Glory be to God, look at the penance for today – and me without my nicks on too!"'

I arrived in Ireland forty-six years later to find the Church and the clergy were no longer held in such respect. Priests told me they did not wear their black suits and dog collars on the streets of Dublin for fear of being jeered or hooted at. The seminaries were empty, and in most parishes there was no question of the church having curates – they were lucky if they had one priest.

But what had survived was the friendliness and humour of the Irish clergy. When organising my visit to Ireland, I had sent an e-mail to Father Bernard Treacy, a Dominican priest, asking whether he would be willing to meet me. It was a tentative request because I also had to explain that I intended to write about the decline in the influence of the Irish Church, a subject he might well have been reluctant to talk about to a journalist. I had met Father Bernard once at a conference in Northern Ireland, after which I had subscribed to the journal he edits, *Doctrine and Life*, but I had no other claim on his friendship. Nevertheless, he sent back a wonderfully warm message, not only offering to meet me but also suggesting other people for me to meet.

Having spent two terms in an Anglican Theological College in Lincoln, I was particularly pleased to see that Father Bernard had arranged for me to visit the great seminary at Maynooth, the only remaining seminary in Ireland. Maynooth College was founded as the Roman Catholic College of St Patrick by an Act of the Parliament of Ireland in 1795. It was to provide clergy for the Irish Church, with the aim that priests would no longer have to go to the continent for training and would therefore not be affected by the revolutionary spirit of the times in Europe. It was crucial in establishing the ethos of the Irish Church, because it trained so many of the parish clergy and those who went on to become bishops.

Some years ago I read a novel by Gerald O'Donovan, a radical Irish priest who eventually left the priesthood. First published in the early twentieth century, the novel, *Father Ralph*, is clearly autobiographical. The novel paints a picture from an insider's perspective of a smug, self-serving Church in its triumphant days, an institution with a conspicuous lack of humility. According to *Father Ralph,* at the end of the nine-teenth century Maynooth was a factory 'fettered by medieval ecclesiasticism' for churning out priests. The students had to dress as though they were already priests, never wearing anything but black, yet seem to have behaved more like school-boys. O'Donovan writes that it was so obvious that one of the lecturers was suffering from the tortures of the rougher students that the soft-hearted Father Ralph felt as if his own mother was being jeered at. Most of the lecturers appear to have been uninspiring and to have positively discouraged independence of mind by dictating notes that they expected the students to memorise. The Church history taught was 'unconvincing' and moral theology was 'crude legalism'.

According to O'Donovan, the leadership of the Irish Church was equally uninspiring. In his book, a radical Catholic comments on one of the portraits of bishops in full episcopal regalia lining a wall of the cloisters in Maynooth. He says to Father Ralph:

> Smugness and self-satisfaction in every line of it. That is the Irish Church all out ... if not the whole Church. Nothing short of a spiri-tual earthquake would make them even question their belief in themselves. They don't know that anything is wrong and they are unteachable. They prefer to be what they are – autocrats, domineer-ing over a sycophantic clergy, holding an ignorant laity in check through fear of eternal damnation.

Sadly for the Irish Church, it didn't heed this sharp criticism of Maynooth. The institution remained autocratic and domi-neered over Ireland, refusing to allow its teachings to be questioned. In his article in the *Irish Times,* John O'Donohue observed that 'no theological consciousness was allowed to develop in Ireland; consequently, when faith in the system was shattered there was no ground to fall back upon'. To make matters worse, the Church remained influenced by the theology that the first priests in Maynooth had already brought back with them from France. They were Jansenists, which meant that they believed in a particularly rigid morality and were deeply suspicious of sex.

The heavy Victorian Gothic architecture of Maynooth symbolises an authoritarian Church. Sister Geraldine Smyth, a Dominican theologian whom I met in Dublin, told me she found the stolid stone buildings of Maynooth so oppressive she almost lost her faith when studying there.

Fortunately, Maynooth itself is now a much more open place. Those portraits of the dour, undoubting bishops still hang on the walls of the cloisters, but, facing them, the photographs of the annual ordination groups tell the story of the change that has come over the college. In its heyday, as many as one hundred priests would have been ordained each year; now, the more recent photographs show much smaller groups. While there are still about as many students of theology at Maynooth as there were when it was churning out priests, these days the majority of them are lay men and women, and the college has become part of the National University of Ireland.

Nor do I think that Father Brendan McConvery, the Professor of Old Testament Studies who showed me round the college, would have fitted into the old Maynooth. He was not wearing black, was very open-minded about the faults in the Church and was clearly at ease with the students we met, bursting into laughter when one of them confessed that he was only studying theology because he didn't get the grades he needed for another university course.

In its heyday, there were enough seminarians at Maynooth to fill the massive and magnificent chapel, which can seat more than

600 people. The building of the chapel was started in 1875 by J.J. McCarthy, who was a pupil of Augustus Pugin, and completed in 1905 by McCarthy's successor, William Hague. A convert to Roman Catholicism himself, Pugin is regarded as the high priest of Victorian Gothic. He believed that Gothic was the only moral style of architecture and once said, 'I feel perfectly convinced the Roman Catholic religion is the only one in which the grand and sublime style of Church architecture can ever be restored.'

In the grandeur and sublimity of Maynooth's chapel, Pugin's pupil outdid his master. Tall pointed arches support the painted roof, soaring high above the rows of mock-medieval choir stalls, which flow down to the nave on both sides. These features, the ornate High Altar and the dim light filtering through the rose window at the west end of the chapel, truly inspire awe – awe of a mighty, majestic, magisterial Church. Maynooth chapel was a fitting place of worship for young men training to become priests who would uphold the authority of the Church. But now the seminarians usually worship in a much smaller, brightly lit chapel, with an altar which is not set apart from the congregation and where the emphasis is not on the authority of the priest but on the unity between priest and people.

Outside the chapel, Father Brendan introduced me to a forbidding, steely-grey-haired priest clothed in clerical black, who was clearly conscious of his presence and prestige as a former pupil of Cardinal Ratzinger, now Pope Benedict XVI. This was none other than Father Vincent Twomey, the author of *The End of Irish Catholicism?*, whom I mentioned at the opening of this chapter. When Father Brendan explained that I had come to Ireland to write about the state of the Church, he simply said, 'Read my book', and walked off. When I did read his book, I was perhaps not surprised to discover that Vincent Twomey was critical of the liturgical reforms designed to make

worship more people-friendly that had been introduced in
Ireland after the Second Vatican Council.

The refectory, or dining room, represents the old Maynooth in
the grandeur of its architecture. It also houses one of
Maynooth's oddest treasures: a silver statue of St George of
England presented by the Empress of Austria in gratitude for
the treatment she received at Maynooth after a hunting accident.
This was perhaps not the most tactful present to send to a seminary dedicated to St Patrick, the patron saint of Ireland.
However, when she learnt of her mistake, the Empress made
amends by sending the seminary a set of cloth of gold vestments
embroidered in Ireland's shamrock green.

Unlike the refectory building, none of the priests with whom
I had lunch reminded me of the old Maynooth. None of them
wore clerical black and all of them openly acknowledged that
the Church needed to change.

After lunch, Father Patrick Hannan, the Professor of Moral
Theology, invited me to his room to discuss my contention that
one reason the Church had lost its influence was its unbalanced
emphasis on its authority to pronounce on matters of morality,
and in particular on sexual morality. The experience of sitting in
a book-lined room overlooking Pugin's quadrangle, and listening to a man with a mind as well stocked as Father Patrick
Hannan's, reminded me strongly of my tutorials as a student in
Cambridge. Small and somewhat Pickwickian in nature, Father
Patrick combined the forensic skills of the lawyer he had trained
to be with the humanity of a pastoral priest. He admitted that
the Church did sometimes get stuck in untenable positions and
that it had given the impression that Christianity was all about
morality. But he added, 'It seems increasingly that people want
to be told what to do. After a certain sense of freedom, humans
become afraid of it. And morality, well – it's the thing that

people ask most questions about. They *want* to know what to do. And of course that's bound to be particularly true of sexuality. It has to loom large in anyone's personality.' He paused before adding with a chuckle, 'Concern with sex isn't confined to the Catholic Church, you know!'

According to Father Patrick, the real problem lay in the fact that, for many, the identity of the Irish Church had become tangled up in the moral authority that it claimed and the form of moral absolutism it preached. Father Patrick thought the Church had given the wrong impression of itself by emphasising a specific Catholic morality or 'God-given law', which was neither discernable by reason nor open to any challenge; whereas – according to its own traditional teachings – morality should be regarded as a feature of common human experience that can be discerned by reason.

Father Patrick explained that 'subjective appropriation' was very much a part of the Catholic tradition and taught as a matter of course in first year divinity classes all over the world. When I asked what he meant by subjective appropriation, he replied, 'Perhaps you could say "conscience". Principles have to be applied and that is where the primacy of conscience comes in. Furthermore, truly moral decisions cannot be based on fear, and the Church has often laid too much stress on fear, such as the fear of punishment in the after-life. According to our own teaching, the prime motive in determining our actions should be love.'

The apparent inflexibility of the Church with regard to its moral authority had made it an easy target for its critics, when it should have been seen to be attacking the very things it often stood accused of. Father Patrick suggested that these were: 'Harshness, a god who is a human law-giver and authoritarianism.' However, he conceded that many priests and bishops still found it easier to talk to people about rules and authority than to discuss their issues with them at a personal and pastoral level.

Even so, the difficulties currently faced by the Roman Catholic Church in Ireland do not spring from an excess of authoritarianism and moral absolutism alone. Over the years, its relationship with the state had become increasing unbalanced, with the state permitting the Church to exercise too much authority for its own good. An Indian Jesuit once said to me, 'When the Church marries the state in one generation it becomes a widow in the next.' This is very true of Ireland.

It would not be going too far to describe the Church I first knew in Ireland as a theocracy, because it had long been allowed to maintain that its law was superior to civil law – the law on divorce being one example. The Church fought hard and, until the 1980s, successfully to prevent divorce being legalised, yet at the same time it was generous in granting annulments of marriage under its own laws. One result was that people who got an annulment and then remarried were committing bigamy under the civil law and thereby breaking the very laws the Church itself purported to uphold. But these bigamous marriages were nevertheless not challenged in the civil courts.

Sister Geraldine Smyth, a theologian of the Dominican order, told me the Church had wielded 'a tyranny over people's sexuality' and created 'a high culture of repression'. When I met Dr Garrett Fitzgerald, the former *Taoiseach*, or Prime Minister, he complained that the Church had thought the state had no right to interfere in family law.

To make matters worse, while imposing its rigid morality on Ireland, the Church was careless about its own morality. It wasn't merely that bishops concealed individual cases of sexual abuse by clergy. Some of the institutions belonging to the Church were run in such a way that abuse became almost inevitable in them. Investigations into orders such as the Christian Brothers, who ran industrial schools for boys, have shown that they sent scouts to schools to look out for promising recruits and then brought those recruits into the order sometimes when they were as young as fourteen. Being chosen was considered a great honour by boys and their parents, so there was no shortage of boys willing to join the Christian Brothers. But they were often whisked away, never to see their parents again.

At an impressionable age, the new recruits were taught that celibacy was the highest state, that the body was the temple of the Holy Ghost and that the sexual urge was sinful. All sexual acts except those intended to lead to procreation were sins, and even those acts, it was pointed out, would not be open to them because they were not allowed to marry. These young boys, who usually had no professional training in childcare, were then put in charge of other boys in the schools who were often older and bigger than they were. Not only were they denied any outlet for their sexuality but they were even denied the comfort of companionship with their colleagues or the boys of whom they were in charge. They were told that 'particular friendships' would come in between them and their friendship with God. This had unintended consequences. One brother, who had confessed to masturbating with boys, saw nothing wrong in it because he had deliberately avoided making friends with them. It's perhaps small wonder that in this culture of repression some of the brothers' sexuality became warped and they abused boys in their care.

For girls recruited into religious orders caring for children and women, the situation was in some ways even worse. Their rules also forbade 'particular friendships', and they were strictly enforced. Their maternal instincts became distorted, and all too often cruelty, as well as repression, pervaded the institutions that these women ran.

The most notorious institution was the Magdalene Laundries, named after Mary Magdalene, the sinner or 'fallen woman' who became a disciple of Jesus. It is believed that as many as 30,000 women may have been confined in these laundries over the institution's 150 years of existence. The women were sent there by the courts or by their families for offences against the harsh code of sexual morality then endemic in Irish society, offences that could be as mild as merely flirting. But the men who were their partners in these so-called sins were usually not punished.

The laundries were run by nuns who tyrannised the women, forcing them to work long hours scrubbing clothes in order, they were told, to wash away their sins. There was no escape, as they were not allowed to go outside the grim walls of the convent.

When news of the sexual abuse scandals broke and the treatment of women in the Magdalene Laundries was revealed, the reports did enormous damage to the Church's standing. The Church now paid the price for putting itself above the law and for insisting that there could be no interference in the institutions it ran. The Church in Ireland has now learnt the hard way that becoming too powerful and misjudging the balance of its delicate relationship with the state leads inevitably from its having too large a role in society to its losing much of its influence.

It would, however, be wrong to suggest that the Church in Ireland is down and out. This was made clear to me as I sat in Father Bernard's central Dublin office, in which a computer was his only concession to modernity. Father Bernard, a Dominican, was joined by his colleague, Father Tom Jordan, and also by John Hayes, who headed the philosophy department in a teacher training college in the western city of Limerick. Father Bernard observed that about fifty per cent of the Irish population still attended Mass regularly, which remains remarkably high for Europe. But he admitted that people in the countryside were much more likely to go to church than those living in cities. However, John Hayes suggested that there might be problems in the countryside soon. He explained that rural

Ireland was changing so fast that the small subsistence farms had already virtually vanished and were being replaced by industrialised farming, yet the small farms had always been the backbone of traditional Irish country life.

I was interested to know how much the Church mattered to young people, so I asked John Hayes about the students at Limerick University. He said a large number of the students in his teacher training college did go to Mass, but went on to explain that this might be because primary school teachers were still expected to act as 'agents of the church' in the countryside. In the other colleges of Limerick University he said Mass attendance was 'almost insignificant'.

Although a large number of parents still bring their children to church for their First Communion, which is often quoted as evidence that Catholicism is alive and well in Ireland, Father Tom was not convinced. 'First Communions are now becoming huge social events,' he told me. 'The socialising, the partying and all that is going up – but the religious content is going down.'

But Father Bernard did not entirely agree. He said, 'I have met priests ministering in deprived areas where regular Mass attendance can be as low as ten per cent. They understand why events like first communion are celebrated with extravagance. They say it's to break out of the routine dullness in which people live their lives. Besides which, you don't have to be regular in attending Mass to take sacraments seriously.'

Father Bernard didn't believe that Mass attendance alone was a true indication of the Church's position in Ireland. Recently he had been asked to conduct a number of baptisms and weddings. Although none of the young couples probably attended Mass regularly, he found they did have a 'real belief in God's providence as bringing them together and as a guiding force in their future'.

*

There are some in the Catholic Church who are campaigning aggressively against the new form of secularism that has no time for religion. The Redemptorist order used to be renowned for fighting sin, with fiery sermons threatening hell fire and damnation for any breach of Catholic morality. Now in their Novenas (nine-day missionary campaigns), they preach charismatic Catholicism and attract large crowds, which create traffic jams in the part of Ireland where John Hayes lives.

A pugnacious new Catholic paper called *Alive*, edited by another Dominican, reaches over 3,000 homes. The edition I bought criticised the European Union for its 'anti-religious direction' and a non-believing professor of genetics for his 'low view of human life'. There was an article praising the 'huge role of the Catholic Church in Western civilisation' and another attacking 'anti-Catholicism', saying it was rapidly becoming Ireland's 'ugly little secret'. All good strong stuff. But, although Father Bernard admitted that *Alive* was having an impact, he said, 'I am unhappy about its aggressive tone, and I do wish some of the stances it adopts were more nuanced.'

However, in spite of these recent developments, there is still a chronic shortage of men entering the priesthood, not only at the Maynooth seminary, where parish priests are trained, but in all the other religious orders too. According to Father Bernard, four men had entered his order recently, but fifteen had died. Nevertheless, he felt that the morale of the Dominicans was holding up, and there was no doubt that he and his colleague Father Tom were in good spirits when I met them. On the other hand, Father Bernard feared that the parish clergy were 'a dispirited lot', distressed by the impact of the recent sex scandals and lacking confidence in the leadership of their bishops.

The morale of the parish clergy isn't helped by a hostile media. In his book *The End of Irish Catholicism?*, Father Vincent Twomey writes: 'It is incontestable that, from the point of view of the Catholic Church, the Irish media can be described as the most hostile media in the developed world.' He describes an interview with a Catholic priest that had been broadcast on the Public Service Broadcaster RTE as like 'an interrogation by the thought police'. Where most of the Irish press was once subservient to the Church – a subservience that enabled the cruelty and sexual abuse of some Church institutions to remain hidden for so long – now there is almost universal hostility towards it. It's as though journalists are taking revenge on an institution that once imposed an unofficial censorship on them. But it's also an example of my profession's tendency to see things in black and white.

The Irish state, which once listened with reverence to the Church, now misses no opportunity to demonstrate its independence from it. It didn't listen when the Church complained about the lack of public holidays marking religious festivals. And it even did its best to prevent a Catholic weekly advertising on the radio; then, when that decision was overturned in the courts, it still insisted that advertisers couldn't claim the Church was doing good. Apparently, now in Ireland advertisements can claim anything from soap flakes to new cars, from chocolate to new homes to be 'good for you' – but not the Church.

Similar obstacles have been placed in the way of establishing a Christian radio station. A Catholic lay woman I talked to, whose husband edits a paper in rural Ireland, was incensed by what she saw as the anti-Catholic bias of the national media and the state. 'Our government – whoever is in power – and all the media are very anti-Catholic in their outlook,' she complained. 'It seems that they can say whatever they like about us and our Church, but we must be tremendously tolerant of everybody else. The use of the word "pluralism" is fine – sure, to be inclusive of ethnic minorities and other religions is very desirable – but does that make "majority" a dirty word now?'

However, David McWilliams, an economist and popular Irish television presenter, has detected signs that the pendulum may be swinging back the other way. He believes that the rampant materialism of a country that has travelled in not much more than ten years from being the 'poor man of Western Europe' to the 'Celtic Tiger', outstripping the economic growth of everyone else, is producing a backlash. In his best-selling book *The Pope's Children*, he claims that many committed secularists who fought against the influence of the Church in the 1980s are now so dismayed by the materialism that has taken its place that they are urging people to 'tiptoe back to the Church'. There is also, according to McWilliams, already 'a revival of religion in Ireland in various incarnations'. He argues that now to be religious is to be radical because 'it involves a rejection of all that is mainstream'. Interestingly, the biggest exhibition on St Patrick's Day in 2005 was the Irish International Mind, Body, Spirit and Healing Arts Exhibition.

Sister Geraldine Smyth is not surprised that people are coming back to religion, because she believes, as I do, that there is 'an irreducible religious instinct in all of us', and only a culture that takes account of this can be balanced. There is, I think, another reason as well.

McWilliams' book *The Pope's Children* is intended to be a celebration of the generation born either side of the visit of Pope John Paul the Second to Ireland in 1979. It is also a critique of the 'Commentariat' – the crusty critics who can see no good whatsoever in the materialism that has replaced Catholicism in recent years. Such a critique is obviously necessary. Those like me who criticise consumerism and materialism need to be reminded that poverty impoverishes the spirit and the mind as well as the body. We need to realise that our ideas about material prosperity might be very different if we ourselves had ever been poor. How people react to affluence has to be their own business. We can only seek to keep the dialogue going in order to present arguments against excessive materialism and to seek a balance between the material and the spiritual in the life of individuals and of communities.

But having accepted this much, a lot of what McWilliams celebrates in his book seems to be unsatisfying in the long run and unlikely to meet the needs of the Irish people's religious instinct, if Sister Geraldine and I are right about that instinct. The materialistic benefits listed by McWilliams include 'borrowing, spending, shopping, shagging, eating, drinking, and taking more drugs than any other nation'.

Ireland appears to have swung from being lean and hungry to wallowing in its own obesity. According to McWilliams, Ireland's 'hard men' were once scrawny lads because of their poor diet, but these days double chins have apparently become *de rigueur* and in their faces 'little piggy eyes are squeezed into sockets among the flab'. He also quotes figures that suggest that thirty per cent of Irish women are now overweight. But on the other hand, Ireland, once renowned for being laid-back, is now a nation of workaholics. Every other shop in Dublin seems to dispense fast food, because Dubliners no longer have time to do more than snatch a snack. Not so many years ago I spent the afternoon in a crowded bar near Cork. When I asked my drinking companions what the area's main industry was, back came the reply with a roar of laughter: 'Unemployment!'

For all their newfound enthusiasm for work, apparently the Irish still find the time and the energy to have sex 105 times a year. Released from Catholic strictures against anything but the straightest of straight sex, Irish people are also now remarkable for their adventurousness. However, McWilliams reveals that this new freedom is not proving much more satisfying than the old ways were, at least from the woman's point of view. Perhaps the Commentariat may be forgiven for questioning how satisfying the new Irish secular ethos will prove to be, although that is no argument for a return to the dead hand of the Church.

*

What has Ireland lost by throwing away so much of its religious culture? The most obvious loss is individuality. When I was recently in Dublin I came across a story in the papers about the decline in tourism. The board for promoting tourism put this down to the fact that tourists no longer regarded Ireland as different from any other western European country. It's lost an aspect of the culture for which it was once celebrated.

For all that he was not a practising Catholic, the novelist John McGahern still missed the old ritual of the Church. In his auto-biographical book *Memoir* he said, 'The Church ceremonies always gave me great pleasure, and I miss them even now. In an impoverished time they were my first introduction to an indoor beauty of luxury and ornament, ceremony and sacrament and mystery.' Mind you, the Church is in part responsible for this loss, because it has now swung too far from its tradition of awe-inspiring worship clothed in mystery and a sense of the transcendental to people-friendly worship that is thoroughly down-to-earth.

The moral philosopher Father Patrick Hannon discerns in Ireland a society made unhappy by ennui and greed; and he regards it as the Church's challenge to point this out and to offer an alternative. A Roman Catholic writer, Dr Desmond Fennell, has analysed Irish society as suffering from 'anomie', that is to say an absence of social norms and values. In a response to Vincent Twomey's *The End of Irish Catholicism?*, he writes:

> Our people – amid the debris of their nation, with the inherited Christian rules declared invalid by the Power and no civic ethic to fall back on – are immersed in anomie. Life, appearing senseless, induces much anguish and depression. Attempts, especially by the young and sensitive, to quench these pains give the republic one of the highest rates of alcohol consumption and drug abuse in the European Union; drive many young men to suicide; drive many girls to reckless sex and guilty abortions. Talk of 'dire need'; there is a famine of foods for the spirit and soul.

Some will immediately think, 'Well, two Catholic writers would say that, wouldn't they?' But when I went to see one of the grand old men of Irish politics, Dr Garrett Fitzgerald, I found he too felt that his country was suffering from anomie after rejecting the Church's rule book. And Garrett, as he is known to all Irishmen, is a Catholic who has by no means always supported the Church's stand. During one of his two spells as *Taoiseach*, or Prime Minister, he attempted to legalise divorce in the teeth of ecclesiastical opposition. He added a clause to the constitution that gave a mother, as well as her unborn baby, the right to life – against opposition by the Church, which opposed the change as a weakening of its stand on abortion. He also undermined the Church's stand on sex by liberalising contraception.

When I met him in his modest house in a residential area of Dublin, he was trying to work out how to arrange the tables for the party in celebration of his eightieth birthday without offending anyone. Always an advocate of a liberal Ireland and what he called 'a non-sectarian nation', he conceded that now he was concerned that Ireland was too liberal, that it had lost one moral code but not found a replacement. 'The Church had such a profound impact on morality, and it wasn't a rational morality,' he said. 'It was dictated by God, the Church claimed, so people didn't think out their morality. Now people no longer accept that morality, what do they have? What are their guidelines?'

'So does that mean you believe that morality has to have a Christian base?' I wondered.

'Oh no,' he replied hurriedly. 'You can have civic morality without the Church, but the domination of the Church and the colonial power meant we never developed it here.'

Garrett was particularly critical of the Church for teaching that morality was derived from God rather than the basic need for humans to live together. 'Acknowledging that we have to live together,' he explained, 'gives you a rational basis for morality a basis which makes you – not God – responsible for it.'

'But that basis is surely not the basis of the consumerism and individualism that have replaced the Church's morality in Ireland?' I asked. 'Aren't they based on the very opposite of the need to live together?'

'Yes,' he replied. 'They're based on pleasure – and pleasure is personal. It's what pleases us as individuals. Happiness comes from our relationship with others. But, you know, the bishops and priests concentrated on personal issues too, particularly family law. They ignored issues of injustice. Why, for instance, did they never take up the issue of tax evasion?' The Church, he felt, had suffered from 'a deficit of morality' and 'an over-emphasis on sex' which led it to ignore or play down other issues. But, in spite of his criticism of the Church's morality, Garrett regretted that its influence had declined so far and fast. He believed the Church had a part to play and this part was 'the prophetic role, which it had abandoned for an institutional role'.

In the newspaper article that first inspired me to set out on my journey to Ireland, John O'Donohue called for 'prophetic reflection'. He had also described his country as having 'driven urgency but little sense of destination'. Those words rang true to me because I too had been through a period of life in which I had a driven urgency to become a successful and well known journalist; but within myself I had always known that this was not a destination in which I would ever be able to rest happily. This was because I couldn't rid myself of what Sister Geraldine had called the 'irreducible religious element' in myself. Now, I felt that the lack of a sense of destination and a sense of meaning were the most profound losses Ireland had suffered – deeper than the anomie, the decline of the once almost universal familiarity with the Church ceremonies, which had left such a mark on McGarhern, and the disappearance of difference. Ireland seemed to me a land that was adrift because it had pulled up the anchor of its rich past and yet had no new course to guide it into the future. It had failed to find the middle way between tradition and change.

On my last evening in Dublin I had dinner with the poet Michael O'Siadhail and his wife Brid. During our conversation he described the role of poetry as 'looking at the past in the present to prepare for the future'.

'That's what Ireland should be doing, that's what we should all be doing,' I said to myself as I scribbled his words in my notebook. 'All three should be connected with each other – the past tradition and history, what they have taught us; the present we have to live in; the future, the changes we have to prepare for.'

The search for meaning in life is very much part of Michael's Irish tradition, and so he was shocked when he first went to Norway and found that people there shrugged their shoulders if he raised the issue. But he believes that the Church has been mistaken in the past when it claimed that it alone knew what that meaning was. When I suggested that the Church's position showed a lack of humility, he said, 'Yes. There can never be only one point of view. No one has a monopoly on the truth. You must say, "I think I am right but I may be wrong. You think you're right but you may be wrong." Because I accept that there can never be one point of view, I wouldn't want my poetry to be read through my lens. I would like readers to find their own meaning.'

Michael believes that today's Ireland is a victim of certainties that have been 'narrowed down'. This has led to the passion for measuring success and achievements, which he describes as 'a mode of thinking that is appropriate in some places and totally inappropriate in others'. The current certainties he particularly disapproves of are those that can be summed up by the phrase 'It doesn't pay so don't do it' and 'the adoration of money'. Although Michael is nervous of nostalgia, he said, 'I may be wrong, but I sense a loss of that Irish sense of questioning; that sense of joy, in the world around us and all its riches. An appreciation that this richness reflects something bigger and greater than me – wonder and awe, huge humility, gratitude too. You're part of it; you're part of the work of it all.'

But the giant cranes looming over Dublin are tearing its heart out in the rush to create an ever busier hive of human activity. The construction sector, the financial sector, the leisure sector and all the rest of them are booming. Servicing these sectors, and simply keeping them going, leaves no time for anyone to wonder what it's all for, or to feel wonder and awe for anything except the never-ending new technologies and the amount of money they generate. What awe there is, is reserved for us humans and our ingenuity; it isn't an awe of the world around us with all its riches.

Ireland's busyness leaves no time for the 'tiny glances of infinity' that first led Michael to 'give in to the wonder of the world' and emboldened him to write poetry. One of his poems, called 'Freedom', seems through my own lens to be warning Ireland against taking its new found liberalism too far:

> Freedom.
> Enough was enough. We flew
> nets of old certainties,
> All that crabbed grammar
> of the predictable. Unentangled,
> we'd soar to a language
> of our own.

Freedom. We sang of freedom
(travel lightly, anything goes)
and somehow became strangers
to each other, like gabblers
at cross purposes, builders
of Babel.

Slowly I relearn a lingua,
shared overlays of rule,
lattice of memory and meaning,
our latent images, a tongue
at large in an endlessness
of sentences unsaid.

'We flew nets of old certainties.' But now Ireland seems enmeshed in new certainties. The Church has been humbled because it became too mighty. There are signs that the arrogance of the secularists is now producing a backlash; that there are the beginnings of a return to religion. But, to paraphrase the words of Karen Armstrong, the danger is that the religious may retreat into a fundamenalist fortress.

When returning from Ireland I thought of the great English twentieth-century poet Kathleen Raine. She was so concerned about what she called the 'spiritual impoverishment' of Western society that she founded the *Temenos Review* and the Temenos Academy. The journal gives space to artists, writers and others who subscribe to the belief that man is primarily a spiritual creature with spiritual needs which have to be nourished if we are to fulfil our potential and be happy. The Academy is a teaching organisation based on the same belief.

Once, when she was speaking in India, I heard Kathleen Raine raise a point that seems to me particularly relevant to the Ireland of today. She attributed the West's spiritual impoverishment to 'a mind set which seems consistently incapable of imagining any ground of reality other than so called matter'. Then she compared this with 'the great edifice of India's spiritual civilisation', and went on to ask the West 'whether we had now advanced to a point where we are ready to learn'. Perhaps the beginning of the current backlash means that Ireland will be willing to learn.

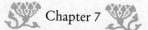

Chapter 7

KHAJURAHO:
THE SENSUAL AND
THE SACRED

WHEN I arrived in Delhi in 1966, one of the first flights I took out of the city was to Khajuraho in central India. This small town, little more than an overgrown village, is famous for its temples with their erotic carvings. I travelled to Khajuraho with my boss of the time, Mark Dodd. We flew in a Dakota plane, which took so long to take off that I turned and said to Mark, 'At this rate we'll have driven there before we're airborne!' But eventually the elderly aeroplane staggered into the air, and some two hours later it deposited us at what passed for Khajuraho airport.

Mark and I found that the western group of temples, which were once hidden in thick jungle, were now surrounded by a park with neatly trimmed lawns, paths and flowerbeds. It seemed to me a tame, man-made setting for monuments that celebrate nature with such intricate carvings of deer, elephants, tigers and lions, dancing peacocks, cuckoos and other birds, and, of course, images of our own natural impulses. But the golden sandstone temples with their tall towers curving gently towards their crown – an urn symbolising the urn that carries the nectar of immortality according to Hindu legend – could not be diminished by their surroundings. The builders had piled blocks of golden sandstone one upon the other in such perfect balance that no mortar or cement was required to hold them in place. The sandstone was soft enough to allow the sculptors to show even the smallest details of each figure, such as single strands of hair.

The portion of the temple walls between the approach to the sanctuary and the sanctuary itself is covered with carvings that show almost every position in which it is possible to have sex. While Mark and I were walking round one of the temples, we heard two young Sikhs discussing a carving of a yogic position in which a man stands on his head and a woman sits on him between his thighs, making love.

One of the Sikhs commented, 'No, that's just not possible.'

Without a moment's hesitation the other retorted, 'Yes, it is – I've done it!'

The Victorian era in Britain was marked by a prudery that hid an obsession with sex and plenty of hypocrisy. It is therefore not surprising that when T.S. Burt, a British military engineer, stumbled upon the temples of Khajuraho in the middle of thick jungle in 1838, he was shocked by the erotic carvings on their walls. The seven Hindu temples he discovered were, he said, 'Most beautifully and exquisitely carved as to workmanship, but the sculptor had at times allowed his subject to grow rather warmer than there was any absolute necessity for his doing; indeed, some of the sculptures here were extremely indecent and offensive, which I was at first much surprised to find in temples that are professed to be erected for good purposes, and on account of religion.' He went on to criticise the religion of the Hindus who had built the temples at least 800 years earlier. In his view, their religion 'could not have been very chaste if it induced people, under the cloak of religion, to design the most disgraceful representation to desecrate their ecclesiastical erections'. He was surprised that the Hindus of his time, such as the porters accompanying him, were delighted by the erotic carvings and 'took good care to point them out to all present'. Fourteen years later a more senior officer, Major General Sir Alexander Cunningham, documented the temples. He considered the erotic carvings 'highly indecent', and 'disgustingly obscene'.

My initial reaction to the carvings was not dissimilar to Burt's. 'How,' I wondered, 'could religion and this blatant sexuality go together?' What could be the religious purpose of this erotica? At that stage in my life, I still held rigid beliefs about sex that I believed were true according to Christian teaching. Everything I had been taught had implied that the sexual impulse was something to be repressed. It certainly wasn't something to be rejoiced in, as the sculptors of the beautiful temples of Khajuraho obviously did.

The Roman Catholic Church maintains that its teaching on celibacy and chastity does not devalue the sexual side of our nature, but what is taught even by Churches that do not insist on clerical celibacy seems to imply that there is something inherently evil in sex. As a schoolboy preparing to be confirmed in the Anglican Church I had to study the catechism, in which I was told I should 'renounce the devil and all his works, the pomps and vanity of this wicked world, and all the sinful lusts of the flesh'. To a testosterone-charged teenage boy, the lusts of the flesh could only mean one thing: sex. And these lusts became the work of the Devil I failed to renounce.

The Christian fear of sex – and the guilt and repression that are its inevitable counterparts – dates all the way back to the earliest days of the Church, when St Paul advised the Christians in Corinth that it would be better for them to live a celibate life as he did, but if they could not cope with that, then they should marry because it was 'better to marry than to burn'.

St Augustine was perhaps the greatest of the early Church

fathers, and another man who had a profound impact on theology, including Christianity's attitude to love and sex. He famously asked God to 'give me chastity and continency, but not yet', which might be taken to imply he thought sex was a bit of a joke. However, that wasn't the case at all. Once he had become chaste, St Augustine condemned all sexual activity. He believed that Adam and Eve's sin in the Garden of Eden consisted of their having sex together, which meant that sex was the true cause of the Fall of man. According to Augustine, any man or woman who wanted to be 'righteous in God's sight' should live a celibate life.

St Jerome, the early Church father who translated the Bible from its original languages into Latin, assessed the value of different ways of living and gave virginity one hundred marks out of one hundred, whereas marriage only got thirty. However, Martin Luther, who founded the anti-Catholic Reformation in Germany, was a bitter critic of celibacy. He married a nun who had managed to escape from a convent into which she had been forced against her will. But even Luther thought sex was such a powerful force for evil that only marriage could protect a person from immorality – and therefore anyone who wasn't married must be a sinner.

It seems to me that this condemnation of sex is theologically flawed because it implies that one of God's gifts to us is evil. It forgets that self-denial can be just as destructive as self-indulgence. It ignores or, at best, underestimates the difficulty of suppressing sexuality. In his book, *A Time to Keep Silence*, Patrick Leigh Fermor describes a conversation with a friend who had been a Trappist monk, and so a member of one of the most austere orders of the Roman Catholic Church. The monk told Fermor that he had experienced 'gruelling struggles with the flesh'. Usually he was too busy with his religious duties and the hard physical toil required of a monk to be troubled by the temptations of the flesh, but then, 'all of a sudden, the surge of restless thoughts would begin. As often as not, profane and carnal visions would be reinforced by the murmurings of religious doubt, and at the end of these alarming onslaughts, from which he emerged unscathed only with the help of prayer and a kind of mental fight, he would feel utterly exhausted.' After winning the first of those battles, the monk asked his confessor whether it was an outright victory, whether temptation was vanquished for ever. The confessor, a wise old monk, shook his head ruefully and assured him that 'no monk, however holy, could say that he was immune for life; the Devil, incensed by defeat, lulled his foe by inaction, and then returned to the attack with sevenfold reinforcements'.

If we go back no further than the Victorian moral code that was still being taught when I was at school in the fifties, we will find that sex was regarded as the number one sin.

Although nobody to this day knows for sure why those erotic sculptures decorate the splendid temples of Khajuraho, after many years in India I think I have come to a better understanding of the possible theology behind them. It's an understanding that has led me to believe that our response to our sexuality should be neither those of the repressive Christian tradition nor the modern licence, in which it seems that everything is acceptable, but a middle way between the two.

When I asked the Indian Jungian therapist Rashna Imhasly-Gandhy whether I was right in believing that Western sexual mores have swung from one extreme to another, from repression to a liberation that has become a licence without boundaries, she said, 'Too true. You have gone from constipation to diarrhoea!' Rashna added, 'For many of my patients materialism has replaced any form of spirituality, so they have no path which can guide them, no collected coherent system of belief to fall back on.'

The Victorian morality I was taught didn't gradually fade into the night: it departed with a bang in the sixties. Now, as my schoolmaster friend Richard Wilkinson has said, the boys and girls at Marlborough would regard the suggestion that they should not have sex before marriage as ludicrous. As for dressing modestly, which was such an obsession with the Victorians that some of them even clothed the legs of tables lest they provoked lecherous thoughts, the aim today seems to be to dress as provocatively as possible. Nudity in films and television dramas is no longer surprising, and it seems almost obligatory to have sex scenes in novels.

The new morality claims that it has liberated women, but it has also exploited them as sex objects. Advertising is the most obvious example of this exploitation, for what is using women's bodies to sell goods ranging from cars to bars of soap other than making them into sex objects? The message of many advertisements to men seems to be that driving a particular car or using a particular soap will make women fall for them, with the not always disguised additional suggestion that women will then want to have sex. In India there is a stricter code on advertising than in the West and more rigorous film censorship, but nevertheless the television coverage of a recent international cricket series was interrupted after almost every over by an advertisement for a male hair gel called 'Set Wet', described by a husky female voice as, 'Sexy – very, very sexy'.

In his book *Growth Fetish*, the Australian economist Clive Hamilton writes: 'In the 1950s middle-class respectability may have been oppressive but it carried with it a certain deference. Women are the subject of far more sexual objectification now than they were in the 1950s, although men have become more adept at concealing it.' Katherine Rake is Director of the Fawcett Society, which was founded in 1866 in order to campaign for women's right to vote in Britain and is named in honour of Dame Millicent Garrett Fawcett, one of the foremost suffragettes in that sixty-year-long struggle. The society now campaigns for equality between men and women. Katherine Rake says that one of the problems now facing the feminist movement is 'the hypersexualisation of our culture, a phenomenon that has developed and snowballed with hardly a murmur of dissent'.

'Hardly a murmur of dissent' is the point. Any suggestion by Church leaders or anyone else that the sexual revolution might be going too fast and too far is derided as old-fashioned, illiberal, and – of course – as wanting to re-impose the old restrictive morality. Once again there is a false alternative here: it is suggested that either you believe in the sexual revolution of the sixties or you want to go back to Victorian times. But Katherine Rake, who certainly has no desire to go back to the repression of the fifties, points out that many women are suffering from the new morality in spite of its claims to have made life better for all by making it freer. She says: 'Against a background of ubiquitous images of women's bodies as sex objects, rates of self-harm among women are spiralling, eating disorders are on the rise, and plastic surgery is booming.' Nor, according to Rake, has the new morality done much to alter the power relations between men and women. According to her, men are still the top dogs.

It is perhaps not surprising that many feminists are calling for 'a new wave of feminism', a wave that will change the power relations between the sexes profoundly. But it would be a mistake to ignore the changes for the good that the years since the sixties have achieved. When I was young, most parents saw nothing unusual in sending their sons to university and their daughters to secretarial college without giving them any choice in the matter. Nowadays, most people would regard that as unacceptable. Although more men than women still get to the top of the tree, the women who do make it are no longer rare exceptions in most professions. My own profession, journalism, was once very much a man's world, but now when I listen to the

BBC's World Service Radio it seems to have become a woman's domain.

Although not all women get paid the same rate as men for doing the same job, more and more are receiving equal pay. In the West, women are also better protected legally than they once were. Taking British law as an example, rape in marriage is now illegal. Sexual harassment and discrimination at work can be challenged. Maternity leave is a right. As regards the situation in Ireland, I have to agree with the Irish lawyer who said to me, 'For all the new problems we now face, I honestly believe Ireland is a happier place now than it was when strict Catholic morality dominated society.' I would certainly not like to go back to the morality of my young days.

Westerners have always tended to be ruled by one form or other of moral orthodoxy, and so it is perhaps not surprising that the sexual revolution has imposed an orthodoxy that is just as pervasive as the Victorian morality once was. However, in India, with its long tradition of heterodoxy, different understandings of sexuality have long lived side by side. There has certainly been a repressive tradition, but India is also the country in which the *Kama Sutra* was written.

Ancient Indians were concerned with the scientific study of human behaviour. They were particularly interested in how life should be lived to achieve four main aims. The first three goals of human life were held to be those of *dharma* (virtue and the following of religious practices), *artha* (economic prosperity) and *kama* (desire, pleasure and love, including the erotic). These led to the final goal of *moksha*, liberation from suffering and from the cycle of death and rebirth.

The title of the *Kama Sutra* shows its concern with the third goal in life. The author, the sage Vatsyayana, drew his material from earlier scientific studies of *kama*. He described sex as it was practised, without flinching from descriptions of homosexuality and adultery, which – although officially frowned upon – were included in his work because he knew that these transgressions from the norm were realities.

The *Kama Sutra* is not a simple sex guide designed to improve performance. Nor does it ignore morality. There are even verses at the end of chapters to tell readers how to behave. For instance, at the end of the chapter on seducing other men's wives, Vatsyayana states that he has described these techniques not so as to encourage or enable adulterers to succeed in their deceptions but to warn husbands in order that they will not be deceived by their wives. The last verse explains:

> This book was undertaken in order
> To guard wives for the benefit of men;
> Its arrangements should not be learned
> In order to corrupt the people.

This might suggest that the *Kama Sutra* is restricted to a purely male perspective on sexuality. It is not. Vatsyayana clearly recognises that women have sexual desires too, and advises them on how these might be fulfilled. His guidance ranges from telling virgins how to get husbands to a discussion of the female orgasm, which, as the psychoanalysts Sudhir Kakar and Wendy Doniger rightly point out in their introduction to their translation of the *Kama Sutra*, is 'far more subtle than views that prevailed in Europe until very recently indeed'. The women described in the *Kama Sutra* are not passive – they are very active. Vatsyayana describes four types of foreplay, in two of which the woman is the active partner. The position portrayed in the carvings at Khajuraho that I mentioned earlier is called 'Climbing the Tree', about which Vatsyayana writes: 'She steps on his foot with her foot, places her other foot on his thigh or wraps her leg around him, with one arm gripping his back and the other bending down his shoulder, and panting gently, moaning a little, she tries to climb him to kiss him.'

In their edition of the *Kama Sutra*, Kaka and Doniger suggest that the work does much more than portray active female sexuality. Rather, Vatsyayana's classic text 'takes a momentous step in the history of Indian sexuality by introducing the notion of love in sex'. There is even advice in one chapter on how to make a virgin bride trust her husband and fall in love with him. Kakar and Doniger see the *Kama Sutra* as 'a tender balancing act' between 'the erotic love and the possessiveness of sexual desire, between the disorder of instinctuality and the moral forces of order, between the imperatives of nature and the civilizing attempts of culture'. They believe that the work is relevant today because the imperatives of nature predominate: 'In today's post-moral world,' they claim, 'the danger to erotic pleasure is less from the icy front of morality than from the fierce heat of instinctual desire. The *Kamasutra*'s most valuable insight, then, is that pleasure needs to be cultivated, that in the realm of sex, nature requires culture.'

The *Kama Sutra* has not always been so well served by its translators. Morality in the nineteenth century put up such a cold front that most translators shied away from revealing the explicit nature of the work. To get round the political correctness and prudery of his day, one German translator went so far as to render the more explicit sections of the text in Latin. By contrast, in the late twentieth century 'the fierce heat of instinctual desire' has all too often turned the *Kama Sutra* into a sexual extravaganza, a book to be leered over and tittered at.

Today, many visitors to Khajuraho still leer at the erotic temple carvings and perhaps all too few trouble to wonder what the erotica might really be trying to communicate to us. There have, however, been various theories put forward over the years about these and similar images. I remember being told that erotic carvings on a temple in Kathmandu were theological lightning conductors, there to ward off the evil eye. Another interpretation often heard is that Khajuraho's carvings represent yogic practices. Some say they represent the stage of life at which a person completes the period of compulsory celibacy required of a student and is allowed – in fact enjoined – to enjoy *kama*. But why would the carvings only represent that stage? Why, for instance, wouldn't they represent the stage in old age when we are told that we should retire to the forest, become an ascetic and meditate? After all, Shiva, the god of Khajuraho, was a great ascetic. Someone has even suggested that the erotic carvings on the part of the wall that joins the sanctuary to the rest of the temple represent a pun set in stone. They celebrate the joining of male and female which is required for human creativity.

For me, art historian Shobita Punja's explanation is the most plausible. In her book *Divine Ecstacy: The Story of Khajuraho* she suggests that the temples and their carvings are the expression of the consummation of the divine wedding – the union of Shiva and Parvati. When Burt stumbled on the temples in 1838 there was only one building that he was not permitted to enter by his Hindu guides. This was probably because it was the only temple still used for active worship. Indeed, it remains a popular temple. It is dedicated to Shiva, and the biggest festival of the year in Khajuraho is the celebration of Shiva's wedding to Parvati on the occasion of Mahashivratri, the great night of Shiva, which falls around the end of February.

Some years ago I went to the festival with Shobita Punja. The village of Khajuraho was packed with pilgrims from the surrounding countryside. Whole families, from great grandparents down to new babies, had travelled to the festival in carts pulled by the diminutive bullocks of the region. They had brought with them their pots, pans, stores and everything else necessary for an overnight stay, and set up camp by the roadside and on every inch of public land. Some families had come to do business. They sat on the roadside with their goods for sale spread out before them. Many were selling items required for worship, such as vermilion, small brown coconuts, pots for the ritual of pouring water, and sweets.

Shobita and I arrived at the temple early on the morning of the moonless night of the festival because I wanted to have a sacred thread tied round my wrist as a token of the occasion. Even then, we found the steep steps leading up the temple crowded with devotees. Inside the sanctuary, a stream of them wound slowly round the narrow passage surrounding the massive *linga* shouting '*Hara Hara Mahadev!*' This *linga,* Shiva's symbol, is a circular pillar about eight feet high and three foot six inches in diameter that almost touches the roof of the sanctuary. Tradition has it that the *linga* emerged by itself and would have burst through the roof and gone on growing for ever if the Raja of Khajuraho had not hammered a nail into the top of it to prevent it gaining any more height!

Everyone wanted to have a *darshan,* or sight, of the god, and to worship him by pouring water on the *linga.* As Shobita had spent a lot of time in Khajuraho, she knew the priest sitting cross-legged at the foot of the *linga* and he readily agreed to tie my thread. While he was doing so and reciting Sanskrit prayers, an over-enthusiastic pilgrim threw water over the *linga* so energetically that it splashed him. He turned round and shouted a crude swear word at the pilgrim before completing my short ceremony as though nothing had happened. In their worship Hindus do not have any place for the sacred silence and solemn whispers of Christian churches; they believe that worship should involve life as it is. So the preliminaries for the wedding of Shiva and Parvati have to be celebrated as boisterously as any village wedding.

The actual marriage ceremony takes place at night and is a replica of a modern wedding. The bridegroom's procession, or *barat,* sets off from the temple priest's house to the accompaniment of a brass band playing not religious music but hits from Bollywood movies. The bridegroom is represented by a huge, conical crown, or *mukut,* sitting on top of an Ambassador car. It is followed by chanting Brahmin priests. Behind them come village women singing their traditional wedding songs. Inside the temple, the Brahmins take their places around the *linga.* The crown is placed on top of the *linga,* which by this time has been washed and decorated like a bridegroom with a new *dhoti* wrapped round its middle, a sacred thread over what would be its chest and the three horizontal marks of a Shiva devotee smeared across what would be its brow. Beside this symbol of Shiva, Parvati is represented by a tiny image buried in a mass of flower garlands. The senior priest's son plays the dual role of chief of Shiva's wedding procession and head of the bride's family. He offers gifts to the teams of Brahmins who conduct the nuptial ceremonies that continue uninterrupted until dawn.

For Shobita, the union of Shiva and Parvati represents 'the ultimate goal of life'. It symbolises the unity of all opposites, and in particular the unity of male and female in nature, and the male and female within us. (Freud and Jung both argue that humans are inherently bisexual.) For Shobita, the temples of Khajuraho are not to be ogled at; they are sermons in stone, teaching us that sex is not to be suppressed nor to be treated purely as a recreation – which is the way it is sometimes described in the West today. Rather, sex is an act of profound significance.

The myth of the courtship and marriage of Shiva and Parvati seems to me to have something profound to say about romantic love. Because of the West's sexual permissiveness an excessive premium is placed on 'being in love'. As there are now far fewer social and religious restraints on making and breaking relationships, we in the West are far more easily tempted to believe that a commitment to a partner is only valid as long as we remain in love with that person and our love is reciprocated.

However, it might seem strange to maintain that too high a premium can be placed on being in love, and I remember how confused I was when, back in the sixties, I read that the Archbishop of Canterbury, Michael Ramsey, had said something similar. After all, the basis of Christianity is love and in the Anglican marriage service couples commit to loving each other. But there is a vital difference between being in love and loving each other, a difference described by the American analyst Robert A. Johnson in his book *We: Understanding the Psychology of Romantic Love:*

> One of the great paradoxes in romantic love is that it *never produces human relationship as long as it stays romantic*. It produces drama, daring adventures, wondrous, intense love scenes, jealousies, and betrayals; but people never seem to settle into relationship with each other as flesh-and-blood human beings until they are out of the romantic love stage, until they *love* each other instead of being 'in love'.

This does not mean that we should avoid romantic love. We can't and we shouldn't, and the myth of Shiva and Parvati does not suggest anything different. Yet the myth does suggest that we should progress from romantic love to loving.

According to the myth, Shiva had withdrawn from the world in mourning for his wife Sati, a form of the great goddess. His absence had allowed a powerful demon to take control of the world and so the other gods went to the great goddess to appeal to her to manifest herself again and woo Shiva back. The goddess was reborn as Parvati, daughter of the mountains. She grew into an intellectually brilliant and beautiful young woman. When she decided to serve Shiva in his meditation, the gods conspired to make him fall in love with her. They sent Kama, the god of desire who – like Eros in Greek mythology – was armed with a bow and arrow. He fired an arrow at Shiva, distracting the god from his meditation and making him aware of Parvati's attractions. In his rage at being thus disturbed, Shiva burnt up Kama with a glance from his third eye. After Kama's death, Parvati felt she had lost all hope of marrying Shiva but was advised that she could still win him if she undertook penances. Her penances enabled her to cleanse herself of all false pride and egotism, and when Shiva felt the time was ripe to test her, she passed the trials he set with flying colours. The two married and their thousands of years of lovemaking started. In the words of the sixth-century Sanskrit poet Kalidas:

> With the day and the night the same to him
> Siva spent his time making love
> And he passed twenty-five years
> As if it were a single night
> And his thirst for the pleasures of loving
> Never became any less in him
> As the fire that burns below the ocean
> Is never satisfied by the rolling waters.

Of course this myth contains many layers of meaning. The union of Shiva and Parvati, for example, restored balance to the universe. But the interpretation I believe is relevant here is that Shiva had to kill Kama, and that Parvati had to undergo penance in the absence of Kama in order to overcome egotistical romantic love. Only then could they be joined in creative and everlasting love, in which the ego is transcended.

However, sometimes Indians seem to go too far in decrying romantic love. I remember meeting a man who had been a member of Lord Linlithgow's bodyguard when the latter was the Viceroy. The man said to me with a mixture of pride and scorn, 'You people fall in love before marriage and out of love afterwards. We fall in love after marriage.' He implied that romantic love was a dangerous diversion. But, unlike the views of the Viceroy's bodyguard, the myth of Shiva and Parvati does not deny the importance of desire. Kama had to fire his arrow at Shiva to make him fall in love, and at the end of the story Shiva is persuaded to bring Kama to life again, so that the work of creation can continue. This myth is also one of many examples of how the Indian tradition is able to combine the sacred and the sensual, unlike either tradition or modernity in the West.

The ability to combine the sacred and the sensual has often been mistaken in the West for a licence to practise free sex. In the seventies, in his ashrams first in America and later back in India, Bhagwan Rajneesh became globally renowned for encouraging his disciples to have sex in the belief that it was a means to enlightenment. He claimed to be following Tantric practices and so it is perhaps not surprising that the Tantric school of Hinduism is widely misunderstood in the West as all about exotic sexual practices.

While making a radio programme about Tantra, I was intrigued to discover that although Tantra teaches that sex is one way through which the purest form of consciousness can be achieved, it is also a path that requires strict self-control and discipline. Madhu Khanna, a Tantric practitioner as well as a scholar of Tantric and other Sanskrit texts, agreed to be our expert for the programme on the condition that we did not concentrate on sex alone, explaining that it was but one way to achieve the purest form of consciousness and was only advocated by one of the Tantric traditions. Madhu suggested that in order to ensure our programme was authoritative we should visit the Tantric centre at Tarapeeth in West Bengal. There we found a small community of Tantrics who spent their lives meditating in a cremation ground set in a grove on the bank of a river.

Smoke was still rising from a funeral pyre when we arrived. We spoke to two Tantric sadhus who lived in small mud huts nearby. Tantrics have a reputation for miraculous powers, and one of the sadhus was very interested in performing 'magic', as he called it. The trick I remember best from that day involved a smoking skull. The Tantric balanced a lit cigarette in the mouth of a human skull and instructed us to watch closely, which was rather difficult to do with the dense smoke from the hut's fire-pit in our eyes. The end of the cigarette glowed and dimmed as if the skull were inhaling.

The second Tantric was a far more serious and impressive man. He sat on a throne of skulls in front of the fire-pit on the floor of his hut, where he performed his rituals. I asked him why he had chosen to spend his life meditating in a place where he was permanently reminded of death. 'That is the point,' he replied. 'In Tantra you learn to overcome fear of anything. So we meditate here to overcome our fear of death, and I sit on a throne of skulls, which many would consider to be a sacrilege.' The Tantric went on to explain that for him death had become a passage, and he had no fear of the transience of existence. 'I live in three times: past, present, and future,' he said.

Tantrics believe they must overcome the fear that lies behind many taboos, including the fear of impurity and pollution. Therefore they can offer hair, blood, fish and meat in their sacrificial rites, as well as other things usually regarded as impure, which means that many of their practices would seem scandalous to other Hindus.

I approached the subject of sex rather gingerly for fear that he would think that I, as a Westerner, had only come to see him because I had heard fascinating reports about Tantric sex. The Tantric laughed at my hesitation and said, 'I knew you would ask about that – and why not? After all, we have to overcome our fear of sex too and I believe that underneath all the Western freedom we hear about – even in this remote place – lies a fear of sex, or at the least an inability to come to terms with it. For us, sex is not to be feared because it is a way to expand consciousness. But then there are special rites for this, and sex has to be refined; rules and discipline have to be followed.'

The Tantric explained how sex was one way of arousing what he called the 'cosmic energy' in all of us and of becoming sources ourselves of that energy. 'You achieve a sense of bliss,' he said. 'How to put it? In our tradition it is described as the purest form of consciousness, like a flash of lightning, tender as lotus fibre, the fine golden thread that binds all believers, the sap of creation.'

In spite of traditions that combine the sacred and the sensual, there is a repressive sexuality that is widespread in India too. Sudhir Kakar has studied this in his book *Intimate Relations*, which he describes as 'a site report, an account of intimate relations as perceived and defined by the participants'. And those accounts make dismal reading. Describing interviews with low caste women who had migrated from villages to a poor locality in Delhi, Sudhir Kakar says they revealed:

> ... sexuality pervaded by hostility and indifference rather than affection and tenderness. Most women portrayed even sexual intercourse as a furtive act in a cramped and crowded room lasting barely a few minutes and with a marked absence of physical and emotional caressing. Most women found it painful or distasteful or both. It was an experience to be submitted to, often from a fear of beating. None of the women removed their clothes for the act since it is considered shameful to do so.

The sexual taboos remained so strong in some areas that the women in these communities didn't have a word for their genitals. As for the more opulent Indian women, Sudhir Kakar has had personal experience of the 'sexual woes of a vast number of middle and upper class women who come for psychotherapy'.

There are parallels with Victorian hypocrisy in India's public life as well, such as the long-running saga of the kiss in Indian films. 'No kissing, please, we're Indians' was the view the censors took when I first came to India, and remained so for a long time. Directors got around this problem by including scenes where female leads somehow found themselves in wet saris which, if not quite see-through, were certainly suggestive enough to titillate the audience. These days, the situation has moved on and the ban on kissing has been relaxed. But that still leaves the question of whether a kiss is always acceptable. A lesbian kiss in Deepa Mehta's film *Fire* provoked demonstrations in Mumbai in 1998 and the trashing of the cinemas that showed the film. Members of a Hindu party protested in their underwear outside the home of an actor who had filed a petition against their earlier demonstrations. Hypocrisy was rife in the southern state of Tamil Nadu in 2005 when a female film star called Khushboo said that men should no longer expect their brides to be virgins. In what the Hindustan *Times* called 'a mad display of priggishness and prudery', no less than twenty-five defamation cases were filed against her, and she eventually issued a public apology for her remarks. Even more incredibly, a minister in the last coalition government headed by the Bharatiya Janata Party objected to the mention of condoms in a campaign designed to make Indians aware of the dangers of Aids.

India's long hangover from the Raj, with its Victorian morality, has helped to stifle the tradition that was able to see the sacred in the sensual. However, the influence of Mahatma Gandhi and the parallel tradition of sexual abstinence that he followed must also bear some of the responsibility for this. The Mahatma and others like him didn't advocate the benefits of abstinence purely for religious reasons, for sacrificing sexual love for a higher love, or for self-discipline. They also argued that abstinence was good for a person and empowered him or her.

When I interviewed India's austere Gandhian Prime Minister Morarji Desai in 1978, he was as open about his sex life as he was about his habit of drinking his own urine. He told me he hadn't slept with his wife since he was in his early thirties, and went on to explain that semen was a liberating force that should be stored, not depleted. There is a common belief in India that if semen is stored its energy can, through yogic practices, be raised up to the head, where it empowers men to achieve union with the divine. Indian mythology has plenty of ascetics who are praised for their asceticism and the powers that come with it. But there are also, I am glad to say, many ascetics in mythology who fall for temptresses, and the gods are happy to see them so humbled.

The values of asceticism are praised in the popular versions of the influential epic, the *Ramayana*. The name of its hero, Rama, was on the lips of the Mahatma when he died. Rama and his wife Sita are worshipped as incarnations of absolute Truth, absolute God. Rama is also known as *Purushottam* – the best of men – and for centuries has been regarded as a model for mankind. To many devotees, Sita and Rama's love for each other, pervaded as it is by ideas of devotion, duty and restraint, represents an ideal relationship. Rama is the perfect son and the perfect prince. He obediently accepts exile from his kingdom, and it is during this period that he and his wife live in the forests as ascetics.

According to the *Ramayana*, the temple town of Ayodhya in north India was the capital of Rama's kingdom, where he returned to rule after his exile and after defeating the demon-king of Lanka, who had abducted his wife Sita. When I visited Ayodhya, I found many different approaches to Rama and they did not necessarily involve revering him as an ascetic. The followers of the Rasik tradition concentrate on Rama and Sita as a young married couple. Some of these devotees try, at a spiritual level, to experience Rama as Sita would have done. This form of spirituality is very similar to the intensely feminine spirituality, with sexual undertones, that is sometimes linked with St John of the Cross, for example. But when I asked the scholar Acharya Kripa Shankarji Maharaj about the tradition, he was not amused. 'Man–woman love is dirty; forget it,' he said. Then, thinking that perhaps he'd gone too far, he went on, 'Well, you can say it's good but not good in a good sense. Love is *ghalat paribhasha*, a dirty word these days.'

The Acharya represents the interpretation that sees Rama as an ascetic and there are some feminists today who argue that this Rama has had malign consequences for women. They maintain that, far from portraying an ideal man–woman relationship, the *Ramayana* presents Sita as a model of a weak, submissive woman. Two feminists, Kamla Bhasin and Ritu Menon, even went so far as to suggest that, 'with Sita as our ideal, can *sati* – widow burning – be far behind?'

The Indian Jungian therapist Rashna Imhasly-Gandhy believes that the *Ramayana* affects the people of India today in much the same way as the Victorian interpretation of Christianity once affected the people of Britain. In a paper on the diversity of Indian myths, she criticises the *Ramayana* because in it Sita appears to subordinate herself to her husband, regarding him as 'a near god'. Looking at the impact of this portrayal on modern India, Rashna maintains: 'Many Indian women even today, like Sita, are subdued in their marital home, their spirit broken, and their minds enslaved. They have learnt to subordinate themselves to the male ego; they must love and worship the man and must believe they are dependent upon him.' But Rashna's is only one interpretation of the influence of the *Ramayana*. I know that while there are many Indian women in villages, towns and cities who would agree with her, there are also many who would not recognise themselves in her portrait.

*

My own favourite myth is the story of Shiva and Parvati, because to me it implies something that I personally feel to be profoundly important: whilst I believe in equality between the sexes, the pivotal role of Parvati in Hindu legend and the fact that Shiva is powerless without her underline for me both the power of the feminine and the different roles of male and female in nature's scheme. Parvati stands not only for women, but for the female aspect in men as well.

The Western sexual revolution may have swept away Victorian sexuality and given women many equal opportunities but, as we have seen, it has not completely diminished male domination. The continued use of women's bodies as sex-objects is obvious evidence of that domination. Maybe it is not surprising that this should be so, as the Western mind has always been predominantly masculine in outlook and the more recent form of feminism, which truly respects the feminine, is perhaps only just beginning to change that.

In the Western world, God has always been a masculine presence. One of the arguments put forward for a celibate clergy by the Roman Catholic Church is the fact that all the apostles were male and so, of course, was Paul, the founder of Christian theology. We have already mentioned the Church fathers, such as St Augustine, but we have not spoken of any Church mothers. It is significant, however, that there have always been plenty of Christian women mystics, but there were no women theologians within the western Church until relatively recently.

Women have been singularly absent from the history of secular philosophy from Plato and Aristotle onwards. Looking down the chapter headings of Bertrand Russell's *History of Western Philosophy*, I do not find a single woman's name listed there. In his book, *The Passion of the Western Mind*, Richard Tarnas sees this masculinity of thought as fundamental to the Western struggle to establish our human autonomy from nature. 'The evolution of the Western mind has been driven by a heroic impulse to forge an autonomous rational human self by separating itself from the primordial unity with nature,' he states. But Tarnas feels that that impulse is weakening and that a longing for the feminine side of our nature is breaking through now that we have – in his words – 'pressed the masculine quest to its utmost one-sided extreme in the late modern mind'.

If that is so, perhaps we should turn once more to the symbolism of Khajuraho, and to the wedding of Shiva and Parvati, in order to begin to redress the balance between male and female, showing equal respect to both.

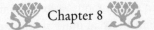

Chapter 8

THE GLOBAL VILLAGE: IN SEARCH OF BALANCE

I N the middle ages, theology was the queen of sciences in Europe. Theologians claimed to know with certainty how society should be regulated, what its goals should be and how those goals should be achieved. But I for one wouldn't suggest that theology should regain her crown; nor would I deny the enormous benefits of the Enlightenment that dethroned her. In Chapter 6, I have already been critical of the Roman Catholic Church's attempt to cling on to power in Ireland well into the twentieth century. I have also seen the impact of theology in Pakistan, where General Zia-ul-Haq came to power in 1978 and where he subsequently imposed military rule in the name of Islam, instructed the recently elected Members of Parliament to stay at home and gagged the press. While theologians did not object to the flawed trial and death sentence passed on the deposed Prime Minister, Zulfiqar Ali Bhutto, theologians did call for the afternoon of public floggings I had the misfortune to witness, during which men who had been found guilty by kangaroo courts of comparatively minor crimes against Islam, such as petty theft, were flogged until blood stained their *paja-mas*. Although I never witnessed a public hanging in Pakistan, some of my colleagues did, publishing photographs of these shocking events.

So, no, I would not recommend that theology should be

restored to her throne. As I understand it, there should be no throne and there should be no dominant discipline; instead there should be a balance between all disciplines. Be that as it may, that throne still exists, and in this chapter I am going to argue that economics now occupies it. The latest god is the market, and we are asked to believe that heaven on earth will be achieved through economic growth. This is not to say that economists, the market and economic growth don't all have a role to play. However, it is to suggest that their current role is too dominant. Economics governs politics, leaving little room for government decisions to be counter-balanced by studies of human behaviour, such as those provided by sociology, psychology, political science and, indeed, religious studies.

Today's dominant economics worships the certainties of market capitalism, globalisation, private enterprise and minimum government intervention. The yardstick it uses to measure its success is growth in GDP, or Gross Domestic Product. When I was young, a form of socialist economics dominated, the rationale of which was almost the mirror opposite of that of today's market capitalism. Socialist economists advocated a major role for the state, distrusted private enterprise and rejected market capitalism. Today, we have seen an all too familiar swing from one extreme to another. Economists, by and large, have failed to seek a middle road and have dismissed socialism out of hand.

No one who lived through the socialist years in India could possibly support a swing back to full-blooded socialism there. When I arrived in India in 1965, eighteen years of socialism and central planning (admittedly assisted by monsoon failures and the cost of two wars) had created an economy of shortages. Consumer goods were in such short supply that foreign diplomats' wives preparing to leave the country found a ready market for their half-used lipsticks and their underwear. Electricity was rationed and there was a long waiting list for telephones. There was a famine in Bihar, and India was so dependent on American food aid that it was said the country was 'living from ship to mouth'.

The private sector survived on sufferance, having to go to the government for permission not only to invest in new projects but even to increase the productivity of existing ones. Large sections of the economy were out of bounds to the private sector. Banking and other financial services were tied up in red tape. I remember being given a cheque for the BBC that had been issued by the Reserve Bank, India's central bank. When I took it to the BBC's bank they refused to accept it, telling me I would have to get it cleared by the Reserve Bank first. Back at the Reserve Bank, I was referred to the officer who 'checks cheques' – who found three reasons to reject a cheque issued by his own bank.

All the same, when Nehru became the first Prime Minister of independent India after the Second World War, there were good reasons for him to espouse socialism, then the dominant economic theory. And after two centuries in which India's economic policy had been run by a foreign government, it's not surprising that Nehru did not want to rely on imports, foreign investments or global markets to establish the state. In any event, global markets were at that time not yet well developed. So it seemed to make sense to build a self-sufficient India and to pull the new nation up by its bootstraps. What's more, Soviet propaganda exaggerating the success of central planning led Nehru to believe that this strategy could succeed. But central planning, together with the administration required for a restrictive currency and trade policy, spawned a massive bureaucracy in a country already bureaucratised by the Raj. The vested interests of capitalists were replaced by the vested interests of those bureaucrats who administered the controlled economy. The politicians, who should have been the bureaucrats' masters, became their partners in twisting controls to suit their own financial purposes.

Indira Gandhi came to power in 1965 and went on to tighten the screws on the economy in order to build her constituency among the poor. Banks were nationalised, a move that was justified by the fact that the banks were owned by industrialists who were funnelling scarce credit their way. However, when Indira Gandhi moved to nationalise the food trade, she bit off more than she could chew. Her proposals only made a bad situation worse, and she was forced to retreat, handing back that particular business to the traders. By the beginning of the 1980s, when Indira Gandhi began to realise that the shackles she had placed on the economy had to be loosened, her earlier aim of bringing 'the commanding heights of the economy' under public ownership had already been largely achieved. About forty-five per cent of the industrial output was produced by the public sector, which included the eight largest companies and twenty-four of the top thirty.

One result of the socialist 'licence permit raj', as it was called, in which the economy was controlled by the state and licences given only to a select few, was that for many years a make of car called the Ambassador enjoyed a virtually unchallenged rule over India's roads. Protected by its exclusive licence from any effective competition, Hindustan Motors' version of the British Morris Oxford 1948 model became a symbol of India's industrial backwardness. Eventually, the car's longevity gave it a global cult status, and Hindustan Motors were able to export it as a collector's item.

Mind you, the aerodynamically challenged Ambassador, which is shaped not unlike a bowler hat on wheels, has proved itself a suitable vehicle for India's pot-holed roads and rural cart tracks. It has a high clearance, which protects its undercarriage from all but the deepest of those holes, and the murderous unmarked speed breakers that villagers lay across roads at will. The Ambassador also has a remarkable capacity. The largest number of passengers I personally have ever seen crammed into one is twelve.

The Ambassador's weakness lay in its finishing. Because Hindustan Motors faced no effective competition and there was always a long list of customers waiting for their cars, they didn't have to bother about putting the vehicles together particularly well and making sure all the nuts and bolts were tightened. There is a certain captain of British industry of my acquaintance who never loses an opportunity to remind me of an occasion when we were bowling along in my own Ambassador and the bonnet flew off. On the positive side, the Ambassador's weaknesses gave rise to a cottage industry, with mechanics dotted all over the country who could patch up any broken-down Ambassador and send it on its way. Although the world came to see the Ambassador as a symbol of India's industrial backwardness, for many ministers and officials it became an important symbol of India, and riding in it became, in turn, a symbol of their patriotism.

Now that the Indian automobile industry has been freed from the restrictions of the licence permit raj, the Ambassador has been dethroned by global models manufactured in India, as well as by a few rival Indian designed cars. While some ministers and officials remain loyal to the Ambassador, that monopoly has also been broken. Nevertheless, Hindustan Motors remains confident that there is a market for the latest modification of the Ambassador. It's better constructed than the old models, as I found when I drove in an Ambassador from Kolkata to Delhi to make a radio travel programme for the BBC. Alarm bells rang only once, when there was a dreadful clang as we emerged from a particularly deep pot-hole. But we found that only the number plate had come adrift.

Figures show the remarkable expansion of the Indian automobile industry once the licensing system started to be unscrambled in 1991, following a macroeconomic crisis. From an almost stagnant output feeding an almost stagnant market, industry has achieved an average annual growth rate of seventeen per cent. Once almost entirely limited to the home market, India is now a global player. It is the largest manufacturer of tractors and three-wheelers, and the fourth largest manufacturer of trucks in the world. If current trends continue, India will be the seventh largest manufacturer of cars by 2016. All this is accompanied by a burgeoning automobile ancillaries industry. In its Draft Mission Plan for the automobile industry, the Indian government forecasts that it will expand within ten years from a turnover of 34 billion to 145 billion US dollars. That industry's growth is now proving so rapid demonstrates the potential that was held back under the old system. But the obvious disadvantages of giving the government too much control over the economy should not cloak the gains that were also made during the licence permit raj period.

Under Nehru, India started to establish the heavy industries necessary to provide a base for its economic recovery. It also created its own nuclear industry. And after Nehru, the country benefited from the 'Green Revolution', which arose from a strategy adopted by the government in 1969. Farmers were encouraged by government incentives and scientists from agricultural universities to sow new breeds of high-yielding seeds. They were shown how much chemical fertilizer and pesticide to use, and were guaranteed a supply of water. Today, this revolution might be criticised for not utilising organic farming methods, but in the 1970s its impact ended the ship-to-mouth supply chain and at long last enabled India to grow enough food to feed her own people.

Because of our Western habit of seeing issues in black and white, advocates of market capitalism sometimes underestimate or ignore the achievements of controlled economies and over-emphasise their failures.

Socialism and government controls over the economy were anathema to former British Prime Minister Margaret Thatcher. Her husband Dennis was shocked when she praised Indira Gandhi during a television interview she gave at the end of one of her prime-ministerial visits to India. Dennis Thatcher and I were watching the interview being filmed and he turned to me and whispered, 'But she's a bit of a lefty, isn't she?' On another occasion, speaking to Australian businessmen in 1981, Mrs Thatcher praised Westernised industrialised economies for increasing average income two-and-a-half times per head between 1950 and 1980. She gave much of the credit to 'the miracle economies of Japan, Germany and France'. Yet she didn't acknowledge that these were three of the most tightly controlled economies.

Turning to the political scene of more recent years, Tony Blair and his colleagues were so keen to put a distance between them-selves and their party's socialist past that they renamed themselves 'New Labour'. Although Old Labour had much to its credit, particularly many of the reforms of the first post-War government, Tony Blair's government swung so far the other way that he was soon being described as the greatest triumph of Thatcherism.

For an outright condemnation of socialism and a one-sided endorsement of market capitalism, it's hard to beat an emotional George Bush speaking to the American National Endowment for Democracy in 2003:

In the middle of the twentieth century some imagined that central planning and social regimentation were a short cut to national strength. In fact, the prosperity, and social vitality, and technological progress of a people are directly determined by [the] extent of their liberty. Freedom honours and unleashes human creativity – and creativity determines the strength and wealth of nations. Liberty is both the plan of Heaven for humanity, and the hope for progress here on earth.

If God is a market capitalist then, surely – in George Bush's book at least – the devil must be a socialist.

Joseph Stiglitz is the Nobel Prize-winning economist who first highlighted the impact of market economics on government decision-making. He was Chairman of President Clinton's Council of Economic Advisors, but since then he has called for a cooling-off period in the shouting match between the advocates of government intervention and the advocates of the market. In his book *The Roaring Nineties*, which analyses the causes of the American boom and bust economy of those years, he puts forward 'a new vision for America'. It's a vision 'which lies somewhere between those who see government having a dominant role in the economy and those who argue for a minimalist role; but also between the critics who see capitalism as a system that is rotten to the core, and those who see the market economy as unblemished, a miraculous invention of man that brings unprecedented prosperity to all'. Stiglitz's vision and agenda 'takes into account the links between the economy and political processes, and between these and the kind of society – and the kinds of individuals – we create'. It's not just, as Bill Clinton thought, 'the economy, stupid!'.

India began to change course in the late 1980s, when economists presented to the government plans for breaking the shackles of the socialist system. Initially, politicians feared there would be a backlash if such plans were to be implemented, as they would be seen as being 'anti-poor'. The politicians were also reluctant to lose the powers they enjoyed in an economy that was so dominated by the government.

The first major reforms came in 1991, when the new Prime Minister, Narasimha Rao, took advantage of an economic crisis to start opening up the Indian economy. When he came to power, India was on the verge of bankruptcy, and the International Monetary Fund (IMF) told Rao that it wouldn't come to the country's rescue unless the government started to relax its control over the economy. So Narasimha Rao was able to tell his ministers that he had no alternative, and his reluctant colleagues were forced to accept that their sacred socialist model had to be overhauled. But the Finance Minister at the time, the distinguished economist Dr Manmohan Singh, although a strong advocate of the reforms, wisely insisted that – even after accepting the need to allow the market to play a bigger part in deciding economic priorities – the government still had a crucial role to play in economic affairs. He argued that a country such as India, with its vast problem of poverty and its stark disparities in *per capita* income, had to maintain a balance between government and the market.

And that remained Dr Manmohan Singh's message when he became Prime Minister in 2004. While continuing to free commerce and industry from outside interference, he launched schemes to provide work for families living in rural areas and to improve education. In 2006, two years after assuming office as Prime Minister, he urged the Annual Conference of the Confederation of Indian Industries to 'give more attention to questions of social and economic discrimination, to the educational and health status of the people', and stressed that 'these are important social responsibilities of both Government and business'.

*

Transport illustrates the strength and weaknesses of the market in India. There is no doubt that the success of the automobile industry is due to its joining the global market and welcoming foreign investment, which brings in the latest technology. There have been enough Indians able to afford cars – or if not cars, motorcycles and scooters – for the domestic market to expand rapidly. However, bus passengers in Delhi still have to travel in decrepit and dangerous vehicles, because public transport can only improve if the government intervenes in the market.

Passengers getting off at the bus stop at the entrance to Nizamuddin East, where I live, often take cycle rickshaws for the last stage of their journey to the railway station at the other end of the colony. Nukun sits by the bus stop, in his shabby rickshaw with its torn seat and narrow uncomfortable saddle. A cotton cloth is tied round the handlebar for mopping the sweat from his brow. His passengers sit under a tattered canopy, but he has no shade as he pounds the pedals, often having to stand on them to keep going. The temperature in Delhi can reach 45°C, but he can't afford to take a break, even when the sun is at its fiercest.

Nukun is a small yet wiry man, with close-cropped black hair and a lined face. I guess he is about forty-five years old. 'No, more like thirty or thirty-two,' he corrects me.

He comes from a village near Morena, in the state of Madhya Pradesh. When I ask him why he came to Delhi, he explains, 'I had to earn money and there was no work in the village, nor do I have any land. I have to keep my family, wife and four children.'

Nukun earns about one hundred rupees a day (which is not much over a pound sterling) if he waits for passengers from seven o'clock in the morning until seven in the evening. He has to pay the rickshaw owner twenty of those rupees, and most of the rest he sends back to his family in the village. That doesn't leave him enough to rent any accommodation, so he sleeps in his rickshaw and eats at a roadside food stall. Yet, for all that, he is dressed in a clean t-shirt and there are no tears in his trousers, which are neatly rolled up above his ankles to prevent them getting entangled in the rickshaw's chain.

Nukun is lucky because he has one of the newer models of cycle rickshaw, 'It's lighter than the old ones,' he tells me, 'but it's still heavy to pull.' Heavy indeed, I found. I tried and had to stand on the pedals to get the rickshaw started. This new model is only a marginal improvement on the old, of which there are still plenty in Delhi. There are no major improvements such as gears or light aluminium frames. The market hasn't provided rickshaw pullers with modern vehicles because they can't afford to buy them for themselves, and the rickshaw owners don't create a demand as there always are plenty of men willing to pull the existing models.

The market hasn't helped people like Nukun when it comes to health either, although it has improved facilities for those with the money to pay for them. Since the economy was opened up in the 1990s, medicine has become big business. The rich of Delhi now demand 'five-star' hospitals, and they get them. Equipped with the most modern equipment and staffed by highly trained doctors, these hospitals have now also entered the health-tourism business. The website health-tourism-india.com advertises orthopaedic surgery, eye care, heart surgery, gynae-cology, cosmetic treatment, dental care, all in India. And why should anyone choose India? The website says 'price advantage'. It has even coined the jaunty slogan 'First World treatment at Third World prices'. Apparently, a joint study by McKinsey and the Confederation of Indian Industries has estimated that the health tourism market in India could be worth one billion dollars by the year 2012.

Without Rita Varma and the mobile clinic she was inspired to run by Mother Teresa, most patients living in the GB Road area of Delhi would get only Third World treatment. Early one summer morning, I sat beside her in the bright white van that she has converted to her clinic, as we drove down the GB Road, the red light area of the city. As we passed, a sex-worker standing in a grubby doorway waved at us; a young man who had just arisen from a night's sleep on the pavement stretched; a dog covered in sores stretched and yawned too; and a barber sharpened an old fashioned cut-throat razor as he waited for his first unshaven customer. But Rita's patients were already up and about, waiting for her in an orderly queue as we drew up.

For nearly three hours her doctors treated patients. One sex worker complained of being tired and was found to have low blood pressure. Another's baby had a bad cough. Many of the men had made themselves ill. Mohammad Aslam had chronic bronchitis from smoking. Kishan, an alcoholic who pulled a handcart in the market, had damaged his liver. Sunil Das, a sweeper, was trying to get off smack. Smack is one of the most common drugs taken by the poor in India. Also known as 'brown sugar', it's low-grade heroin, which has been heavily adulterated with anything from citric acid to rat poison.

Rita had been allocated a building in which she will be able to establish a permanent clinic. When I was taken to view it, I saw at first hand why these men and others like them were driven to drink and drugs. Squeezed between the dilapidated building and the yard of Old Delhi Railway Station were two rows of tin and cardboard shacks – the homes of rag-pickers. The area was littered with waste paper and garbage, and, with their grubby sacks slung over their shoulders, the rag-pickers were setting out for a day's scavenging. A man crouching under a handcart smiled furtively at me when I noticed him trying to light up a blend of smack and tobacco.

The only individual with a secure job seemed to be a grey Langur monkey, who leapt nimbly from a ledge of the building onto the cross-bar of a bicycle, tucking his long tail neatly over the handlebar. The cyclist told me with pride, 'He's going on government duty!' The duty of the langur and his minder was to 'fight the monkey menace' posed by the red-brown Rhesus macaques. Rhesus macaques are terrified of langurs and therefore the latter patrol the Rhesus-infested corridors of the highest offices of the government of India in the grand, pink sandstone secretariat buildings that flank the approach to the President's palace. Langurs also patrol Parliament, where many red-bottomed Rhesus macaques scamper around the corridors, although they have never yet, at least as far as I know, managed to get into the Chambers of the Upper or Lower Houses.

The defeat of socialism and the victory of the market have led to another economic imbalance: the triumph of globalisation, which turns the whole world into a market. It's significant that globalisation came to prominence in the 1970s, just as socialism was collapsing, which makes it part of the swing from one economic extreme to another. It has become another economic certainty.

After 1991, when India started to seek foreign investment, the United States insisted that the new globalisation had to mean the return of Coca Cola. Coke had closed down its Indian operations in 1977 rather than agree to the Janata Party government's demand that it reveal the recipe for its soft drinks. The members of the newly elected Janata Party wanted to prove that they were even better socialists and patriots than their opponent, Indira Gandhi. The expulsion had been very popular. Kicking Coke out had become a symbol of India's independence and her refusal to cow-tow to the United States. So Coke's return was bound to be seen as a surrender. I remember asking an American diplomat why his country was insisting that Coca Cola should be allowed back at this early stage, when it was a gift to the opponents of the reforms who were already making life very difficult for the Prime Minister and his Finance Minister. The diplomat replied, 'We say all in or none in.'

But it hasn't been 'all in'. There are still restrictions on foreign companies in some sectors, and businessmen from abroad continue to complain about the complexities and corruption involved in investing in India. That said, a visit to any market in Delhi will demonstrate that no one now needs to buy second-hand clothes or used lipstick from diplomats leaving the country. International brands of consumer goods are widely available and Indian brands that are just as good have also been developed. Indeed, modern India could market itself as a retail therapy destination, as well as a centre for medical tourism, because there are plenty of First World brands available at Third World prices.

India has certainly benefited from globalisation. At first, it was its IT, business-process outsourcing and call centres that found a ready international market. Now, Indian manufacturing is also becoming an international player. But there are many voices who say that we need to look at the issue of globalisation again. They question whether globalisation has been fair to the poorer nations, whether it leads to greater rather that less inequality, whether it allows governments sufficient autonomy to do what they see as best for their own people, whether it is a threat to an open society and, finally, whether it brings with it the threat of a monoculture.

Some Indians are suspicious of this questioning. The Indian Prime Minister Dr Manmohan Singh's spokesman, Sanjaya Baru, is an economist too. When I told him that I was reading some interesting critiques of globalisation in preparation for writing this book, he commented dryly, 'I am suspicious of these Westerners who don't want us to gatecrash their exclusive club.' I can well understand that suspicion, especially as there are already murmurings in America and Britain about job losses to Indian call centres and business-process outsourcing. When businessmen in those countries lose out to India, they say they've been 'Bangalored'.

But those critics whose works I have read, and who have experience of putting economics into practice, do not see globalisation in black and white terms. They recognise that there is a certain inevitability about it, that it can bring benefits to developing as well as developed countries, but it must be balanced against other considerations and it must not become an overriding principle.

Jeffrey Sachs, who acted as Special Advisor to Kofi Annan, the former Secretary General of the United Nations, and who has also worked in many developing countries, including India, was an advocate of Big Bang globalisation in Russia after the collapse of the Soviet Union. The Big Bang resulted in a free-for-all, a mad scramble to grab the state's assets, and the worst form of crony capitalism. Sachs changed course, and by 2005 he had published his book *The End of Poverty: How We Can Make It Happen in Our Life Time*, which warns against becoming too dependent on the economic theories that underpin globalisation. Describing the task of eliminating poverty as 'a collective one', he goes on to say: 'Although introductory economics text books preach individualism and decentralised markets, our safety and prosperity depend at least as much on collective decisions to fight disease, promote good science and widespread education, provide critical infrastructure, and act in unison to help the poorest of the poor.'

In *The Roaring Nineties*, Joseph Stiglitz also warns that 'economic globalization has outpaced political globalization ... nor have we yet come to a clear vision of which decisions ought to be made at the national level, and which at the global level'. He lists a number of 'myths that desperately need debunking' about the economic prosperity of the 1990s. One myth is 'that American-style globalization will inevitably lead to global prosperity, benefiting financial markets in America and also the poor in the developing world'.

Many leaders in Britain and the United States nevertheless seem to believe that myth and assume that it gives them the right to lecture developing countries on free trade, as though they themselves have never practised protectionism. In 1981, Margaret Thatcher told an audience in Mumbai, 'In a way one of the great contributions that we in Britain try to make to international prosperity is to keep our markets open, and to persuade other countries to keep their markets open.' Perhaps she had forgotten, or perhaps she didn't know, that cheap cotton goods produced in the northern English city of Manchester had destroyed the Indian textile industry. And perhaps she wasn't aware of the quotas that still restricted Indian textile exports to Britain at the time.

As one of the most successful practitioners in global financial markets, the international financier and philanthropist George Soros should understand globalisation if anyone does. He was stimulated to write his book *On Globalization* because of what he saw as 'an unwitting alliance between market fundamentalists on the far right and anti-globalization activists on the far left'. By taking extreme positions, and by allowing themselves to become involved in a shouting match, they are – according to Soros – muddying the issues and undermining those international institutions who should hold the balance between the two sides in the globalisation argument. George Soros argues, 'We need stronger international institutions, not weaker ones. We need to form a different coalition whose aim is to reform and strengthen our international arrangements, not to destroy them.'

Much of the debate about globalisation hinges on the question Joseph Stiglitz raises about getting the balance right between decisions that ought to be made at the national level and those that ought to be made at the global level. The international institutions George Soros wants strengthened are there to maintain that balance. It's not surprising that agriculture is among the most difficult subjects that one of those institutions, the World Trade Organisation, has to deal with.

If you pass through the Indian countryside in a train, you will see land neatly parcelled into small fields. Recently, when I was in a village in northern India, I asked a farmer with ten acres of land whom in his view should be classified as a big farmer. 'Well,' he replied, 'in this part of India there are no farmers with more than twenty acres, so we call them the big farmers.'

A few weeks after that visit, I was gazing out of the window of a Eurostar train as we shot through northern France at a speed no Indian train gets anywhere near emulating yet. I was struck by the sight of mile after mile of yellow corn. The landscape was flat; there was barely a tree in sight, and no hedges, no fences, no sign of fields. 'And France,' I thought to myself, 'is said to be a land of small farmers.' They must have been located in other parts of the country, because all the agriculture I saw was typical of modern mechanised manpower-free farming. 'How,' I wondered for the umpteenth time, 'can there ever be a level playing field for peasant and mechanised agriculture?'

India justifiably maintains that if the global market is given too much freedom, and Indian agriculture is not adequately protected, there will be a catastrophe, because its cities are already choked with villagers who, like the rickshaw puller Nukun, can no longer earn a living working on the land. And at the opposite end of the scale, the mechanised farmers of America want to retain the subsidies that effectively keep produce from the developing world out.

But balanced globalisation could still help a country like India. A few years ago, when I was in Punjab, I was told that two problems might lead to a revival of the separatist movement. They were the lack of jobs for the young and the lack of water for farmers. I argued that perhaps Punjab didn't need so much water, but that wasn't a point of view that would ever appeal to a farmer. Nevertheless, because India has tried to feed itself rather than trading in agricultural produce, Punjab has been growing rice, and this needs a great deal of water. The Sikh farmers have sunk wells so deep that the subsoil water level is dangerously low and much of the land is suffering from salination. If Punjab had gone in for horticulture and exported its products, then India could have bought its rice from Thailand, which is a country that is suited to growing this crop.

Retail is an example of the dilemmas globalisation can pose. The British, American and other governments put pressure on India to open its retail trade to supermarket chains such as Walmart and Tesco. The supermarket chains promise that 'modern efficient retailing' will reduce prices for consumers; that they will pay remunerative prices to farmers, helping those farmers to improve the quality of their produce; and that they will provide millions of new jobs. But what sort of jobs are these? And what about those jobs that will be lost in the process, such as the jobs of the vast army of small shopkeepers they will put out of business?

My local grocer is proud of his trade. He tells me, 'This is no easy business. I have to keep stock of 5,000 different items manually, and I know the price of most of them in my head!'

'So what's the price of a packet of ginger biscuits?' I ask him.

'Sixty-four rupees,' he says confidently. And, when I check, there it is – printed on the packet by the manufacturers – sixty four rupees. In his shop there is none of that marking it up to the nearest hundred in order to make life easier for the cashier, nor that trick of stopping just short at ninety-nine to deceive the customer into thinking something is cheaper.

The Indian small shop is a true convenience store. My grocer offers free credit and home delivery, no matter how small the purchase. Similarly, my butcher cuts all his meat to order before his customers' eyes, holding his knife in the traditional Indian manner, between his toes. The neighbourhood fishmonger sits behind a knife shaped like a scimitar, fixed horizontally to the floor just a few inches from his legs. He fillets my fish on the blade without losing a millimetre of the flesh. If the grocer, the butcher, and the fishmonger are put out of business by firms such as Tesco and Walmart, who have already decimated small shopkeepers in their countries of origin, these Indian shopkeepers will lose not only their jobs but their source of self-respect. And that really can't be replaced by stacking shelves in a supermarket or swiping bar-codes at a till.

Retail is the second largest source of employment in India after agriculture, and a large percentage of those working in shops are self-employed. These small shopkeepers form a notoriously volatile section of society that is particularly prone to nationalism. They are the backbone of nationalism, which all too easily tips over into the Hindu nationalism of Togadia.

Globalisation already feeds that nationalism because nationalists portray it as a threat to Indian culture. They say it's a campaign by Western industrialised countries and their allies, the multinational corporations, to impose a materialistic culture on India – a culture that would have no time for the Indian spiritual tradition that the BJP and, even more overtly, other Hindu organisations associated with the BJP claim to be protecting. This claim that globalisation is an alien culture, not just an economic doctrine, has some basis.

The Australian economist Clive Hamilton, a political scientist who has headed his country's foremost public interest think tanks, observes in his book *Growth Fetish*: 'At its heart globalisation is not so much about the deepening of global economic and financial networks or the extension of the international reach of corporations. It is about the restless spread of the ideology of growth and consumer capitalism.' He goes on to describe globalisation as 'a culturally specific ideology, constituted as an independent force [that] has spread and colonised the world'. According to Hamilton, the very situation has arisen which Nehru feared – the old colonial powers have emerged in a new shape to dominate the world. That fear led Nehru down the self-reliant socialist path and convinced him of the need for the Non-Aligned Movement, in which over 100 states declared themselves as not formally aligned to any major power block.

Hamilton's view of globalisation should not just be dismissed as far-fetched scaremongering. Anyone who lives in India cannot but be aware of the force of the ideology of globalisation, and the direction from which it is coming. It involves much more than merely the return of Coca Cola and the arrival of other multinationals. Indian business is following the outsiders' example. Reliance Industries, a vast Indian conglomerate, has announced plans to create its own version of a Tesco or Walmart. It's talking not just of setting up supermarkets but also of establishing a direct product line 'from farm to fork', as Reliance's Chairman Mukesh Ambani put it when he announced his retailing plans.

Except for the government-controlled television and radio networks, the press and the electronic media are now run by proprietors who, like their counterparts in Britain, regard shareholder value as the supreme value. Media proprietors aren't likely to act as effective watchdogs, warning about the dangers as well as the advantages of globalisation, because advertising is their main source of revenue and advertisers want to promote global brands. But they do protest when international media groups claim that globalisation means they should be allowed to enter the Indian market.

So television networks that slavishly imitate the style of Western TV help to promote the consumerism that goes with globalisation. Relentless advertising pushes goods and services, the majority of which are out of the reach of the poor. Bank advertisements urge viewers to borrow money and offer credit to buy goods, though only those considered credit-worthy need apply. The branded clothes culture has also swept through the middle classes, with fashion houses from even the very top of the range, such as Louis Vuitton, opening shops in the big cities.

However, India is fighting back on several fronts, one of the notable examples being fast food. Chains selling Indian fast food have spread throughout the country. One of my favourites, Saravana Bhavan, which serves South Indian dishes, even has outlets in eight other countries, including Britain and the United States. On a weekend evening near Connaught Circus, in the heart of New Delhi, I have often joined the families outside Saravana Bhavan's restaurant queuing for a table to eat south Indian fast food. Just down the street, MacDonalds is generally half empty.

The government is under constant pressure from developed countries to globalise more rapidly. There is a stream of what are always described as 'high-powered' visits by ministers from abroad, who represent their countries' business interests, and there is ceaseless diplomatic activity in Delhi, which has one of the largest diplomatic corps in the world. Foreign businessmen demand changes in the laws on investment, employment, the environment and anything else that they think stands in the way of making life easier and more profitable for them. Added to this is the continued pressure from the international financial institutions such as the International Monetary Fund (IMF), the World Bank and the Asian Development Bank.

Indian politicians do not put up a very effective resistance to this pressure. There seems to be a consensus among them that the spread of the present dominant Western global culture is inevitable, and there is not much they can do to resist or even influence it. When there is resistance, it usually springs from the short-term political interests of a party which, for instance, thinks that a particular privatisation will be unpopular with voters, or a minister who doesn't want to lose control of a particular part of his empire. Only the Communists actively resist globalisation, and their resistance usually does more harm than good, because it is based on discredited dogma. And even the Communists are softening their stance on globalisation in the states where they are in power.

There is, however, one influential politician who has consistently warned that India must pursue the middle path and must not be swept off its feet by globalisation. He is, as I have already noted, Dr Manmohan Singh, the Prime Minister since 2004. When I interviewed him for the *Alumni* magazine of Cambridge University, where he got a brilliant first as an undergraduate, I found the same softly spoken, modest person I had met in earlier encounters. Dressed in a white *kurta pajama*, with his trademark blue Sikh turban, he admitted that he was uneasy about anything that smacked of a personality cult and was not a great public speaker. 'But,' he added with a smile, 'I am improving.'

Although Manmohan Singh still describes himself as a socialist, he told me that he had learnt from the great Cambridge economist Nicholas Kaldor that capitalism could be made to work. As Finance Minister in the early 1990s, when he launched the economic reform programme, and as Prime Minister, this is a goal that he has been trying to achieve – to make capitalism work, but to make it work in order to meet India's particular needs. This has meant making 'calibrated reforms', introducing reform gradually; taking a step, watching and waiting, before taking the next step, in the same way that trade in the rupee has gradually been liberalised. (The rupee is still not fully convertible.) But this softly softly approach has earned him the wrath of both the globalisation and the anti-globalisation lobbies. He remains philosophical about this, and once told a journalist, 'When you take the middle path you get hit from the left and the right.'

But do we need to be a little more radical than Dr Manmohan Singh? Some years earlier I had, with some trepidation, given a lecture on a small cruise liner about the need for market capitalism to take a dose of compassion. The first person to come up to me after the lecture was a leading light in the Conservative Party in the north of England. The second person was the head of a property firm. Both, not surprisingly, disagreed with me. When a third person came up and told me he had just retired from teaching economics at the London School of Economics I thought to myself, 'I'll have to hide in my cabin for the rest of the cruise!' But when we sat down together he was very sympathetic. Instead of exposing my limited knowledge of his subject, he said, 'I think what you're talking about is moral economics and you needn't despair. Don't forget how lonely market economists were during socialism's heyday – now it's the socialist economists who are lonely. There is no reason why the turn of the moral economists shouldn't come and the market economists become lonely again.'

When I mentioned this recently to an Indian economist, Rajiv Kumar, I was delighted when he said, '"Moral economics" – that's a very good statement.' But then Rajiv Kumar is an unusual economist. As an economics undergraduate at St Stephen's College, Delhi, he compared all the privileges students enjoyed with the way most Indians had to live and determined to do something about what he saw as 'this injustice'. But he didn't just join leftist university politics (as most students who felt that wrong should be put right might have done). Instead, he became a Naxalite.

The Naxalites are an underground group who describe themselves as Marxist Leninists. Mao is their inspiration and they believe that the entire political and economic system in India should be uprooted. They set up alternative governments in remote parts of India where the official writ barely runs, and try to introduce communist egalitarian societies there. Landlords are one of their main targets, as Naxalites believe they should be annihilated.

When Rajiv went to work with the Naxalites in a village in Bihar, he was told there was no landlord, only a 'big farmer'. Some of the brick kiln labourers he was working with used to be employed on the farmer's land from time to time. This experience marked the beginning of the doubts about Naxalite doctrine that eventually led Rajiv back to the study of economics. But it wasn't until he went to Oxford as a post-graduate that he finally lost his faith in Marxism. Describing his conversion, he said, 'I read a book called *The Secret Life of Plants*, which proved to me there is something beyond matter – there is a spirit; there is an energy; plants speak and are alive.' Suddenly he realised the limits of the economics he had believed in.

I talked to Rajiv in his office in Delhi, where he is now the Director of the Indian Council for Research on International Economic Relations, a leading think tank. When I asked him what 'moral economics' meant to him, Rajiv said, 'If you're an economist it means there's a profession called "economics", which you get from the West. That doesn't have anything to do with religion. My case is different – I now recognise I am a spiritual person.' He hesitated and then continued almost as if he were slightly embarrassed, 'I'm trying to become a spiritual person through the practice of Sahaja Yoga. You might be surprised to hear it was founded by Shri Mataji Nirmala Devi Srivastava, the wife of a member of the Indian Civil Service (ICS) who was knighted by the British government. Because of her teaching, some of the human values like compassion are beginning to become more important in my economics – not just profit maximisation, or purchasing power and things like that.'

For Rajiv Kumar, moral economics doesn't necessarily mean doing away with market economics, but it does mean a guided market. He compared the market to a donkey, saying, 'If you walk behind it and let it lead you, you will get kicked. If you ride on it and direct it, it can take you where you want. It's a set of rules which enables you to distribute goods and services efficiently. To get it to deliver what you need you must specify your objectives and work to develop consensus for them.'

'And what should India's objectives be?' I wanted to know.

'Japan and Korea got the market to deliver good education, and India should set that as one objective – a vital service the market can deliver. When it comes to goods, the market should deliver the cheap goods the poor want and can afford. Our export-led growth tends to meet the needs of the elite and disconnects from the domestic economy, which will demand cheap goods.'

Like Rajiv Kumar, Joseph Stiglitz doesn't believe that globalisation has necessarily been directing the market the right way. Towards the end of *The Roaring Nineties*, he argues:

> We [America] have been pushing a set of policies that is increasing inequality abroad and, in some cases, undermining traditional institutions. There is an alternative vision, one based on global social justice and a balanced role for the government and the market. It is for that vision we should be striving.

But this doesn't mean completely rejecting globalisation. Elsewhere Stiglitz notes, 'We cannot go back on globalisation, it is here to stay. The issue is how we can make it work.' Another Nobel Laureate economist, the Indian Amartya Sen, has also said: 'The one solution which is not available is stopping the globalisation of trade and economies.'

So what is the solution and how can globalisation be made to work? The answers may lie in keeping the correct balance between decisions made at the global and the national levels, in strengthening the international organisations (which are there to maintain that balance), in ensuring that the market doesn't lead us by the nose, and in keeping the role of the market and the government in balance. To maintain that balance there need to be regular reviews and discussion, not the sort of shouting match between market fundamentalists and anti-globalisation activists that George Soros has warned us against.

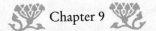

Chapter 9

GURGAON: NEVER-ENDING GROWTH

IN 2004, when the leaders of the ruling Bharatiya Janata Party (BJP) decided to call an early general election, I wrote an article for BBC On Line suggesting that in so doing they had taken the temperature of India incorrectly. They had used gross domestic product as the thermometer of the nation's health and the reading was very favourable – somewhere near eight per cent growth per annum. The BJP believed that this reading of the national temperature meant that 'India is shining', words that they took as their election slogan. But they forgot that the sun was only shining on the beneficiaries of that growth rate: the middle class and the rich. Life was still anything but bright for those living in rural India, where farmers were committing suicide because they couldn't pay their debts. Nor was the prospect particularly sunny for the urban slum dwellers who were threatened with eviction to make way for development projects that promised little or nothing for them. Eventually the farmers, the slum dwellers and the many others who saw the BJP's slogan as a bad joke did just as I had predicted and refused to return the ruling coalition to power.

The BJP leaders had been seduced by a 'certainty', one which, like globalisation and market capitalism, had come to be a dominating force in the economic debate once socialism had gone out of fashion. That certainty is the belief that maintaining and, if possible, accelerating the rate of growth measured by GDP should be the overriding ambition of every government. At first glance it would seem difficult to criticise the BJP for measuring the nation's health by this method. Redistributing the present wealth of the nation is never going to remove its poverty, in spite of Mahatma Gandhi's famous saying that, 'There is enough for everyone's need but not everyone's greed.' The Mahatma's words might be true if the wealth of the entire world were redistributed, but that seems a pipe dream given the reluctance demonstrated by richer nations to fulfil the targets they set themselves for redistributing wealth through aid, debt relief and pro-poor trading terms. So isn't growth the only answer to providing for everyone's needs?

The Indian economist Surjit S. Bhalla has no doubt about the importance of economic growth. In his book *Imagine There Is No Country: Poverty Inequality and Growth in the Era of Globalization*, Bhalla puts what he believes is the success of the last twenty years down to growth and maintains, 'Growth is good, growth makes the world go round. Growth is a many-splendoured thing.' He argues that these years have been 'the twenty best years in the history of poor people' and so denies the validity of what he admits is the received wisdom that there has been a large increase in world inequality. The book ends with Bhalla posing the question: 'Can growth alone be sufficient for poverty reduction?' He answers firmly that, yes, it can. What's more, he dismisses the need for 'actions beyond the economic domain' to combat poverty. 'Growth is sufficient, period' are his final words.

On the other side of the argument stands Australian economist Clive Hamilton, the author of *Growth Fetish*. He says: 'Growth fosters empty consumerism, degrades the natural environment, weakens social cohesion and corrodes character. Yet we are told *ad nauseam* that there is no alternative.' Hamilton's argument is that we should not be concerned about wealth but about contentment. He would no doubt support the King of the small Himalayan kingdom of Bhutan, who measures his country's health by its Gross National Happiness.

In 1997, the fiftieth anniversary of India's independence, I attempted to measure the nation's happiness by making a series of short films about Indians in different walks of life. The series was called *Faces of India*. One of these faces was that of Budh Ram, the Dalit, or former untouchable, whom we first met in Chapter 3. He lives in a village in eastern Uttar Pradesh, a part of India that could not be described as in the vanguard of progress. In 2006, Gilly and I went back to see what India's increased economic growth over the last nine years had meant to Budh Ram personally.

We met Budh Ram, a small bird-like man with stick-thin legs, shuffling along the road from the village in a pair of shoes at least four sizes too big for him. 'I've just finished working in the fields,' he said, 'so I suggested to my son that we should go to the stall on the main road for one of my *nashas* – a cup of tea.' A *nasha* is an intoxicant, and Budh Ram has two – tea and *bidis*, a packet of which was stuffed into his shirt pocket. *Bidis* are the cheapest thing to smoke in India and are made from pungent tobacco wrapped in the leaf of a *tendu* tree. 'They're a little more harmful than tea. They do give me a cough,' Budh Ram admitted ruefully.

Budh Ram agreed to forsake his tea on this occasion to drive with us to the edge of the village. The lanes were far too narrow to drive right up to his hut. And a hut it most definitely was, built of mud, with two tiny rooms separated by a thin partition and a porch of scruffy thatch precariously perched on bamboo poles. In terms of housing, India's nine years' of economic growth seemed to have driven Budh Ram downmarket. When we last met he had been living in a more substantial mud house with a small enclosed compound. 'My family has split up,' Budh Ram explained. 'This is why my wife and I live here now.'

A *charpoy* was brought out. 'It's the same one we sat on when you came before. It's only lost a few strings, like I have lost a few more hairs,' Budh Ram explained, smiling and rubbing his shaved head. His cheeks had sunken because he had lost some of his teeth since I last saw him. A chair was produced for me, but it was very much on its last legs so I decided to stick to the charpoy. Inevitably, the whole of Budh Ram's family, along with other Dalits from the village, gathered round. The women sat in silence, with their heads and much of their faces covered by their saris. Young boys wearing only tatty shorts sat beside them.

In 1997, we had filmed Budh Ram singing a song bemoaning the fact that India had found freedom fifty years ago, yet his family had still not found freedom from poverty. He had accompanied himself on a child's keyboard. He apologised for not singing this time. 'Now I don't have so much of a voice. The spirit is willing but the body is weak; I must be between seventy and seventy-three.'

'You still have the strength to work at the backbreaking task of transplanting rice seedlings,' I pointed out.

'What else can I do? All my family have to be labourers – there are no other jobs.'

We were sitting next to an emerald-green field of newly transplanted rice. Budh Ram owns a small patch of land, but it's not enough to feed all his family. When asked, he seemed a little confused about exactly how many family members there were, but in the end there was a general consensus that twenty-seven of them were still living in the village.

Reminding Budh Ram of his song, I asked him whether he had found freedom from poverty yet. 'Some, just some,' he replied.

I teasingly suggested that the Indian villagers were always complaining. Budh Ram laughed. 'You journalists want us to complain, so I have to, don't I?'

This annoyed a member of our audience, who angrily told Budh Ram, 'We've got a lot to complain about and it's our right to complain because there isn't anything else we can do about it!'

'All right, all right,' Budh Ram conceded. 'But it's true we've got something since the Sahib was here last.' He went on to list the midday meal of dhal and rice that was now provided by the government for children. There were also two more schools now, and old age pensions for some – but not for him – and eighty houses had been built for Dalits, but again not for him. Although the staff did at least turn up to teach in the schools, Budh Ram felt that the education was poor. 'The rich get the good education,' he objected, 'and that is why they stay ahead of us.' Nevertheless, one of Budh Ram's granddaughters had become the first member of the family ever to pass the tenth standard exams, which are school leaving exams for those who are not going to take the university entrance level exams.

Advocates of growth as the panacea for countries like India maintain that the wealth generated will trickle down to the poor, but it was quite clear that little or no wealth had trickled into the pocket of Budh Ram or any of the other men listening to our conversation. All were still obliged to work as labourers, but as the farmers were not doing very well, there was less work around. When I asked Budh Ram whether he had a television set, he laughed yet again. 'Why? Have they started giving them away in the bazaar? Anyway, you can see my house – where is the room to put the television set?'

Nearby, buffaloes buried their noses deep in a brick trough while whisking away flies with their tails. One buffalo was so keen to get at her food that she tried to climb into the trough but got stuck in the process. No one seemed particularly worried about her. Thick curd made from the buffaloes' milk was produced as our snack. It prompted me to ask Budh Ram about his diet. The staple foods were still rice and dhal, he explained, but continued, 'That is an improvement from the days when we used to pick out the grain from the dung dropped by the bullocks on the threshing floor, wash it and eat it.'

Budh Ram believed that the basis of his family's economic problems was the lack of jobs – a complaint that is echoed in every Indian village. He said that all the money was in the cities, where people could afford to pay out bribes to secure jobs. He was referring specifically to government jobs, which most villagers in eastern Uttar Pradesh believe are the only ones worth having. A government job gives a man status as well as security, even if he is only a police constable or office clerk. Moreover, there is next to no industry in Budh Ram's district of Ghazipur, so there are no opportunities in the private sector.

I asked about a new government scheme that guaranteed work for one hundred days a year to one member of every family living below the poverty line. This scheme was designed not only to give employment but also to improve the rural infrastructure, as the beneficiaries were to work on projects designed to improve roads, irrigation and other local assets.

Budh Ram dismissed the scheme as just another way of putting money in the pockets of local officials and contractors. 'The money has reached the office of the Block Development Officer,' he claimed, 'but then he gives the list of people registered as below the poverty line to a contractor who draws up a false list of names, so that he can show on paper he has employed below-poverty-line people. But in fact he uses machines to do his work because they are cheaper.'

I didn't expect a Dalit from his *biradiri* to have any sympathy for the contractors, but one of Budh Ram's relatives intervened to say, 'What can they do? They have to pay so much in bribes to officials to get the contracts that they can only afford to do the work cheaply.'

Budh Ram was philosophical about the situation. He had given up on politics and stopped actively supporting the Dalit party, the BSP. Now he devoted his free time to worship and to listening to readings of the scriptures. Apart from his tea and *bidis*, the temple that the Dalits had built for themselves in the village had become the centre of his life. In that temple the Dalit saint Ravi Das is worshipped as God. According to Budh Ram, 'He is the pole of truth.'

Before we left Budh Ram and his extended family, there had to be a photo call. Yet every time we photographed him he kept his mouth firmly shut. We couldn't understand why he wouldn't smile. Eventually a big smile broke out on his face and he explained, 'I was trying to hide my missing front tooth!'

As we walked out of the village, Budh Ram summed up his position on the growth of India's GDP: 'We did get some freedom from poverty in my generation; we have got something. We hope the next generation will get full freedom.'

Budh Ram's wish does not seem likely to come about if economists just rely on India's growing wealth trickling down into the pockets of the next Dalit generation. This hasn't even taken place in a rich country such as the United States, where Ronald Reagan was a strong advocate of trickle-down economics in the 1980s. The former president supported cutting taxes in order to enable the rich to create more wealth, believing that some of it would find its way down to the pockets of the poor. In fact, the rich got richer and the poor got poorer.

As far back as 1958, the American Fabian socialist economist John Kenneth Galbraith issued a warning against trickle-down economics. In his famous book *The Affluent Society*, he argued that private affluence led to public squalor. Unfortunately, we have still not heeded that warning: in cities around the world the gap between private affluence and public squalor can be observed by anyone with the eyes to see. According to the United Nations report 'State of the World's Cities 2006/2007', 998 million people now live in slums around the globe. Significantly, the last fifteen years, which have marked a period of high growth rates in Asia, have seen an unprecedented rise in the number of slum-dwellers.

In the sixties, when Galbraith was America's much-loved Ambassador in India, it was quite difficult to find slums in Delhi. But now you can't avoid them. Some forty years ago, Delhi was an open city. Now, in my part of the city – Nizamuddin East – we demonstrate the gap between private affluence and public squalor by living behind bars, in a gated enclave, like the residents in almost all other prosperous parts of New Delhi. I protested when the gates first went up, but I was told by a member of the local Resident's Association that they were necessary to keep the slum dwellers out.

In recent years, there has been a tendency all over the world for prosperous individuals and organisations to increase the divide between private affluence and public squalor by relocating to new areas. The big Indian companies and multinationals have fled from overcrowded Delhi to Gurgaon, which is about twenty miles away. There, they have built a city of skyscrapers in what used to be a small town, once just the headquarters of a rural district administration.

Microsoft India has offices in Gurgaon. I invited myself to lunch there to continue a discussion I had begun with the Chairman, Ravi Venkatesan. Like many of the new breed of India's captains of industry, Ravi's first degree was from one of the prestigious Indian Institutes of Technology. From there he went to the United States, where he got another degree in engineering, and then an MBA from Harvard. Before joining Microsoft he was chairman of the Indian subsidiary of Cummins, the diesel engine manufacturers.

I had first met Ravi in Mumbai, after a Microsoft sales meeting at which I had spoken. I had told the meeting I was not convinced that IT would necessarily make the way governments in India worked so transparent that corruption would be drastically reduced. India is obsessed with the evils perpetrated by corrupt politicians and bureaucrats but seems incapable of doing anything about them. I related the story of a meeting I had attended in Chandigarh, a city designed by Le Corbusier and the capital of two states, Haryana and Punjab. There, too, I had expressed my doubts about the ability of computers to foil the cunning Indian *babu*. After I had spoken, a smartly dressed young man stood up and said, 'I agree with Mark Tully. I am a police officer and my policemen are very happy with IT. They are now taking their *hafta*, or weekly bribes, by e-mail!'

The next morning, over a hotel breakfast in Mumbai, Ravi said it was good to hear counter-cultural views, but he thought that I was underestimating the power of computers. He was convinced that the IT revolution was going to be bigger than the Industrial Revolution. I thought to myself, 'Then I am a Luddite, because I refuse even to have a mobile phone', and secretly vowed to get one. Wanting another opportunity to counter my Luddite views with a refreshing dose of Ravi's enthusiasm, I asked him whether we could continue our conversation some time. That was how I came to be sitting in the Microsoft canteen.

Microsoft India is clearly more egalitarian than many older Indian companies. There was no directors' dining room and I could see that Ravi didn't expect or receive the VIP treatment that most company chairmen in India regard as their right. Even the food in the canteen could be described as egalitarian; a group of staff who wanted something a little special for a celebration had to bring along their own meal.

After we had eaten, Ravi opened his laptop and brought up a diagram illustrating three potential futures for India. There were three arrows pointing away from a crossroads. In one direction was an arrow with an elephant on it labelled 'Bolly World'. The arrow rose sharply and then bent downwards. Bolly World,

Ravi explained, was the future if India continued on its present path, with rapid economic development only benefiting a minority of the population. On the other side of the diagram, an arrow pointed straight into the sunrise. There was another elephant on the arrow, but her tail was up and she was balancing the globe on her trunk. This elephant was labelled '*Pahle Bharat*', or 'India First'. She symbolised an India in which everyone puts the nation first, determined that the entire country should benefit from its development. The third arrow shot straight down into the darkness and the elephant sliding down it was called '*Atakta Bharat*', or 'India Getting Stuck'. That dismal elephant warned of the possibility that the entire global economy might slow down, offering far fewer opportunities for the export of Indian goods and services that is fuelling the current rapid GDP growth, while within the country itself there would be little development and the little there was would be uneven.

The elephants, I told Ravi, represented much that I believed in personally: the imbalance in the present development of the Indian economy; the need for business to create a market that included everyone; and the need for global growth – but growth that offered benefits to poor nations as well as rich ones. So Ravi showed me leaflets describing Microsoft projects designed to ensure that it would be the 'India First' elephant who trumpeted her way into the future. The goal of one project was to take the benefits of IT to grassroots communities by providing Community Technology Learning Centres. Another aimed to empower students, their teachers and the development community, among others, by improving their existing skills. The scheme would give them more access to the latest technologies, and their training would be tailored locally. Then there were two further projects designed to deal with particular weak spots in the Indian economy. One was aimed at energising the rural economy, which is lagging behind its rapidly developing urban counterpart. Another was designed to help make India's small and medium-sized enterprises more globally competitive. While explaining these projects to me, Ravi was keen to stress that Microsoft was not going it alone, nor was this purely a private sector enterprise that had nothing to do with the government. The emphasis in all the projects was to be on private–public partnerships, on bringing the individual, businesses and the government closer together.

The anti-growth and anti-capitalism lobbies would almost certainly dismiss Microsoft India's schemes as disguised self-interest, and there is obviously an element of self-interest in them. A bigger and more balanced Indian economy would naturally mean more opportunities for Microsoft India. But a balanced view of India's needs would accept that business interests must play a role in creating wealth. Microsoft's founder, Bill Gates, has already shown through his Bill and Melinda foundation, which is dedicated to reducing inequity in the United States and around the world, that his interests are wider than just profit and loss and shareholder value alone.

But what exactly is the development path the 'India First' elephant should follow? Ravi surprised me by saying, 'It would be a tragedy if India imitated the West.' He continued: 'Just look at one example, road transport. If India based its economy on that – with such a huge population – imagine the energy and environmental problems it would create.'

If India were to accept without question that the Western precedent is the only way to develop, then by 2050 the number of cars in India might well exceed the number in the United States. India is a far more crowded country than the US. Whereas there are thirty-two Americans per square mile of America, there are some 840 Indians per square mile of India. If India surrenders to the road lobby, there will simply not be enough space to drive all those cars, let alone park them.

There is also the question of all the energy that an increased number of cars and the lifestyle that goes with them would consume. At present, the average citizen of North America uses twenty-five times more energy than the average Indian. It would therefore take an awful lot of energy-saving measures and a gigantic breakthrough in the discovery of new non-fossil fuels to prevent a crippling shortage of oil and an environmental disaster if India's growth were to follow the present Western pattern. As the situation stands, energy consumption in India and China is already pushing up the international price of oil.

Of course, America and other industrialised countries also have to change their ways if we are to avert fuel and climate chaos. In the near future, their politicians will have to stand up to their road lobbies and wean their people off their addiction to the motor car. Rich countries simply can't expect a country such as India to roll over and say, 'It's fine for you to go on consuming energy at the rate you do. We will find an alternative growth pattern, so that you don't run out of oil'! The industrialised nations must show that they are taking the search for the Holy Grail of sustainable development seriously and are prepared to make whatever changes in their own lifestyle are necessary if they are to ask India to restrict its energy consumption. Sustainable development has been defined by the World Commission on Environment and Development as 'development that meets the needs of the present without compromising the ability of future generations to meet their own needs'. We will surely compromise future generations if we don't take note of the evidence all around us that our insistence on the primacy of GDP growth imposes far too much strain on nature. We will compromise future generations if we don't redefine our needs and reduce our greed.

However, the prevalent modern economics teaches us that it is attachment to things, the desire to possess and consumerism that power the engine of growth. We are told that the economy is in good shape when consumerism is rampant, when the tills in the High Street are ringing merrily and banks are pouring money into the housing market. But, as I have suggested, it would seem that the main beneficiaries of high house prices are the speculators and estate agents. The most vulnerable people in the housing market, such as young couples trying to buy their first home, don't regard the prices they are asked to pay and the mortgage they are burdened with as a good idea at all. The jingling tills in the High Street only reveal that people have been persuaded to waste their time and money buying things they don't need unless they really do find retail therapy effective. In his book *The Hungry Spirit*, the British management guru Charles Handy says, 'If we go on growing at our present rate we will be buying sixteen times as much of everything in one hundred years' time. Even if the world's environment can tolerate the burden, what are we going to do with all that stuff?'

In early 2004, Britain witnessed consumerism on the rampage in what the Independent newspaper called 'The Battle of Edmonton'. Consumerism ran riot and retail rage erupted when the furniture chain store Ikea opened the doors of its new shop in Edmonton, north London, for the first time. Some 6,000 people crowded into the store, lured by incredibly cheap offers on sofas, beds and other furniture. Tempers flared, fights broke out and people lost all sense of self-respect. Competing customers pulled at both ends of sofas, shouting, 'It's mine, it's mine!' They sat on chairs others were trying to take away, and lay on beds to claim them. About six customers were injured and twenty suffered heat exhaustion even though the Battle of Edmonton was waged on an English winter's night. Interviewed about the overwhelming response the next day, a senior executive of Ikea confessed, 'We're in total shock ...'

The Battle of Edmonton is an embodiment of greed on the rampage, but without greed there can be no consumerism. And greed is a particularly corrosive vice because it is never satisfied. In the *Bhagavad Gita*, the god Krishna says to Arjuna,

'... enveloped is wisdom by this insatiable fire of desire, which is the constant foe of the wise'. In his commentary on the *Gita*, the Hindu philosopher Radhakrishnan uses two quotations to illustrate the meaning of Krishna's remarks. The first is from the Hindu *Laws of Manu*: 'Desire is never satisfied by the enjoyment of the objects of desire; it grows more and more as does the fire to which fuel is added.' The second quotation is from the seventeenth-century philosopher Spinoza: 'The things which men, to judge by their action, deem the highest good are Riches, Fame or Sensual pleasure. Of these the last is followed by satiety and repentance, the other two are never satiated.'

In theory, Christianity has always rejected the desire for possessions. When Jesus sent the apostles out, he told them to 'provide neither gold nor silver nor brass in your purses. Nor scrip for your journey, neither two coats, neither shoes, nor yet staves: for the workman is worthy of his meat.' Yet – perhaps not surprisingly – the medieval Church had great difficulty in coping with the followers of St Francis when they took these words literally.

In his book *The Dignity of Difference*, Rabbi Jonathan Sacks notes that Judaism has traditionally had a more balanced attitude towards property. Wealth is seen as God's blessing, and to be enjoyed as such. As for the opposite extreme of asceticism and self-denial, these qualities have little place in Jewish spirituality according to Chief Rabbi Sacks. However, Judaism does not encourage greed, because it balances an individual's right to property with the concept that we all hold our possessions in trust from God. Wealth and possessions held in trust have to be used or spent as God would like them to be, which is why charity is obligatory and can be enforced by law in Judaism. So too can *zakat*, or charity, in Islamic law. But consumerism has no such obligations.

*

Consumerism can lead to imbalances with nature too, because we humans give priority to our need for economic growth over everything else, including nature's own need to grow. The world's worst industrial disaster was the result of a poison gas leak in Bhopal on 3 December 1984, caused by the manufacture of a highly toxic pesticide. The pesticide was supposed to provide a short-cut to agricultural growth, but in the event it damaged far more than pests. The manufacturers, Union Carbide India, appear to have been oblivious to the dangers the manufacturing process posed both to nature and to human life.

One of the most sickening sights I saw in my career with the BBC in India was in the Bhopal slum known as 'Jayaprakash Nagar' after the poisonous gas had leaked from the pesticide plant. The slum was just across the road from the plant. Bodies of humans, cattle, goats and dogs littered the narrow lanes. Inside the shacks, sitting on their mud floors, men women and children coughed, choked and gasped for breath, making their sore eyes sorer by rubbing them. Some moaned with pain, others moaned with grief. All were stunned by the disaster that had overtaken them, and terrified of its potential consequences. There was no room at the city's main hospital for those who managed to get there, and so they were laid out on the hospital's lawns. The doctors were desperate because Union Carbide could not or would not tell them the composition of the poisonous gas, nor advise them correctly on how the patients' symptoms should be treated. Dead bodies were piled on carts to be taken to burial grounds and crematoria.

Reviewing the disaster and its consequences ten years later, Paul Srivastava, an American academic born in Bhopal, called on all of us to 're-envision the relationship between humans and nature in ways that can prevent more Bhopals on our only too fragile planet'. Organic farming, including organic pesticides, is a re-envisioning of that relationship. The opponents of organic farming argue that chemical fertilisers and pesticides give a higher yield, but yield is, like GDP growth, a very narrow measure which takes no account of broader benefits such as long-term health of the soil and indeed the health of those who eat the food.

Just how narrow a measure GDP growth can be was brought home to me when I met economists from the Justice Commission of the Conference of Religious of Ireland, or CORI. The Justice Commission has been set up because the religious, that is the priests, nuns, and brothers who belong to religious orders in Ireland, do not accept the divisions between the prosperous and the poor they see in their country. The religious are particularly concerned about the divisions created by Ireland's rapid economic growth. One of the economists, Father Sean Healy, ridiculed the way we measure growth. 'Would you believe it?' he said. 'The key measure is GDP. Well, if you increase the number of children in care you increase GDP. And if you have an oil spill you increase it too.'

'Why should that be so?' I asked, somewhat bewildered,

'The expense of bringing up a child in a family doesn't register as part of GDP, because it can't be costed. So it can't be added to the total value of goods and services produced by Ireland. The cost of a child in care is €2,000 a year, and so that sum is added to the total GDP value. As is the cost of clearing up an oil spill.' Father Sean went on to explain that a mother who went out to work increased the GDP two-fold; firstly by her earnings and secondly by the money she paid to a child-minder.

Father Sean Healy is not alone in criticising the way that the various contributions to GDP are added up and then conclusions based on this sum total. Clive Hamilton has noted that John Maynard Keynes, John Hicks and Simon Kuznets, who first developed the system of national accounting, repeatedly warned against using measures such as GDP as indicators of prosperity. In 1934, Kuznets cautioned Congress against inferring the welfare of the United States from the measurement of national income. Neither Congress nor any other part of the government in the United States paid any attention to his warnings, and by 1962 Kuznets was calling for the system of national accounting to be rethought. He wrote, 'Distinctions must be kept in mind between quantity and quality of growth, between its costs and returns, and between the short and the long run ... Goals for more growth should specify more growth of what and for what.' Kuznet's advice was still not taken.

I have already observed that it would be doing the poor of India a great disservice to suggest that their country's economy did not need to grow. But, as the economist Rajiv Kumar said to me, 'Whilst growth is necessary it is not sufficient.' If we question the very nature of growth, we may be drawn to question the underlying myth that distorts our thinking: the myth of progress. We might ask whether we really can go on growing forever, as so many politicians suggest we must.

Our modern-day belief in progress is not dissimilar to the Christian belief in providence, according to which God guides history and human affairs towards the achievement of His purpose. As the hymn says, 'God is working his purpose out as year succeeds to year'. But of course there is an essential difference between the Christian doctrine and this modern belief. The evangelists of progress and economic growth would have us believe that we human beings can work out our purpose as year succeeds year. They lack the humility to question human ability to direct the world aright and they assume that the universe is constructed for our purposes. In contrast to this, many Christians have the humility to accept that humankind's dominion over the Earth has been given by God, that it is not ours by virtue of our own superiority and that we on our own cannot achieve its purpose – which anyhow is God's, not ours. Personally, I prefer a theology in which God does not give us dominion over the world but instead makes us partners with nature.

There is another problem with the concept of growth and progress that underpins much of our thinking: it is taken as given, as though it could be justified rationally or, in other words, taken as a certainty. But in his book *Heresies*, John Gray, Professor of European Thought at the London School of Economics, has suggested that our current faith in progress is in fact a substitute for the religious impulse, which he believes is 'hard-wired in the human animal'. According to him, the repression of the religious impulse is responsible for the mistaken view of progress.

> Screened off from conscious awareness, the religious impulse has mutated, returning as the fantasy of salvation through politics, or – now that faith in politics is decidedly shaky – through a cult of science and technology. The grandiose political projects of the twentieth century may have ended in tragedy or farce, but most cling to the hope that science can succeed where politics has failed: humanity can build a better world than any that has existed in the past. They believe this not from real conviction but from fear of the void that looms if the hope of a better future is given up. Belief in progress is the Prozac of the thinking classes.

It is the effectiveness of that Prozac, the certainty of our belief that science and technology ensure progress, that has led us to accept technology so blindly, to forget that almost every advance in technology has a down- as well as an up-side. Advances in nuclear science are an obvious example. These advances have given us nuclear energy, medicine and power, but they have also given us nuclear waste and nuclear weapons capable of creating disasters worse than any of the natural ones that God gets blamed for. Because the original nuclear powers have been unwilling to abandon their nuclear capability, they now face the terrifying prospect that these weapons themselves might fall into the hands of rogue nations or terrorists.

We invent a technology but then fail to use it in a balanced manner, and so it takes us over. The motor car, for instance, has taken us over. We didn't realise its failings until it was too late. We have been given such freedom to use cars that we have become addicted to them and now seem incapable of limiting their use. Today, motorists regard the freedom to drive as a fundamental right that supersedes all other considerations, including the damage they are doing to the environment and to society; and politicians in democracies are terrified to take on the motorist.

Similarly, communications technologies are advancing so quickly these days that no one has time to consider the harm as well as the good that they might be doing. Certainly, our newfound technologies are generating an enormous amount of superfluous communication. We probably all have our own favourite story of futile mobile phone conversations. Mine concerns the young lady I sat next to on a one-hour train journey, during which she spoke to her boyfriend four times. The last time she called him, we were just outside the final station. Her only purpose in calling him appeared to be to inform him, mile by mile, about the progress of her journey.

Maybe I am just prejudiced because I dislike so much about the consumerist society. Maybe I am unrealistic. Perhaps the British businessman working in India was right who, after listening to me speak, said, 'You are an old-fashioned socialist and a romantic about India.' Maybe there really is no alternative to economic growth driven by consumerism if we are to overcome the problem of poverty? The economist Rajiv Kumar ventures that there is an alternative:

> Don't let consumerism create demand; rationalise it so that it creates the sort of wealth a society needs, like education and health services. In the case of America this means you don't expand and expand in

the hope of trickle-down solving problems of deprival, but you recognise your priorities. Trickle-down never works. The problem is that in economics you never teach welfare; you only teach GDP and per capita income.

The Prime Minister of India, Dr Manmohan Singh, who heads a Congress Party-led coalition, also believes there is an alternative. In an interview he gave to India's *Economic Times* at Gandhi's ashram at Wardha, he described the Mahatma as, in many ways, 'the most modern Indian we have had'. He noted that Gandhi told Indians: 'We are not only Indian but we belong to the whole world. It is one family.' The Prime Minister went on to say, 'We must have the resilience and strength to stand up and uphold our beliefs and not be swept off our feet in the wake of integrating with the rest of the world at a time when the process of globalisation is sweeping all over.' The Prime Minister went on to urge Indians to 'copy the West in production and raising productivity, and not in consumption'.

According to Dr Manmohan Singh, India does not need consumerism; it needs the opposite – a dose of Gandhi's austerity: 'We cannot afford to have a situation of excessive and wasteful consumption ... we must adopt Gandhiji's principles of simple living and high thinking.' Another distinguished economist, I.G. Patel, who was once Director of the London School of Economics, warned his fellow Indians: 'We ignore his [Gandhi's] vision only at our peril.'

So there is an alternative. It's the man Indians often ignore when they turn their back on their own tradition and imitate the West. Now more than ever, Gandhi's basic principles need to be brought back into the dialogue on India's future. Gandhi told those who did have wealth to hold it in trusteeship for others and not to spend it on themselves. That's not unlike the Jewish belief described by Rabbi Sacks that we all hold our possessions in trust from God. Mahatma Gandhi said, 'Economics is untrue which ignores or disregards moral values.' One of his moral principles was 'non-possession'. For him this had been 'a positive gain'. 'Though I preach poverty,' he said, 'I am a rich man.' This, of course, is the opposite of modern economic growth based on consumerism. Gandhi also said that wealth should be created at the bottom level, the village, not trickle down from the top.

Unfortunately, Gandhi – like almost all prophets – is without honour in his own country, or perhaps I should say he is a prophet honoured in theory as the 'Father of the Nation' but ignored in practice. The historian and biographer of Gandhi, B.R. Nanda, said he felt embarrassed whenever foreign visitors asked him, 'What is Gandhi's legacy for present-day India? Why do we hardly hear him mentioned?' I believe that Gandhi is not mentioned because he has been taken too literally. I am sure, for instance, that neither Manmohan Singh nor I.G. Patel would suggest that India should follow Gandhi's economic advice to the letter. Instead of encouraging a nuanced understanding of the Mahatma, his disciples have canonised him, turned him into a saint. Gandhi always insisted that he wasn't a saint, and even said, 'Nobody in this world possesses absolute truth. This is God's attribute alone. Relative truth is all we know.' But his followers have put him on such a high pedestal that they have given the impression his words and his example enshrine absolute truths and that we should take them as gospel truth. I am reminded of Kipling's poem, 'The Disciple':

> He that hath a gospel
> whereby heaven is won
> (Carpenter or cameleer,
> Or Maya's dreaming son)
> Many swords shall pierce Him
> Mingling blood with gall;
> But his own disciple
> Shall wound him worst of all!

If Gandhi is taken too literally, it's all too easy to debunk him. How could independent India take seriously a man who said he didn't believe in industrialisation 'in any case for any country', and who regarded cities as 'evil things'? It may be a pity that middle-class India is shedding the sari for jeans, and *dhoti kurta* for shirt and trousers, but surely Gandhi's intention can't have been that Indian men should take renunciation so far that, like him, they shed all their clothes to wear only a loin cloth?

I remember Malcolm Muggeridge, the irreverent writer and television presenter, debunking Gandhi's celibacy. At one point, Gandhi had taken his pursuit of *brahmacharya*, or celibacy, to such an extreme that he took girls to bed with him in order to test his control over his sexual urges. Muggeridge recalled that, when speaking to an audience of Gandhians in Delhi, the Mahatma defended this behaviour by saying, 'My meaning of *brahmacharya* is this. One who, by constant attendance upon God, has become capable of lying naked with naked women, however beautiful they may be, without being in any manner whatsoever sexually excited.' Muggeridge said the practice reminded him of the story of an old man in bed with a young woman who said, 'Pass me my false teeth. I want to bite you!'

It would seem that in many ways Gandhi was his own worst enemy. I once described him as 'too good a man'. He was such an extreme ascetic that many must be tempted to say they can't live like him and therefore he has no relevance to their lives. Although a devout Hindu, he was not one to take the middle road when he expressed his ideas, which has made it all too easy for the establishment and the press, hell-bent on promoting their own concept of growth as the panacea to all society's ills, to ridicule him and his beliefs as romantic and unrealistic.

So, what if we were to peel away the crust in which the Gandhians have encased their hero, to try to understand the symbolism of Gandhi's language instead of taking him literally?

What is he saying about our needs? In his own words, 'Renunciation does not mean that if one has wealth it should be thrown away and wife and children should be turned out of doors. It simply means that one must give up attachment to these things.'

Yet the principle of non-attachment has a limited appeal in a world that is steered predominantly by Western values. As the Western nations are among the richest, they also appear to be the most successful, so it's not surprising that the elite in a country such as India should be tempted to follow their lead. And there is no sign that most Westerners want anything to do with the ideas propounded by Gandhi. Instead, Western businessmen continue to extol the virtues of consumerism and to demand the right to spread its principles as a condition for investing in developing countries. Western politicians preach the virtues of a way of life they regard as freedom. The Western media disseminates the attractions of an energy-guzzling way of life. In its messages there is no suggestion that the West needs to do some major rethinking.

If the West won't listen to the Mahatma, perhaps it will listen to another man greatly admired there, the Dalai Lama. In his *Ethics for the New Millennium* the Dalai Lama says:

Although I never imagined that material wealth alone could overcome suffering, still, looking towards the developed world from Tibet, a country then as now very poor in this respect, I must admit I thought it must go further towards doing so than is the case ... The extraordinary achievements of science and technology have advanced little more than linear, numerical improvement ... progress has meant hardly more than greater numbers of opulent houses in more cities with more cars driving between them. Certainly there has been a reduction in some types of suffering, including certain illnesses. But there has been no overall reduction.'

But the dominant Western 'science', economics, does not take account of suffering, nor do mainstream business models consider it to be a cost. The only costs they worry about are those which directly affect profits and shareholder value.

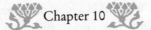

Chapter 10

DARJEELING: COUNTING COSTS

THE huffs and puffs of the little b-class engine grew longer and longer, her breathing became more and more laboured, and the effort to keep her pistons moving backwards and forwards seemed greater and greater. Black smoke poured out of her funnel and steam hissed from her aged, leaky joints as she crawled up the steepest section of the narrow gauge Darjeeling Himalayan Railway, which climbs to a height of 7,400 feet. Since she was now more than one hundred years old, it was hardly surprising that she found hauling the school train from Kurseong to Darjeeling such strenuous work.

At about six-thirty on a winter's morning, everyone was well wrapped up, with woollen balaclavas being the preferred protection for heads and ears. Schoolboys dressed in neat uniforms with satchels on their backs jumped on the train as it passed. One fell in his effort to scramble on board, and another was kicked off by a large boy who thought the carriage was already crowded enough.

Squeezed into one corner of a carriage, I remembered the days when I used to jump on and off this train myself on my way to boarding school in Darjeeling. I would boast to my friends, 'My father owns this railway', which wasn't quite true. He was a director of the company, and I still have his tiny golden *kukree*, which can be used as a brooch or a tie pin. On the back is inscribed 'DHR Pass No 73 Director'. Now, as we made our way slowly but surely past the Castleton tea garden, with its small bushes clinging to the steep slopes, I thought of the tea garden where my sisters and I used to stay during midterm breaks. I still believe the fragrance of tea leaves being roasted in a tea estate factory is finer than any perfume.

My father was a partner in a firm based in Kolkata, which managed not only the Darjeeling Himalayan Railway but a variety of companies, ranging from coal mines to construction, from insurance to jute manufacturing. The company portfolio also included some tea gardens, and his youngest brother, Grafton, was the manager of one of them. Like all good planters, Grafton held those who worked in the head office in Kolkata in contempt, believing that no one there knew anything about tea, and resenting them whenever they issued instructions to the men on the ground who did. When I came back to India as an adult, I stayed with Grafton. I remember him recalling the occasion when my father, on a visit to the tea garden, asked why a roller was dirty. Grafton replied scornfully, 'Because it's just been used!'

On this visit to Darjeeling I was delighted to find that battles between planters and head offices were still being fought, and that recently one head office had suffered such a severe defeat that it had withdrawn from the fray. It wasn't just because, having spent most of my own working life a long way from head office, I was naturally disposed to support the planters. To my mind, this particular battle provided evidence that modern business methods based on the so-called 'management science' taught in various business schools were not infallible.

The business community has run one of the most successful sales campaigns of the last twenty years, persuading most of us that businesspeople have the answer to everything, that their methods can be applied to running anything from biscuit-making to broadcasting, from the civil service to schools. As Colin Hines says in his book *Localization: A Global Manifesto*, big business leaders and international financiers have become 'the new masters of the universe'. But I found that the science of management had come unstuck in Darjeeling.

Liptons, one of the biggest names in tea, is a company owned by Hindustan Lever, the Indian subsidiary of the multinational Unilever. It had recently sold all its gardens and was now engaged only in marketing tea, rather than growing it. While in Darjeeling, I asked a planter who had worked for Liptons why this had happened. He asked me not to give his name, explaining, 'I wouldn't want to be black-listed by a company as powerful as Liptons. You never know, I might need to sell tea myself one day – planting is a pretty precarious business nowadays.' Then he continued, 'The trouble was that they had this standard pattern of management. In theory, all multinational managements are bottom up, but in practice – in Liptons at least – the input from the planters on the ground got blocked before it got to anyone who mattered.' Management had required planters to achieve quarterly targets set by accountants, although in tea no two quarters were ever alike.

'Supposing there was a drought,' the planter said. 'Then inevitably output was down, but you were still expected to achieve the same bottom line – so you had to cut costs. But then that would affect output in the longer run. That was the heart of the problem: Hindustan Lever's management system couldn't cope with an agro-business. They needed quick results, but in our line of business doing everything on a short-term basis means long-term losses. So in the end they cut the losses they had incurred and ran. Liptons' management system simply couldn't cope.'

When I sent an e-mail to Hindustan Lever's head office asking why they had sold their gardens, their explanation was, 'The sell-off of our plantations businesses was part of our company strategy to focus on the branded packet tea segment.'

*

The exalted position now held in society by businessmen and -women is another of the swings from one extreme to the other that I have been writing about in this book. The elite members of the Indian Civil Service and the gentlemen officers of the Indian Army used to refer to my father and other businessmen like him in Kolkata by the derogatory term 'box-wallahs'. When I was at university in the late 1950s, the brightest and best wanted to become civil servants, diplomats, doctors or lawyers. Business was not a career option for them. In the India of the sixties, I found that the ambition of most students was to get into the Indian Administrative Service (the equally elitist successor of the Indian Civil Service) or the diplomatic service. But now in India the business schools have become the most sought after post-graduate training institutes and the MBA the post-graduate degree to boast about, particularly if it's an American one.

Modern business methods require constant assessment to measure performance, no matter how difficult performance might be to define. While this may be a comparatively simple assessment to make when you are manufacturing a clearly defined product, such as a motor car, it's far less easy when your product is school children, university students or hospital patients. League tables based on exam results, for instance, are now used to judge the efficiency and effectiveness of schools in the UK, as though a good education were limited to exam success alone. Nevertheless, parents have become convinced that this is the valid measurement of a school.

By one of the many strokes of good fortune I have enjoyed in writing this book, I was told of the inaugural address given by Professor Rebecca Boden when she took up her chair at the Business School of the University of Wales Institute in Cardiff. Professor Boden is an academic whose basic discipline is political science but who has also worked for the British government as an inspector of taxes, so she has had practical experience of government accounting. In her speech, she talked about the targets, league tables, accounts and performance indicators that dominate public life in Britain today and the damaging effect they can have. To illustrate that this is not an entirely modern problem, she quoted a letter from the Duke of Wellington to the Foreign Office in London written when he was commanding the British Army in central Spain during the wars against Napoleon:

> Whilst marching from Portugal to a position which commands the approach to Madrid and the French forces, my officers have been diligently complying with your requests ... we have enumerated our saddles, bridles, tents and tent poles, and all manner of sundry items for which His Majesty's Government holds me accountable. I have dispatched reports on the character wit and spleen of every officer. Each item and each farthing has been accounted for, with two regrettable exceptions, for which I beg your indulgence.

One of the exceptions was one shilling and nine pence unaccounted for in the petty cash of an infantry battalion. The other was confusion about the number of jars of jam issued to a cavalry regiment during a sand storm. Wellington ended his letter by asking whether it was his job 'to train an army of uniformed British clerks in Spain for the benefit of accountants and copy boys in London or perchance to see to it that the forces of Napoleon are driven out of Spain'.

Many of today's schoolteachers, doctors and other providers of public services must feel like writing similar letters to their respective ministries. But Rebecca Boden went on to argue that the accounting and assessments they are required to provide are far more damaging than the sort of bureaucracy inflicted on the Duke. She discussed the case of schools and prisons in detail. Speaking of the tests that children now have to undergo and which are used for drawing up school performance league tables, she listed their chief adverse results as the following:

- They reduce teaching time.
- What is taught reflects only what children need to know for the tests.
- Pedagogy becomes moulded to teaching children only to pass the tests.
- Tests cause children stress and anxiety.
- Teachers are adversely impacted and deskilled.

According to Boden, this causes 'extreme anxiety amongst some kids – especially girls'.

Assessment is a key aspect of management, and it is my belief that the increasing tendency to try to assess everything arises from the conviction that management is all important. And I am not alone in this belief. In his book *Blair's Britain*, Mark D. Chapman claims:

> Blair, and perhaps even more importantly Brown, have come to see management not simply as a means to an end but as an end in itself, as something which is the principal function of good and responsible government acting in the best interests of its citizens. Perhaps most crucially good management is like the British weather – it cannot be changed. It lies beyond the scope of the politician and has to be left to the experts.

In other words, politicians in Blair's Britain appear to have handed over their obligation to take decisions to company directors and management consultants

There is now such faith in the business methods of the private sector that it is widely assumed that the public sector cannot be equally efficient and so everything the government owns should be privatised. It was the former British prime minister Harold Macmillan who first described privatisation as 'selling the family silver' and he had a point. Private enterprises don't buy public sector undertakings unless they are confident they can get a

higher return on the money they pay for them than any investment in shares or bonds would produce. This means that, in the
longer term, the public will lose on the deal.

It has to be said that where there is competition, privatisation
does often increase efficiency and profitability. I was always
sceptical about the privatisation of the railways in Britain, but I
have to admit that it seems to have made them more competitive
and thereby increased the number of passengers taking the train.
Whether the engineering and maintenance standards of the
private companies are up to those of the old British Rail is more
questionable.

When it comes to privatising genuine monopolies, the situation is altogether different. In 1988, British private companies
were given exclusive concessions for sanitation and water
supply. They were guaranteed there would be no competition.
The concessions were sold at knock-down prices and on such
generous terms that even the *Daily Mail* newspaper, that most
ardent supporter of Mrs Thatcher and her Conservative government, called the privatisation the greatest act of licensed robbery
in British history. Since then, the price of water has soared and
many of the assets of the companies have deteriorated.

In 2006, the pipes of Thames Water, the largest supplier, were
leaking enough water to fill 344 Olympic-size swimming pools
every day, and this at a time when Britain was facing the threat
of a drought. But while the leaks got worse, the financial return
got better, with the company announcing a thirty-one per cent
increase in profits. Not surprisingly with profits like that to be
made, many of the original companies have been swallowed up
by multinationals, and now Britain's most essential asset – water
– is owned by French, German and American companies.
All this is the result of blind faith in the private sector and its
business methods.

The wastage of Britain's water is also the result of the narrow
calculations that business uses to make its decisions. A

spokesman for Ofwat, the British water regulatory body, which is meant to act as a watchdog to protect the public's interest, was asked why this wastage was being tolerated. He explained that it would cost too much to plug the leaks. Since business culture believes that the only way to people's hearts is through their purses, he went on to say, 'This is the way the bills will be cheapest for the consumer.' He didn't say that cutting the company's profits might help in that direction too. But he did admit that the level set by Ofwat at which it would be economical to plug leaks was 'purely a financial mechanism', and even went so far as to acknowledge, 'We may have to question whether it's the right one.' It could never be the right one because when decisions are taken on such a narrow financial basis, inevitably social and environmental costs are ignored.

Riddled with corruption and crawling with superfluous staff as many of the nationalised organisations in India are, no one could argue that they have given their proprietors – namely the public – value for money. Of late, the new competition with the private sector has made some of the nationalised banks more customer-friendly. And the threat of privatisation has improved the performance of some nationalised manufacturing companies. The nationalised company generating electricity from thermal power and the nationalised company making heavy electrical equipment have already shown that there are exceptions to the rule that all the industries in the public sector are unprofitable. But when I discussed this issue with the economist Rajiv Kumar, he warned me, 'The exceptions are islands. Nothing should be written which suggests that there is anything to say for most of the public sector in India!'

The major problem with the Indian public sector is that the nationalised companies are treated as milch cows by politicians, providing not only money and perks but also opportunities to please their constituents by employing some of them. The politicians fight privatisation to protect their own interests and yet, supported by the trade unions, mutter socialist mantras and manage to convince the poor they are fighting for them.

There is one outstanding exception to the rule that politicians inevitably have a malign influence on Indian public sector organisations, and it's a surprising exception: the railways. The Indian railways are a little like Lord Jagannath's chariot in Puri. They roll on at their own speed, crushing anyone who gets in their way. They are the world's largest employer, with far too many employees. Their management structure is hierarchical, based on the Buggin's turn principle, by which long service rather than merit is rewarded by promotion, and tied up in the red tape of government procedures. Political pressures distort management decisions.

A former railway minister told me the story of the Chattisgarh express in central India. It was said to be the slowest express in India, so he decided to speed it up by cutting out some of the stops. After taking that momentous decision, he went abroad for two weeks. By the time he came back, the MPs of all the constituencies where the service had been cut had seen to it that their stations had been restored to the Chattisgarh express timetable. With the railways carrying more than 5,000 million passengers every year, any minister attempting drastic measures such as cutting staff, jacking up fares, cancelling uneconomic services or closing branch lines would do so at the risk of being thrown out by the voters. The most that could be hoped for was that the railways would somehow muddle through in India's own peculiar way.

However, in July 2001 an expert group headed by one of India's leading economists warned that the national railways were about to hit the buffers. They were facing what the group termed 'a terminal debt trap'. And, indeed, in 2001 the railways failed to pay a dividend to the government. Then, to the surprise of everyone, there came a turn-around. Within four years of the group's report, the railways were generating a handsome profit. This hadn't been achieved by increasing fares or the charges for carrying freight; it had been achieved by improved use of the railways' capacity. More passengers were carried by making the trains longer – the more popular trains are now nearly three quarters of a kilometre in length, which is not always good news for those at the back of the train as many platforms are not long enough to accommodate them. Reducing some fares also helped to increase the number of passengers. Freight was increased by allowing wagons to carry heavier loads. And, rather than telling freight customers to take it or leave it, railway bosses made a concerted effort to offer services that were tailored more closely to the needs of manufacturers and other business proprietors.

Some of the cobwebs left behind by the British Raj were swept away at last. The nineteenth-century list of freight tariffs, voluminous enough in itself but also complicated by a mountain of corrections that had piled up over more than one hundred years, was reduced to a few pages. The timetable bequeathed by the Raj had only ever been tinkered with in the past, but now wholesale change is afoot to create more efficient and faster trains. As an example of this, when I first came to India it took twenty-four hours to travel from Delhi to Mumbai or Kolkata, but soon I will be able to get into a comfortable sleeper after office hours in Delhi and reach either of those cities before offices open the next day. There are to be new tracks dedicated to freight trains, which will more than double their average speed. At present, 'crawl' would be an appropriate word for their average speed, which is eighteen miles an hour.

The revolution in the railways could not have been achieved by anyone but a politician who understood that normal profit calculations, cost-cutting and measures to increase efficiency would not work in such a politically sensitive public sector undertaking. What's more, that politician had to be a populist in order to sell the reforms to the public.

The reforming minister in question, Lalu Prasad, was certainly a populist, and was renowned for his rustic wit, but he was equally notorious for the inefficiency of his administration in Bihar, the state he and then his wife had presided over as Chief Minister. When his party lost the state election in Bihar, Lalu was given the railways ministry in the central government as a compensation prize, and it appeared that, with his appointment, the railways were being saddled yet again with a minister who would treat them as a milch cow. But Lalu, who came from a farming caste, had different ideas about cows. He told the senior management of the railways that 'if you don't milk the cow fully it falls sick'. Metaphorically speaking, the railways are now yielding more milk than before because they are making better use of their capacity. Lalu observed, 'The wagon is the bread-earning horse of the railways; load it adequately. Make it run and don't stable it.' Wagon turn-around time has decreased markedly. Lalu rejected the standard management strategy of downsizing, saying, 'It may make Indian railways thinner but not necessarily healthier.' And, indeed, the Indian railways are now not much thinner than they were, but they are more healthy. Still, it remains to be seen whether the momentum generated by Lalu will be maintained by his successors.

It seems to me that one of the weaknesses of the business culture and its 'management sciences' is that it is too certain; it doesn't allow for questioning, and it often ignores the voice of experience. That is not to say that experience necessarily means accepting the status quo, but those who have learnt from experience often have as much to say that is relevant as those who have acquired their knowledge from text books and college courses. All need to be heard and all need to be taken into account if the way any company, institution or service is managed is to improve in a manner that takes into account broader considerations than the narrowly defined efficiency of the business world. This was the nub of my argument when, in 1993, I found myself challenging the best known British high priest of business methods, John Birt (now Lord John Birt), then the Director General of the BBC.

John Birt's message to Britain was straightforward: there was absolutely nothing positive to be said for the BBC's system of management, even though it had evolved out of years and years of experience. The Corporation, he asserted, was a 'bloated, bureaucratic monolith' and it was 'wasting licence payers' money on a massive scale'.

To add weight to his argument that the BBC needed radical changes, he also attacked its output, and in particular its journalism. In his autobiography, he describes the way he felt about BBC journalists:

> [they were] ... a huge cohort – chiefly in their forties or fifties – for whom news and current affairs were a process. They covered and responded to events. They were competent and experienced, but they had long since ceased to think enquiringly. They were in a groove, serving time. They were mostly male and macho, and drink played an important part in their lives. The place was awash with Australian Chardonnay.

There were, according to Birt, many bright lights in this darkness, some 'glorious individual exceptions' who were 'generally in their twenties and thirties'. Arguably ageism and, the other side of that coin, adulation of youth, appeared to be very much part of the management doctrine at the time and many of the older staff were let go. One of the most respected elder statesmen among BBC journalists, the former political editor John Cole, spoke of 'a prodigal erosion of staff loyalty resulting from early retirements and redundancies'.

The market was to be at the centre of the new BBC. In his autobiography, Birt says he converted the BBC from 'a command economy' to a 'trading institution'. Command economies are usually associated with Soviet-style central planning, trading institutions with market capitalism. By his own admission he had gone from one extreme to the other.

Controversy raged in the press. At one stage, six of the best-paid BBC journalists, some of whom had been brought into the Corporation by John Birt, wrote a letter to the *Times* in which they said, 'So far within the BBC many of the voices of those hostile to John Birt, too cowardly to give their names, have been anonymously quoted in the press. We feel it is time for some of us to offer our public support for John Birt and for the difficult and radical changes he is making.'

At the time I had been asked to give the main lecture at the annual meeting of the Radio Academy, one of the major events of the year for radio in Britain. I had been given a platform to stand on at the very moment when the charges against John Birt's critics needed to be challenged, so – with my belief in karma – it seemed to me that I had to stand on that platform and mount that challenge. Maybe this was presumptuous thinking on my part, but it seemed obvious at the time.

Indeed, some of my critics did think I was presumptuous, arguing that, as Delhi correspondent, I was out of touch with what was taking place. But when I decided to make the speech, I naturally spoke to many other members of staff, and a group of advisors soon formed who helped me to shape it. We were so up-to-date on what was happening in the BBC that, as we were putting the final touches to my speech, we managed to get a copy of the one that John Birt was intending to give at the Radio Academy meeting the day after mine.

Because of my Indian-style belief in balance, the theme of my speech was 'evolution is better than revolution'. For me, evolution means seeking for balance between tradition and change, whereas revolution means tearing up the past. I maintained that John Birt's revolution was doctrinaire and that the doctrine was being applied too rigidly.

In my view an internal market called 'Producer's Choice' was one of the main planks of John Birt's sweeping changes. It was a system designed to make producers and their bosses aware of all the costs they incurred and to give them the freedom to buy in services from outside if necessary, instead of using BBC facilities. Everything a producer did, including borrowing a book from the library or consulting the pronunciation unit, had to be costed and charged to his or her budget. In my speech, I said that, although it was too early to judge Producer's Choice, the system had started badly. Indeed, I argued, had Birt been more flexible, had he listened more to his staff, Producer's Choice might not now be largely discarded as part of a new 'common sense' approach to managing the BBC's finances. Zarin Patel, the BBC's Group Finance Director, said that the new approach was all about 'changing the culture and enabling the BBC to spend less on bureaucracy and processes and more on content and output'. She described some of the practices Producer's Choice involved as ridiculous, and wanted staff to 'focus on the things that really matter and not have to think about signing for fifty pounds here and fifty pounds there.'

I admit that some of the worst fears I and others expressed at the time of my speech were not subsequently realised. The BBC has since survived John Birt and, indeed, there are some ways in which it is a stronger organisation after him. I'm quite envious of the BBC journalists today who have benefited from the money Birt put into news and, in particular, his belief in the importance of foreign news. All the time I was with the BBC in Delhi, little or no money was spent on our equipment. These days, the BBC's Delhi offices and studios are as well equipped as any in London.

On the debit side, I still believe that my basic criticisms were justified. In his autobiography, John Birt says that when the governors came to choose his successor they felt 'the BBC needed cheering up'. That seems to me to be an admittance that there was concern at the highest level about staff morale. Perhaps because he seemed to be so certain he knew best, John Birt lost some of his most senior colleagues during his time as Director General. Even Marmaduke Hussey, the Chairman of the Board of Governors who backed Bird through all the controversies surrounding him until almost the end, eventually fell out with him.

All that is in the past now. I remain grateful to John Birt for the generous way he referred to me in his autobiography. And I am also grateful to him for not standing in the way of my doing some work for the BBC when I resigned my contract a year after my speech.

So if all this is in the past, why write about it now? One reason is that it was those events at the BBC which first made me realise that Indian thought, of which my understanding was growing, might have something useful to say about the business culture that was sweeping Britain at the time. India had taught me to be increasingly suspicious of certainties and wary of an unflinching commitment to any point of view.

For me, John Birt stood for the opposite of India's open-mindedness, and he revealed as much by his reaction to my speech. In his autobiography, he said that I had opposed even the notion that any significant change was needed. Yet I had acknowledged the need for change more than once and even ended my speech by saying, 'We in the BBC must demonstrate that we are willing to change.' To Birt, it seemed anyone who questioned the way he was changing the BBC was opposed to change, full stop. It was a black and white issue.

In these pages, I'm arguing for the need for balance, and it seems to me that Birt did not balance tradition with change. In his enthusiasm for change, did he denigrate the ethos and traditions of the BBC, which had gained it the reputation of being the best broadcasting organisation in the world? In his enthusiasm for management, did he give a higher priority to making the BBC the best managed broadcasting organisation than to making it the best broadcaster? Early in his BBC career he told the Royal Television Society that 'the BBC should never be the prisoner of fashionable thought', but was he himself a prisoner of fashionable management?

Birt's doctrinaire approach to running the BBC so delighted the management consultants McKinsey's that they appointed him as an adviser to their global media practice when he left the Corporation. While he was Director General, the BBC had spent large sums of money buying advice from McKinsey's.

As I have said before, *India's Unending Journey* is also a book about humility and nowhere in his autobiography does John Birt appear to question himself.

But then John Birt is not alone in his self-confidence. It comes from the culture he embraced. It is a culture that believes business is a science whose findings are as conclusive as those of the physical sciences and therefore, like them, should not be questioned. In their book *The Puritan Gift: Triumph, Collapse and Revival of an American Dream*, brothers Ken and Will Hopper are critical of the concept that running a business is a science. While Ken Hopper has extensive experience of manufacturing, Will is in the financial world. The two are scathing about the MBA degrees awarded to students of management, and attribute many current ills in society to the teaching in business schools. They point out that even some leading business school professors express doubts about the value of the degrees they offer. For example, they quote Henry Mintzberg, a professor at McGill, as believing that 'all MBA graduates should have a skull and crossbones on their foreheads along with warnings that they are not fit to manage'. Similarly, after retiring, Russell L. Ackoff, who had been a professor at Wharton, describes the principal achievements of a business school education as:

> First, to equip students with a vocabulary that enabled them to talk authoritatively about subjects they did not understand. Second, to give students the ability to withstand any amount of disconfirming evidence. Third, to give students a ticket of admission to a job where they could learn something about management.

This is not to argue that there is no point in a business education; rather it is to warn that an MBA doesn't know everything that there is to know about business, that everything he or she does know is not applicable in all situations, and that the voice of experience is sometimes worth listening to.

Among the outcomes of the business school culture listed by the Hopper brothers are collegiality being replaced by the worship of an all powerful Chief Executive; rounded experienced managers being replaced by money managers; and so-called management science driving out 'implicit management', which takes account of past experience.

Business and market economics go hand in hand in exalting competition above all other virtues, but, curiously, competition often reduces competition, with big fish swallowing the smaller ones. However, this is not always so. A minnow of a one-man operation took on the whales of the detergent market in India – the multinationals Unilever and Procter and Gamble – and grew rapidly into the multi-million pound company Nirma, which now employs some 14,000 people.

These days, businesses don't believe only in the benefits of competition with their rivals. Internal competition too has become a key component of corporate culture. Just as external competition keeps companies on their toes, internal competition keeps the staff on their toes – or so the received wisdom goes. 'Never let the staff feel secure' seems to be the motto. So short-term contracts replace staff jobs, lest security should make staff lazy. The threat of redundancy also hangs over employees. Whenever savings are to be made – and it's naturally part of corporate lore that every manager should be 'making savings' – employees are usually among the first costs to be cut. Often only the most senior managers are able to buy their security through contracts that guarantee they'll be richly rewarded even if asked to leave the company.

Staff assessments sound great in theory – and of course management has a duty to keep an eye on its staff. In theory, there is nothing wrong with relating pay rises to employees' performance. But who makes those assessments and by what standards are the staff judged? To my mind, both questions were answered succinctly by a BBC journalist attending a meeting about the introduction of performance-related pay. He said, 'As far as I can see, this is a charter for sycophancy.'

At the other extreme, the Indian government is a patent example of an employer who appears to be unable to make any meaningful assessment of its staff. Government departments, institutions and nationalised companies would all benefit from an element of competition among employees, along with some threats to their security to prevent them becoming complacent. As it is, the laziest clerk can climb to the top grade of his cadre, and the most corrupt policeman can be reasonably certain that he will reach retirement.

The farmers' leader from Uttar Pradesh (UP), Charan Singh, became Home Minister in the government that came to power after Indira Gandhi's defeat in 1977. A strictly honest man himself, the prevention of corruption was one of his hobby-horses. He once complained to me that it was very difficult to discipline a corrupt officer of the Delhi Police, who were administered by his ministry. 'I can't dismiss him,' he sighed.

'All I can do is transfer him. That was some sort of punishment when I was Chief Minister of UP, because it's a huge state and I could transfer an officer from the very hot south to the cold remote Himalayas in the north or from the borders of Delhi to a really rural district on the border with Bihar. In Delhi what can I do? Transfer an officer from central to south Delhi, and what meaning will that have?'

What is the aim of all this competition? The business community says it is to cut costs so that products and services become cheaper. Price is one of the biggest selling points, with businesses competing with each other to convince customers that their product is cheapest. In England one retail chain advertises that it is never knowingly undersold. In India, where the mobile phone market has become extremely competitive, you would need a double doctorate in maths and law to deconstruct the rival offers and work out which deal really is the cheapest.

So surely no one can object to the benefits of competition? Who wants to pay more money to fill their supermarket trolley or phone their family if competition can help to keep the prices down? But the price tag on a product does not represent its real cost. There are social, environmental, health and other costs involved in its production, distribution and marketing that are not accounted for. Because marketing has made us so obsessed with the price of everything, Barbara Panvel, the coordinator of the Centre for Holistic Studies, a network I belong to, agreed to launch a project to calculate in financial terms the real price of what we buy. She warned me that in some instances prices couldn't be compared directly because business calculations left out many costs that it would be difficult to put a financial value on.

The project is called 'Counting the Costs'. Molly Scott Cato, an economist who lectures at the Business School of the University of Wales in Cardiff, wrote the first paper for it. At the top of her paper Molly quotes the poet William

Wordsworth's words 'high Heaven rejects the lore of nicely-calculated less or more' in relation to business lore. She goes on to say, 'The purpose of this project [Counting the Costs] is to confront global capitalism on its own terms, to challenge it to explain why, if it is so efficient, it has failed to notice that so much of the energy expended is dedicated to repairing damage it is creating.' When I first read that, my mind went back to the words of the Irish economist who told me that clearing up oil slicks was good for GNP. Molly suggests, 'It is one of the direst indictments of developed economies that people are so dissatisfied that they need to find a multitude of means of escape.' She then goes on to look at the evidence for this dissatisfaction and to assess the cost of the various escape routes Britons take, after rightly warning about the dangers and limitations of doing this.

Molly's evidence for the dissatisfaction in Western society includes a survey by a reputable organisation which found that one in three Britons is actively considering a move abroad. The ways people try to escape from life if they stay in Britain include gambling, smoking, drugs and alcohol abuse. Molly quotes a Cabinet Office estimate that alcohol abuse alone costs 20 billion pounds sterling per year in terms of health disorders, disease, crime (including domestic violence), anti-social behaviour and loss of productivity at work. Molly also discusses depression, because she sees it as 'a response to an oppressive social and economic system'. She calculates that in 2002 the cost of prescribing the most common anti-depressant drugs was 7 billion pounds. At the end of her paper, Molly Scott Cato calculates that the overall cost of Britain's dissatisfaction, within a society that calculates values in terms of price, profit and loss, is about fourteen per cent of the whole of government spending.

Back in the days of the Industrial Revolution, the philosopher and economist John Stuart Mill warned against the evils of a society which, in terms of its values, resembles a modern business-culture dominated society. He wrote:

> I confess I am not charmed with the ideal of life held out by those who think that the normal state of human beings is that of struggling to get on; that trampling, crushing, elbowing, and treading on each other's heels, which form the existing type of social life, are the most desirable lot of humankind, or anything but the disagreeable symptoms of industrial progress ... the best state for human nature is that in which, while no one is poor, no one desires to be richer, nor has any reason to fear being thrust back by the efforts of others to push themselves forward.

Britain is sufficiently wealthy today to ensure that no one need be poor, so there should be no need for a culture of thrusting and crushing – but this is exactly what modern management seems to be all about. Perhaps that's not surprising, because the culture of modern management doesn't share Mill's concern for the lot of human beings. Its goals are far narrower than that.

But it was not always so. Puritan ethics inspired the management of the new industries and manufacturing processes that arose in the nineteenth-century United States in what has been described as the second industrial revolution. Puritans believed that the aim of creating wealth was to establish the Kingdom of Heaven on earth, not merely to create shareholder value. Before the first Puritans set sail for America in the seventeenth century, John Winthrop, who was to become the founding governor of the new colony, told them New England was to be 'as a City on a hill'. None of the Puritans listening to that sermon would have missed the reference to Jesus' words to his disciples, 'Ye are the light of the world. A city that is set on a hill cannot be hid.'

As time went by, the Puritan aim of creating wealth became the secular Great American Dream. No matter how much non-Americans, and I'm sure many Americans, may squirm when they hear presidents of the United States repeatedly referring to America's greatness, no matter how strange people like me might find the fact that the Stars and Stripes flies over so many homes in the United States, these are signs that the Dream remains alive. But what has happened to the industry and commerce that was to make that Dream real? In their book, Kenneth and William Hopper maintain that American business has lost its way since the 1970s because its roots in Puritan culture have dried up. They believe that 'if the whoring after false managerial gods is abandoned in favour of the pursuit of true ones the uneven distribution of wealth that occurred in the United States in recent decades can be halted and perhaps even reversed'. The false gods are 'financial engineering' and the main beneficiaries are 'financial engineers'.

One of the other Puritan values the Hopper brothers describe in their book is the importance of collective action and cooperation in any activity. They quote John Winthorp telling the New Englanders, 'We must knit together in this work as one man ... we must make each other's conditions our own, rejoice together, mourn together, labour and suffer together.' That is the opposite of the rat race modern management culture believes in. The rat race reflects the individualism of modern times, which is not properly balanced by responsibilities to others.

It can certainly be argued that a fundamental weakness of modern management and modern market capitalism is their lack of moral purpose. Whatever can be said against socialism, no one can deny that it has a moral purpose – to remove poverty and to create an egalitarian society. Modern management culture encourages shareholders, directors, managers, and staff to believe that the purpose of economic activity is to make them wealthier.

However, the *Bhagavad Gita* warns that those who 'take action with their eyes on the rewards for themselves will never enjoy serenity, fearlessness, peace, harmony, or the supreme happiness'. It's not that the *Gita* recommends withdrawal from the world or renunciation, as some have suggested; rather, Sarvepalli Radhakrishnan called it 'a mandate for action'. It is the mandate the god Krishna gives to the warrior Arjuna when he begs to be allowed to renounce action and withdraw his army from the battlefield of Kurukshetra, where he has come to fight to regain his kingdom. 'What use is it going to be getting back our kingdom?' Arjuna laments. 'I do not see any good in slaying my people in the fight.' But Krishna insists that it is his duty to fight because the battle is between good and evil. He tells Arjuna, 'To action alone hast thou a right and never at all to its fruits; let not the fruits of action be thy motive; neither let there be in thee any attachment to inaction.' In his commentary on the *Gita*, Radhakrishnan notes, 'This famous verse contains the essential principle of disinterestedness. When we do our work, plough, or paint, sing or think, we will be deflected from disinterestedness if we think of fame or income or any such extraneous consideration. Nothing matters except the good will, the willing fulfilment of the purpose of God.'

There is a well-known Christian prayer of St Ignatius that says much the same thing as Krishna tells Arjuna in the *Gita*. Ignatius prays to the Lord to teach him, 'to give and not to count the cost, to fight and not to heed the wounds, to toil and not to seek for rest, to labour and not to ask for any reward save that of knowing that I do Thy will.'

While writing this book I have often wondered what my reward will be – not so much the financial reward as the comments I'll receive. I've worried that they will be hostile, and I've worried, as I did before giving the lecture on the BBC, that no one will be interested in what I have to say. But then my mind goes back to someone to whom I was devoted when I was a teenager.

Philip Francis was the vicar of the small country parish in Cheshire where my siblings and I lived as children after returning from India. There are many historic parish churches in Cheshire, but All Saints Marthall was neither particularly old nor particularly beautiful. Nor could it have been called a prestigious post for a parish priest.

Philip, a small, rather insignificant figure with a wisp of hair standing up on his otherwise bald head, emerged from the vestry Sunday after Sunday to preach to the same handful of faithful church-goers. He was a humble man, and some of his parishioners seemed to think of him as Churchill did of Clement Atlee: 'He has plenty to be humble about.' Philip was unmarried, not because he was a celibate priest, but because he had never found anyone to marry. His career was going nowhere. He was never going to hold any higher office in the Church than that of parish priest, and only in small insignificant parishes. If success in his job was to be measured, as it often was in the Church, by 'bums on seats', the number of people attending Sunday Services meant that he was a failure. But to me he wasn't a failure at all. He was an inspiring example of someone who laboured and yet who did not seek for any reward; someone who truly practised the Christian virtue of humility.

The memory of Philip Francis came back to me while I was writing this chapter because it is a critique of a competitive culture obsessed with rewards. Of course there has to be a balance. We can't have a society without competition and rewards. We are never going to have a world of people like St Ignatius and Philip Francis. But that does not mean we should go to the other extreme and accept that rat-racing is the natural sport of human beings.

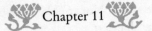 Chapter 11

VARANASI: THE UNITY OF OPPOSITES

I STARTED this book in the temple town of Puri, remembering my childhood holidays there. I am ending it in the holy city of Varanasi on my seventy-first birthday, because this city symbolises for me all that the adult years I have lived in India have taught me. Varanasi is, for me, a city where communities remain different but live together, where there is not one but many different certainties.

For many Hindus, Varanasi is the archetypal sacred place, yet almost one-third of its population is Muslim. It is Shiva's city, yet many gods are worshipped here and different religions practised. It is also the city where the Buddha said he would not concern himself with matters of ultimate reality, such as whether God exists or not.

Accommodating diversity is second nature to Varanasi, which is even known by more than one name. Internationally, its best-known name remains Banaras (Benares), a corruption of the much older name the Indian government has now restored: Varanasi. According to one popular tradition, the name is derived from the geography of the sacred city, most particularly the area between two small rivers that flow into the Ganga: the Varana in the north and the Asi in the south. But this being India, where tradition is respected, the most popular name of the city is still Kashi, the city of light – its oldest name.

For all its sanctity, Varanasi symbolises a balanced life in which worship, work and pleasure all play a role and earning money is an obligation but not an obsession. God and Mammon are both given their due, for as well as being a place of pilgrimage, Varanasi has a long history as a commercial centre. As the city of Shiva, it acknowledges the pleasures offered by Kama, the god of love, and also the danger of his arrows.

Varanasi has learnt to preserve tradition and accommodate change. It is one of the oldest living cities in the world – as old as Jerusalem, Athens or Beijing. But there is a difference between Varanasi and those ancient sites, which the American scholar Diana Eck, who has studied the city's traditions, religion, and culture carefully, has observed. In her book, *Banaras, City of Light,* she says:

> If we could imagine the silent Acropolis and the Agora of Athens still alive with the intellectual, cultural, and ritual traditions of classical Greece, we might glimpse the remarkable tenacity of the life of Kashi. Today Peking, Athens, and Jerusalem are moved by a very different ethos from that which moved them in ancient times, but Kashi is not.

Varanasi has been destroyed and rebuilt many times. Those who come here expecting to see its long history enshrined in ancient buildings will be disappointed. Varanasi as it stands today is only some 200 years old. Its ancient traditions have been challenged by centuries of Muslim rule and by the Christian missionaries of the British Raj, but they have survived. Varanasi is certainly not immune from one modern challenge, which is particularly threatening to a city with such an old Hindu tradition and such a large Muslim population: the explosive cocktail of religious fundamentalism and politics. The right-wing Hindu Bharatiya Janata party (BJP) and associated organisations such as the Vishwa Hindu Parishad (VHP), or World Hindu Council, have for years been trying to whip up Hindu fury by demanding that a mosque that stands right next to the most important of all

Varanasi's Hindu temples should be pulled down, saying that the Mughal emperor Aurangzeb pulled down an earlier temple to build the mosque on that site. There were serious Hindu–Muslim riots in Varanasi in 1991, and five months before I arrived back in the city in 2006 there was a threat that rioting would erupt again.

Shortly after six o'clock in the evening on Tuesday 7 March 2006, a bomb exploded in the courtyard of the temple dedicated to Hanuman as Sankat Mochan, or 'Hanuman who averts dangers'. According to myth, the popular monkey god was the devoted follower of Rama and helped him to rescue his consort, Sita, who had been abducted by the demon Ravana, king of Lanka. That evening, there was a particularly large gathering in the temple because Tuesday is Hanuman's day.

The temple explosion was followed by a bomb blast at Varanasi's main railway station, just before the departure of the overnight express to Delhi. A rumour spread that a bomb had also exploded on the train itself, but that was found to be untrue. However, the police did find other bombs, which they were able to defuse. Three of these were also in the Hanuman temple complex; another was on the most popular ghat, a section of the banks of the Ganga, where the evening *aarti*, or worship, was due to begin; and yet another was in a restaurant frequented by foreign tourists. With politicians and the police already blaming Muslim organisations based in Pakistan for recent attacks elsewhere in India, and particularly given the timing and the targets of the attacks in Varanasi, it was inevitable that suspicion would fall on Muslim organisations here too. So there was a very real danger that Hindus would respond by attacking Muslims.

Indian television channels were unintentionally doing their bit to provoke rioting as well. As soon as they could get their outside broadcasting units to the sites of the blasts, they began showing continuous live coverage, consisting largely of clips of the bloodiest scenes they could film. These clips were repeated time and again, along with interviews with distressed relatives of the injured and the dead and with other angry citizens. Overwrought presenters bombarded hapless reporters on the scene with questions. On one channel a presenter, beside himself with excitement, jabbed feverishly at a map of Varanasi, gabbling in his excitement, 'There was a bomb found here, a bomb found here, and a bomb found here!' But all the viewers could see was his back, because he was standing right in front of the map. I remember commenting that if anyone was going to turn this situation into a communal riot, it was going to be the television networks.

One person who did keep his head amidst the chaos was Veer Bhadra Mishra, the Mahant, or Head Priest, of the Sankat Mochan temple. He realised that it was absolutely crucial to get routine worship in the temple started again as soon as possible. This he achieved in a remarkably short time. He also issued a statement calling on people to be peaceful. His appeal was supported by the Muslim leader Mufti Abdul Batin Nomani. All the press agreed that it was the two religious leaders who ensured that Varanasi remained calm. In contrast, politicians of the BJP tried to disturb the peace by pestering the Mahant to allow protesters to hold a *dharna*, or sit-in, within the temple premises. The Mahant, however, insisted that the temple should not be used for any purpose that was not strictly religious. So it was the religious leaders who frustrated the bombers, while some politicians tried to do the terrorists' work for them by inciting Hindus to violence.

I decided to ask both religious leaders whether they believed that Varanasi's traditions had helped them to keep the peace. Abdul Batin Nomani is known as the Mufti of Varanasi. He has an office in a mosque deep inside a Muslim area of Varanasi. When I went to meet him, his brother led me through a maze of alleys, which were narrow even by Varanasi's standards and in which I would certainly have got hopelessly lost on my own. The alleys widened to accommodate shops in which butchers stood hacking at great hunks of buffalo meat and doing good business because it was the eve of the festival of Eid, the end of the month-long fast of Ramazan. The alleys narrowed again, and eventually we came to a building that I didn't immediately recognise as a mosque because other buildings pressed in on it so closely.

Once inside, I was taken down to a bare cellar, where I sat cross-legged on the white sheets that covered the concrete floor. Soon the Mufti came in and sat behind his small low desk, the only piece of furniture in the room. There wasn't a white hair in his black beard, and his face seemed remarkably unlined for a cleric holding such a senior office. With his thick spectacles, he looked more like a scholarly student than one of the most important Muslim leaders in Varanasi. The Mufti explained that his office was traditionally held by a member of his family and he had inherited it when his cousin died.

I started by asking the Mufti whether he thought that the culture of Varanasi had helped to maintain peace after the explosions. He seemed nervous, uncertain as to how to answer, and asked me to repeat the question. Then he replied, 'Through Allah's grace all religions live here in India without discrimination. All share each other's happiness and sorrows, and this tradition continues. It is still maintained by the peace-loving non-Muslims. But one group wants us to fight. As long as they are not successful it's fine, but if they are, then there is danger.'

The Muslim cleric had already established relations with Veer Bhadra Mishra, so when he heard about the explosion in the temple he went straight to the Mahant to 'console and comfort him at his time of pain'. The two men had also visited hospitals together. 'After all, our loss is common and equal in the bomb blast,' the Mufti explained. 'It was a dirty deed. It was terrorism. It had no sanction under Islam. But by God's grace we have peace.'

One of the Mufti's neighbours, a businessman by the name of Khaliquzzaman, joined us in the cellar. Older and more experienced than the Mufti, he soon took over most of the talking. The businessman praised the Mahant for issuing a statement that showed 'great self-restraint, condemning the act but not saying a word which might inflame the majority'.

I wanted to broaden the discussion, so I asked what the two men thought about the controversies in Europe over Muslim women wearing head scarves. The businessman replied, 'If you say to one person in a community "don't cover your head", then that person becomes a symbol, and there is a reaction and it will be prolonged. It is necessary to protect all good religions.'

'What about Western culture?' I asked.

Khaliquzzaman replied, 'Materialism and worldliness are the main characteristics of Western culture, as we understand it. There is a lack of spirituality and no fear of God. We are afraid of it coming to India and becoming so strong that it turns us into consumers, full of greed and with no generosity in us towards others. Then the moral restrictions of our religion will be set aside and there will be an excess of lust, desire, and killing for gain. Instead there should be an equilibrium in society with everyone practising their own religion and maintaining their values.'

At the top of the many steep steps leading from the Ganga to the home of Veer Bhadra Mishra, there is one of the thousands of small temples dotted all over Varanasi. When I reached it, breathless after the climb, I asked an attendant how I could arrange to meet the Mahant. I was told that I should wait on the far side of his house, where he would complete his morning worship. When that was over, I could ask for an interview.

A tall *peepal* tree spread its branches over a cluster of shrines outside the doorway to his house. Although there was a large ochre-coloured image of the monkey god Hanuman in one of the shrines, the monkeys here were not being shown any respect by an elderly man armed with a big stick. In spite of being lame, he moved with remarkable alacrity from shrine to shrine, waving his stick and shouting at the animals. They scampered away, only to return as soon as their pursuer moved on to another shrine. I admired the old man's perseverance and his energy, even though his exertions seemed rather pointless. But I was wrong there, for eventually the monkeys got bored with the sport and wandered off down a narrow alleyway.

When the Mahant emerged, he was dressed as always in a white *kurta* and *dhoti*. His white hair was neatly cut and his white moustache trimmed. The Mahant is now well into his sixties and smiles often but speaks rather solemnly, with deliberation. After paying his respects to the *linga*, the symbols of Shiva, in the shrines and to Hanuman, he came over to me and, with his usual immaculate politeness, said in his magnificent, deep voice, 'How good of you to come to Varanasi.' After a little more polite chatter, he agreed that we should meet in the afternoon.

The west bank of the Ganga at Varanasi is divided into thirty-six paved areas, or ghats, each with steep steps leading from them up into the city. The ghats vary in importance. Some of them are musts for pilgrims because of their spiritual significance, but the ghat at the top of which Veer Bhadra lives is important for historical reasons. It's named after the sixteenth-century poet Tulsi Das and is said to be the place where he wrote his retelling of the *Ramayana* epic. Because Tulsi Das chose to offend the Brahmin elite by writing in the everyday language of Hindi rather than the language of ritual, Sanskrit, his retelling of the *Ramayana* became immediately popular. To this day it is still immensely influential in north India.

The Mahant has not always lived on Tulsi Ghat. As a child he lived in a village in a district east of Varanasi. Recalling his childhood when we spoke later that day, he remembered that Muslims and Hindus used to attend each other's festivals and weddings. Their food traditions were different, so separate meals were provided by the hosts for the guest community. He added that Muslims were invited to his own wedding. 'Hindus and Muslims were living very happily,' he told me, 'but that has come under threat for political reasons. If only politicians would stop exploiting people, the tolerance of this society would find a way for us to live together. That is why I was determined that after the explosions took place we should not allow ourselves to be exploited. Politicians exploit because they want us to divide on lines of caste and religion so that they can rule over us. There should be institutions to see that good candidates are selected for elections and we are not ruled by muscle power and money.'

Veer Bhadra put his concerns about the future to me more forcefully than the Mufti had. 'Can we not see that we are dividing society?' he asked with anguish, continuing, 'This is a nation of so many languages, twelve philosophies, as many gods and goddesses as people. It is still being held together by the institutions of the British. We have been independent for sixty years now and we still have not found the way this country should be run.'

In addition to being the Mahant of the temple, Veer Bhadra is a former professor of civil engineering, specialising in hydraulics, at Banaras Hindu University, one of India's largest universities in India. Now retired, he sees no conflict between his science and his faith. To him, they belong to two different faculties: one to reason and the other is what he calls 'the heart'. Both are necessary. 'The interface between them,' he told me, 'is the key to a happy life. Science and faith are like two banks of a river. If one crumbles there is a flood and disaster.'

Science and faith come together in his concern about the River Ganga. As a scientist he knows how serious the problem of pollution is. Although he takes a ritual bath in the river every-day, he told me, 'Every moment I am reminded that this water is not safe.' For twenty years now the government has unsuccess-fully attempted to clean the Ganga. As an expert in hydraulics, Veer Bhadra believes they have failed because they have favoured expensive sewage treatment plants over more tradi-tional and cheaper technology, which passes the sewage through ponds treated with purifying algae. All this matters deeply to him. 'For me,' he says, 'this cleaning of the Ganga is a sacred responsibility given to me by God. We Hindus have a relation-ship with the Ganga that is unique. We come from all over India to see her, to touch her, to dip our body in her and sip her water. For us the Ganga is a medium of life. Environmentalists are busy trying to save plants and animals, but in Varanasi human beings like us are an endangered species because her water is so polluted.'

I told the Mahant about the boatman who had rowed me down the Ganga on the previous night, the night of Diwali, the festival of lights. Large crowds had gathered on Dasashwamedh Ghat to take part in the evening *aarti*, at which the Ganga is worshipped. *Diya*s, small clay saucers with flickering wicks, floated on the surface of the river like stars in the night sky. Bare-chested priests facing the river held brightly burning tradi-tional temple lamps high above their heads and then rotated them in strictly choreographed movements. Bells intended to awaken the gods clanged incessantly in the temples. I asked the boatman which temple he worshipped in and which god or goddess he worshipped. 'We boatmen live in the lap of the Ganga,' he replied, 'so we worship her and no one else. And when I'm finished I will light my Diwali *diya* in this boat.'

Although Jawaharlal Nehru, India's first Prime Minister, was a non-believer, he acknowledged the place the Ganga has in the hearts of Indians by asking that a handful of his ashes should be sprinkled on her waters when he died. In his will he said, 'The Ganga, especially, is the river of India, beloved of her people, round which are intertwined her racial memories, her hopes and fears, her songs of triumph, her victories and her defeats. She has been a symbol of India's age-long culture and civilization, ever changing, ever flowing, and yet ever the same Ganga.'

To me, the Ganga's place at the heart of this ancient culture is a mark of India's traditional respect for nature – her understanding that we are all a part of nature and dependent upon it. The pollution of the Ganga is a reminder of what happens when, in our rush to develop, we abuse nature, for that is what pouring sewage and industrial waste into her is. Scientists might argue with some justification that if India had implemented either the government's expensive plans or the Mahant's more traditional methods effectively, the Ganga would be much cleaner. That may be so, but this shouldn't be taken to mean that we can abuse nature freely in the misguided belief that technology can be relied upon to repair all the damage later. The more we believe that, the more we will be inclined to ignore the need to lead our lives in balance with nature.

I stayed in a hotel on the southernmost ghat, where the Asi river forms the boundary of the sacred city. The Ganges View is a very special hotel in a very special location. There is no bar, and no television set in the small rooms, which are beautifully decorated and furnished. The food is strictly vegetarian, which means in this instance that there are not even any onions or other root vegetables. It is the custom for guests to take off their shoes as they enter and walk around the hotel barefoot. The proprietor, Shashank Singh, is an authority on Varanasi and a connoisseur of art. The hotel was his family house, and Shashank has preserved its atmosphere, together with many of his family customs, including worshiping Hanuman every day in a small temple at the top of the steps leading to the hotel. There are always interesting guests. This time I met a young British theatre director who was going to stage the *Ramayana* in London and a writer who was researching a book about the sun.

The only disadvantage of the Ganges View is that it's not very easy to have a lie-in. Even before sunrise there is a lot happening on the ghat and it's rather noisy. Men and women come down to bathe early so that they can worship the sun as it rises. The priests, known as *ghatias*, sit under their straw umbrellas for protection from the sun and minister to the pilgrims' needs. They look after the bathers' clothes while they bob up and down in the Ganga. When the bathers come out, the *ghatias* put a red mark on their foreheads and provide a comb and a mirror for them. Groups of women chant as they make offerings to a *linga*, and little children scamper over the steps of the ghat, trying to extract money from tourists.

During the festival of Diwali, the ghat by the Ganges View Hotel was noisy throughout the night too. The machine-gun-like stutter of firecrackers and the explosions of even louder fireworks, known appropriately as bombs, accompanied by choruses of '*Hara Hara Mahadev!*' made sleep impossible. The next night there was another festival, and an image of the black-faced goddess of destruction Kali arrived to be immersed in the Ganga to the accompaniment of raucous recordings of hymns set to film music, with the volume turned up to maximum. They say there is a festival every day in Varanasi, and some even say there are seven days in a week in the sacred city but eight festivals.

This succession of festivals brought to mind what I believe to be a sad loss in British life – the punctuation mark that used to be provided every seventh day by Sunday, and the festivals that marked the seasons of the year. In Britain, we still have Sundays but they have become shopping sprees. So many activities now go on for twenty-four hours a day, seven days a week. We still have festivals, but deprived of their religious significance they also seem to have lost their seasonal flavour. When I recently interviewed the Bishop of London, Richard Chartres, he told me he tried to keep a Sabbath every week so that he could be with his family on Friday evening and Saturday. 'I think it's crucial to maintain the rhythm of the day, the week and the year,' he said, adding, 'The ecological crisis is a reflection of the loss of that rhythm. It's really a crisis of an impaired awareness of order, and unless you begin to re-engage with and respect the deep rhythms and deep structures of life you will not solve it.' Varanasi, with its daily round of worship in both temples and mosques and its year punctuated by perhaps more than 365 festivals, is in no danger of forgetting that rhythm.

For all its long history of being a city of God, or perhaps I should say gods, Mammon has not been ignored in Varanasi. When the Buddha came to preach here, he found a prosperous business centre, and the city remained so because it was at the crossroads of important trade routes. One traditional description of Varanasi is 'the Forest of Artha'. Along with *kama*, the principle of pleasure and love, *artha* is, as I have explained in Chapter 7, one of the four aims of a traditional Hindu life. *Artha* is the goal of material prosperity. However, as Julius Lipner notes in his book *Hindus*, 'The pursuit of *artha* and *kama* were set in an ethical context very early on. They were never recommended as goals to be sought for their own sake irrespective of an ethical code of practice.' So traditional Varanasi would not approve of the prevailing business practices, which appear to have no ethical or moral motives and promote the pursuit of goals entirely for business's own benefit.

Apart from pilgrimage and tourism, the best known business in Varanasi is traditional handloom weaving. The city is particularly renowned for its beautiful silk brocade saris. Suhail Bhai, a Muslim whose family has been in the industry for generations, unpacked some of his prize examples to show me the skill of Varanasi weavers. He carefully unfolded a hundred-year-old blouse woven with gold thread and a collection of mauve, maroon, scarlet, golden and lemon-green saris with motifs of vines, flowers and the Indian mango pattern known in the West as paisley. There was even his wife's blue and gold wedding outfit.

Suhail Bhai explained that one of his best saris would take one and a half months to weave, but the real trouble now was finding the weavers to do the work. According to him, many of the weavers had been tempted away from traditional methods to work on power-looms, because the emphasis nowadays was not on quality but on quantity. That wasn't the only problem he faced. 'Our dyers, who are renowned for their skills, are now dying synthetic cloth,' he complained. 'And there is too much competition from cheap Chinese cloth.'

Harshpal Kapoor, a Hindu merchant who deals in silk yarn, told me that traditional weaving was also being hit by changes in the clothes that modern Indian women are wearing. 'There is a decrease in the demand for saris, which were what Varanasi was famous for. In my young days only Punjabi women wore *shalwar kameez*, but now you see them everywhere. And of course there are all those jeans the younger women are wearing too. But,' he added hurriedly, 'still no wedding can be performed without a sari.'

To my mind, one of the strangest modern indicators of economic well-being is threatening the Varanasi tourist and pilgrimage businesses. While economists struggle to control inflation, and businessmen never cease their cost-cutting and price-slashing, we are told the economy is doing well when the property market is inflating. Economists maintain that it is good for us if it costs more and more to buy a house. Property prices are now soaring in Varanasi, with speculators buying land on the far bank of the Ganga. The land on the opposite bank to the ghats is still relatively undeveloped, having only one or two small buildings on it. If the speculators are eventually allowed to build there it will be architectural barbarity. It will be as sacrilegious as destroying the view of the Taj Mahal by allowing construction on the opposite bank of the river Yamuna. It will be commerce run riot, a total surrender to the property market, as was the surrender to the developers when the high-rise buildings that diminish St Paul's Cathedral in the heart of London were built.

I have written in Chapter 7 about the myth of Shiva's wedding to Parvati. After their marriage, Parvati persuaded Shiva to come down from the mountain top and live in a city. That city was Varanasi. So it's not surprising that Shiva's *linga* is to be seen everywhere – on street corners, under trees, in houses and in temples. These emblems may be inches high or feet tall and set in the grandest or most humble surroundings, but they always stand in the circle representing Shiva's union with Parvati, who represents the female power without which he can do nothing. There are said to be thousands of *linga* in Varanasi, but it might be better to say that there are countless numbers of them, because I can't imagine anyone ever counting them. If they did, they would be bound to come across one they had missed when they completed the task, or hear of yet another that appeared while they were counting.

The *linga* that attracts the most worshippers is in the principal shrine of Varanasi, the golden temple dedicated to Vishvanatha, Shiva as 'Lord of the world'. It is approached down a long, dark alley where daylight only occasionally breaks through. The alley is lined by shops that cater to *artha* rather than *moksha*, the 'liberation from earthly desires' that should be the ultimate aim of Shiva worshippers. Jewellers are particularly prominent here, and there are also plenty of garment shops with life-size plastic models dressed in clothes that demonstrate only too clearly the decline of the sari. But pilgrims are reminded of their ultimate destination by the many small temples and shrines along the way.

I stopped short at the large silver Ganesh, the elephant-headed god and son of Shiva, who guards the entrance to the main temple. Non-Hindus are not allowed inside and I wasn't about to argue with the police, who have become even more officious since the Varanasi bombs. 'No cameras, no pens,' they shouted, as they frisked those they did let in.

Even when they worship Shiva as 'Lord of the World', pilgrims have to be reminded that he is nothing without his female power. All those who pray at the Vishvanatha temple are obliged to go on to the nearby temple of Annapurna. The scholar Diana Eck translates 'Annapurna' as 'She of Plenteous Food' and points out that in popular art Shiva is often shown as so dependent on this female deity that he is depicted beseeching her for alms. As I have suggested in Chapter 7, it seems to me that this relationship between male and female, in which neither is complete without the other, has something profoundly important to teach us today.

But for all its long history of sanctity, Varanasi is not perfect. It's clearly not heaven on earth for many of its citizens. My visit in 2006 coincided with the municipal elections. Flags of different political parties were strung across the streets, and candidates were campaigning at roadside meetings. I couldn't help wondering why anyone should bother to vote in elections for such an apparently powerless institution as the municipality. The roads were pot-holed, the traffic chaotic even by Indian standards, and the garbage from a dump had spilled onto the main road running parallel to the ghats. The Ganga was still polluted, and on Asi Ghat there was only one meagre hose pipe available for cleaning off the clay, in many places three feet thick, deposited by the Ganga during the monsoon. Speculators may be licking their lips at the prospect of profitable land development, but beggars were still sitting patiently by the roadside, hoping at least for a handful of rice from the worshippers passing to and from Asi Ghat. The large number of cycle rickshaws was an economic indicator too, for no one who can earn a half-reasonable wage would choose to pull a rickshaw. Nevertheless, one rickshaw puller told me, 'At least here I can fill my stomach; I couldn't do that in my own city of Patna.'

The boatman who had rowed me down the Ganga during Diwali was, like many poorer Indians, amazingly well informed about politics. He knew the form in the municipal election and the forthcoming State Assembly election too. I asked why the municipal elections were being contested so fiercely when the municipality didn't seem capable of doing anything for anyone. He replied, 'Because the municipality has money to spend, and where there is money to spend there is money for those who get elected to steal too.'

A longstanding member of the local BJP, which has been running the Varanasi municipality, told me there wasn't any money. He blamed Varanasi's dilapidation on the Samajwadi Party governing the state of Uttar Pradesh, saying that they had not released funds for the municipality. When I asked him why he was campaigning so energetically in what were only municipal elections, he replied, 'They will be taken as a guide to what is going to happen in the state election. They are a sort of launching pad.'

'What sort of a launch are they going to give you?' I asked.

'Not very good. We are in power in nine municipalities now and I think that is likely to come down to four, which will not include Varanasi.'

Not surprisingly the BJP leader did not want me to use his name.

So democracy does not appear to be the ideal solution in Varanasi, nor is it necessarily the panacea that many Western leaders claim it is when they lecture less developed countries on following the democratic example. But that is not to suggest that Churchill was wrong when he said that, for all democracy's faults, he didn't know a better system. What is wrong is to assume that any criticism of democracy is inevitably anti-democratic. It's right, surely, to recognise that no democracy is perfect, that all can be improved on.

But despite all that is far from ideal in Varanasi, for me the city still represents much that is essential to living a balanced life; most particularly to living a life in which there is a place for the transcendent as well as the concerns of this world. Richard Lannoy, who is one of the most profound modern Western writers about India I know, has written in the preface to his book *Benares: A World Within a World*: 'Living among the people of this extraordinary city opened my eyes to levels of psychological and spiritual awareness which we in the West, with our most externalised preoccupations had thrust into the unconscious.' I have not spent as long in Varanasi as Richard Lannoy, nor would I claim to be anywhere near as spiritually aware as he is; nevertheless, Varanasi makes me aware through parables of much that I believe to be important. The relationship between the Mahant and the Mufti teaches me that it is possible for communities to live with each other while respecting their differences. The Shiva legend reminds me of the importance of restoring a balance between men and women that grants them equality but does not obscure their differences. The threat to Varanasi's economy and heritage adds to my conviction that GDP is an inadequate measure of progress and that the market must not rule our lives. The sanctity of the Ganga symbolises our relationship with nature, and its pollution is an indication of how poorly we have sometimes treated our partner. The Mahant, with his views on the importance of science and religion, and the combination in him of a priest and a scientist, represents the need for non-rational as well as rational understanding of reality.

Varanasi's attitude to death is also for me a parable. Richard Lannoy says, 'Benares has a way of persuading one to confront hidden, but universal, human proclivities. This is especially apparent in the city's unflinching attitude to mortality.' In the West we try to hide death. In Varanasi we cannot fail to be reminded of it. Traditionally, cremation grounds in India were sited outside towns and cities because Hindus regarded them as polluted places, but in Varanasi they are in the heart of the city. When I floated in a boat down the Ganga after dark and saw the flames of funeral pyres still burning on the two cremation ghats, I was reminded that Varanasi is probably the only city in the world where cremation grounds are tourist attractions. Those tourists who are too squeamish to face the two ghats, or who prefer not to be reminded of death, will still almost certainly see a funeral procession passing through the streets on their way to these cremation grounds, with the mourners chanting, '*Rama nam satya hai, Rama nam satya hai*' ('Rama's name is Truth, Rama's name is Truth').

In Varanasi death is transformed into liberation. The dead are brought from far and wide to have their last rites performed on the ghats, for there, according to Hindu tradition, the dying are guaranteed to secure the goal of *moksha*, freedom from the cycle of birth, death and rebirth. On one of the ghats, I once saw a frail old woman drawing her last shallow breaths as she lay on a low cot looking towards the river. She was surrounded by her relatives, who had brought her there to die. As I watched she gently passed away.

Why do we try to hide death in the West? I suspect because we don't want to be reminded that the things modern life cherishes are ephemeral. Fame, wealth, possessions only last one lifetime. I suspect it is also because most people no longer have the comfort of religion; they no longer believe, as St Paul did, that death cannot separate us from the love of God. In a materialist society death is the end. The awareness of death in Varanasi reminds me that I am part of nature and, like all living things, I will die; that all I take pride in is only temporary; and that there is going to be one time when I will have to trust in God, not in myself. It is a parable about humility.

The final parable Varanasi offers me lies in its unique position as the only one of the world's ancient living cities whose original culture and faith are still intact. To find out how that has happened and why it remains important, I went to see a Swami, or Hindu teacher, who speaks in parables. Swami Avimukteshwaranand Saraswati is one of the two principal disciples of the Shankaracharya of Joyotispith and Dwarka, two historic and highly respected Hindu offices. The Swami wore the traditional saffron robes, which also covered his head, and a necklace of bulky rudraksha beads round his neck. There was a statue of Saraswati, the goddess of learning, in one corner of the room where we spoke. Like the Mufti, the Swami seemed remarkably young to be holding a high religious office in India and to be the head of a *Math*, or monastery.

When I asked him how Varanasi's culture had survived, a smile lit up his broad handsome face. He was clearly a man who enjoyed discourse. 'A tree that bends in the wind will not break,' he said. 'We have one rule: there has to be liquidity in our traditions and our teaching. To be flexible like that tree you need to accept that there are many ways to God. There are many rivers flowing into the sea, and they are different; some twist and turn, some are straighter, but they all want to merge in the sea. So with God's grace there are many ways we can reach God. Don't pay attention to the way but to the goal. If the goal is good the way will be good.'

'But this requires humility, doesn't it?'

'Yes,' the Swami replied, tapping the small desk he was sitting behind cross-legged. 'It's like the guru who asked his disciple, "Do you know the Truth?" The disciple replied, "I know," and the guru sent him away to think again. Back came the disciple and this time he said, "I don't know," but he was sent away again. Finally he returned saying, "I don't know whether I know or not." That, you see, is the humility I mean, the humility to admit the limit of our knowledge.'

I told the Swami that this was what I was trying to say in my book. He smiled again, 'So you are saying that you know, aren't you?'

'In a way yes and in a way no,' I replied, getting myself tied up in knots.

The Swami was amused at my confusion. 'There are some people who do discover the truth,' he said. 'But the trouble is that when you discover the truth, you become part of it, there is no other, and you no longer have a self left to tell the truth. You are like the man made of salt who said he wanted to find out how deep the ocean was but by the time he reached its bed, he had dissolved into the ocean.'

I thought the time had come to bring the discussion back onto a more practical plain, so I asked the Swami why he was so confident that Varanasi would not be swept off its feet by modern materialist culture. He came up with another parable.

'Materialists are like the man who is driving at night with his headlights on but no light inside the car. He can see what is outside but he can't see what is inside. A materialist society is not a society at all.' He continued, 'It is nothing more than a bazaar. I believe a time comes when people realise there is such emptiness within themselves that they turn to what will fill them. Hunger starts small and it's only when you are fully hungry that you go to a restaurant. When they are totally empty, people will go back to their old ways to fill that emptiness.'

*

Varanasi and India have taught me to respect the faith I was born into. For me to become a Hindu would be to deny that Christianity is also a way to God and to reject the teaching in Swami Avimukteshwaranand Saraswati's parable about the many rivers flowing to the sea. The Swami told me, 'Your well-being lies within your own tradition.' I was born a Christian and I believe that by remaining a Christian I am respecting fate and tradition, both of which are such important aspects of a balanced life. There is also a question of loyalty to the Church and to the priests and others who have kept my faith alive at those times when I had almost abandoned it. Bede Griffiths, whose whole life was dedicated to God in a way mine certainly has not been, wrote of a marriage of East and West. He didn't divorce the West and marry the East.

Varanasi demonstrates that a marriage of East and West is possible. For me, as someone brought up as a Westerner yet much influenced by India, it also confirms that if the marriage is to take place the West must be flexible in its thinking and suspicious of certainties. It must seek for balance between the material and the spiritual, between reason and other means of perceiving reality, between tradition and change, between individuals and society, between humans and nature. It must have the humility to live respectfully with different faiths and cultures, and to be prepared to learn from them too. That, of course, means that the East also has to have the humility to learn from the West. Throughout this book I have argued that we should not fall into the error of assuming that the East has got it all right and the West has got it all wrong. For me, India acknowledges that we can never find absolute answers to the most important questions in life, but we must go on asking them. This is why I have called my book *India's Unending Journey*. It is a journey that we can all learn from.

FURTHER READING

Armstrong, Karen, *A History of God* (Vintage, 1999)
— *The Battle for God* (HarperCollins, 2001)
— *A Short History of Myth* (Canongate, 2006)

Badrinath, Chaturvedi, *Dharma, India and the World Order* (Saint
    Andrew Press & Pahl-Rugenstein, 1993)
— *The Mahabharata: An Inquiry in the Human Condition* (Orient
    Longman, 2006)
Beames, John, *Memoirs of a Bengal Civilian* (Chatto & Windus, 1961)
Bhalla, Surjit S., *Imagine There Is No Country: Poverty Inequality and
    Growth in the Era of Globalization* (Institute for International
    Economics, 2002)
Bharati, Swami Veda, *God* (The Himalayan International Institute of
    Yoga Science and Philosophy, 1979)
Birt, John, *The Harder Path* (Little, Brown & Co, 2002)
Brar, Lt Gen K.S., *Operation Blue Star: The True Story* (UBS, 1993)
Brendon, Vyvyen, *Children of the Raj* (Weidenfeld & Nicholson, 2005)
Brown, Judith M., *Gandhi: Prisoner of Hope* (Yale University Press,
    1989)

Cato, Molly Scott, *Market, Shmarket: Building the Post-Capitalist
    Economy* (New Clarion Press, 2006)
Chapman, Mark D., *Blair's Britain* (Darton, L. & T., 2005)
Clarke, Richard, *And Is It True?* (Dominican Publications, 2000)

the Dalai Lama and Bstan-'Dzin Rqy, *Ethics for the New Millennium*
    (Riverhead Books, 2001)

Dawkins, Richard, *The God Delusion* (Bantam Press, 2006)
Dupuis, Jacques, *Towards A Christian Theology of Religious Pluralism* (Orbis, 1997)

Eck, Diana, *Banaras, City of Light* (Arkana, 2003)

Fermor, Patrick Leigh, *A Time to Keep Silence* (John Murray, 1994)
Ford, Adam, *Faith and Science* (Epworth Press, 1999)

Galbraith, John Kenneth, *The Affluent Society* (Penguin Books, 1999)
Goodall, Dominic (trans. & ed.), *Hindu Scriptures* (J.M. Dent, 1996)
Gopal, Sarvepalli, *Jawaharlal Nehru: A Biography* (3 vols.) (OUP, 1984)
Gray, John, *Straw Dogs* (Granta, 2003)
— *Heresies* (Granta, 2004)
Griffiths, Bede, *The Marriage of East and West* (Canterbury Press, 2003)

Hamilton, Clive, *Growth Fetish* (Pluto Press, 2004)
Handy, Charles, *The Hungry Spirit* (Arrow, 1998)
Hannon, Patrick, *Church, State, Morality and Law* (Gill and MacMillan, 1992)
— *Moral Decision Making* (Veritas, 2005)
Heifetz, Hank (trans.), *The Origin of the Young God: Kalidas' Kumarasambhava,* (The Regents of the University of California, 1990)
Hines, Colin, *Localization: A Global Manifesto* (Earthscan Publications, 2000)
Hopper, Ken and Will, *The Puritan Gift: Triumph, Collapse and Revival of an American Dream* (I.B. Tauris & Co Ltd, 2007)
Hughes, Gerard, *The God of Surprises* (Darton, Longman & Todd, 1996)

Imhasly-Gandhy, Rashna, *The Psychology of Love: the Wisdom of Indian Mythology* (Roli Books, 2001)
Iyengar, B.K.S, *Light on Life* (Rodale, 2005)

Jaffrelot, Christophe, *The Hindu Nationalist Movement in India* (C.Hurst, 1996)

Johnson, Robert A., *We: Understanding the Psychology of Romantic Love* (Harper San Francisco, 1983)

Kakar, Sudhir, *Intimate Relations* (University of Chicago Press, 1990)
— *The Ascetic of Desire* (Overlook Press, 2002)

Lannoy, Richard, *Benares: a World Within a World* (Indica Books, 2002)
Lipner, Julius, *Hindus: Their Religious Beliefs and Practices* (Routledge, 1994)

McGahern, John, *Memoir* (Faber and Faber, 2006)
McWilliams, David, *The Pope's Children* (Gill & Macmillan, 2006)
Miller, Barbara Stoler (trans.), *The Hermit and the Love Thief* (Columbia University Press, 1978)

Nanda, B.R., *Mahatma Gandhi: A Biography* (OUP, 1958)
— *In Search of Gandhi: Essays and Reflections* (OUP, 2002)

O'Donovan, Gerald, *Father Ralph* (Brandon, 1993)
O'Muyrchu, Diarmuid, *Religion in Exile* (Gateway, 2000)
O'Siadhail, Michael, *Poems 1975-1995* (Bloodaxe Books, 1999)

Pande, G.C., *Foundations of Indian Culture* (2 vols.) (Motilal Banarsidass, 1984)
Punja, Shobita, *Daughters of the Ocean: Discovering the Goddess Within* (Viking, 1996)
— *Divine Ecstasy, The Story of Khajuraho* (Viking, 2003)

Radhakrishnan, Dr Sarvepalli, *The Hindu View of Life* (Allen & Unwin, 1926)
— *Eastern Religions and Western Thought* (OUP, 1939)
— *Bhagavadgita* (George Allen and Unwin, 1948)
— *The Principal Upanishads* (OUP, 1953)

Rama, Swami, *Living with the Himalayan Masters* (The Himalayan Institute Press, 1978)

Ramanujan, A.K., *Speaking of Siva* (Penguin, 1973)

Ram-Prasad, Chakravarthi, *Eastern Philosophy* (Weidenfeld & Nicolson, 2005)

Richman, Paula (ed.), *Many Ramanayas: The Diversity of a Narrative Tradition in South Asia* (OUP, 1991)

Sachs, Jeffrey *The End of Poverty: How We Can Make It Happen in Our Life Time* (Penguin Books, 2005)

Sacks, Chief Rabbi Jonathan, *The Dignity of Difference* (Penguin Books, 2005)

Sen, Amartya, *The Argumentative Indian* (Penguin Books, 2006)

Singh, Karan, *Hinduism* (Criterion Publications, 1987)

Soros, George, *On Globalization* (Public Affairs, 2004)

Stiglitz, Joseph, *The Roaring Nineties* (Penguin Books, 2004)

Tacey, David, *The Spiritual Revolution* (Brunner Routledge, 2004)

Tarnas, Richard, *The Passion of the Western Mind* (Pimlico, 1996)

Toynbee, Polly, 'Narnia represents everything that is most hateful about religion' in the *Guardian* (5 December 2005)

Twomey, Vincent, *The End of Irish Catholicism?* (Veritas Publications, 2002)

Vatsyayana, Mallanaga, *Kama Sutra*, eds. Sudhir Kakar and Wendy Doniger, (OUP, 2002)

Ward, Keith, *God, Chance and Necessity* (Oneworld Publications, 1996)

— *What the Bible Really Teaches* (SPCK, 2004)

Williams, H.A., *The True Wilderness* (Continuum International Publications Group, 2002)

Zaehner, R.C., *Hindu Scriptures* (J.M. Dent & Sons, 1938)

— *Hinduism* (OUP, 1982)

INDEX